Options for Swing Trading

OPTIONS FOR SWING TRADING

LEVERAGE AND LOW RISK TO MAXIMIZE SHORT-TERM TRADING

MICHAEL C. THOMSETT

OPTIONS FOR SWING TRADING
Copyright © Michael C. Thomsett, 2013.

All rights reserved.

First published in 2013 by
PALGRAVE MACMILLAN®
in the United States—a division of St. Martin's Press LLC,
175 Fifth Avenue, New York, NY 10010.

Where this book is distributed in the UK, Europe and the rest of the world, this is by Palgrave Macmillan, a division of Macmillan Publishers Limited, registered in England, company number 785998, of Houndmills, Basingstoke, Hampshire RG21 6XS.

Palgrave Macmillan is the global academic imprint of the above companies and has companies and representatives throughout the world.

Palgrave® and Macmillan® are registered trademarks in the United States, the United Kingdom, Europe and other countries.

ISBN: 978–1–137–28256–9

Library of Congress Cataloging-in-Publication Data

Thomsett, Michael C.
  Options for swing trading : leverage and low risk to maximize short-term trading / Michael C. Thomsett.
    pages cm
  Includes bibliographical references and index.
  ISBN 978–1–137–28256–9 (alk. paper)
  1. Stock options. 2. Speculation. 3. Investments. I. Title.

HG6042.T46165 2013
332.64—dc23   2013001692

A catalogue record of the book is available from the British Library.

Design by Newgen KnowledgeWorks (P) Ltd., Chennai, India.

First edition: September 2013

10 9 8 7 6 5 4 3 2 1

Printed in the United States of America.

Contents

Acknowledgments — vii

Introduction: Problems of Risk in Most Trading Systems — 1

1. Options: Trading Basics — 7
2. Swing Trading: The Basics — 27
3. Dangerous Waters: Risk Inherent in Comprehensive Swing-Based Strategies — 61
4. Marginal Potential: Leverage Limitations in Swing Trading with Stock — 75
5. Elegant Solutions: Options to Address the Risk and Leverage Issues — 85
6. In and Out: Entry and Exit Criteria for Swing Trading — 99
7. Powerful Timing Tools: Expanding Swing Signals with Candlestick Reversals — 133
8. Flexing Your Muscle: The Power of Options Close to Expiration — 165
9. Swings Maximized: Timing the Swing with Ex-dividend Date — 179
10. Strategy # 1: Long-Option Approach, a Basic Solution — 193
11. Strategy # 2: Long/Short-Call Strategy, Uncovered Short Side — 213

12. Strategy # 3: Long/Short-Call Strategy, Covered Short Side	227
13. Strategy # 4: Long/Short-Call Strategy, Ratio Writing on the Short Side	245
14. Strategy # 5: Long/Short-Put Strategy	267
15. Strategy # 6: Short-Option Strategy	281
16. Strategy # 7: Synthetic Option Positions Strategy	295
17. Strategy # 8: Multiple Contracts and Weighting with Ratio Calendar Spreads	307
18. Strategy # 9: Expanded Iron Butterfly Swing Trading	327
Epilogue—The Big Picture: Swing Trading and Your Portfolio	339
Notes	347
Bibliography	349
Index	351

Acknowledgments

I extend my thanks to the numerous individuals who responded to my articles and blog posts on LinkedIn, Twitter, SeekingAlpha, and CBOE on topics found in expanded form in this book. Your observations, questions, and criticisms were appreciated. Also, thanks to the management of StockCharts.com for allowing the free use of their charts in this book. The publishing and editorial staff at Palgrave Macmillan deserve special acknowledgement for their professionalism, enthusiasm, and dedication to creation of high-quality projects, with special thanks to Laurie Harting, Lauren LoPinto, and Joel Breuklander. Finally, my deep gratitude to my agent, John Willig, for his energetic and unfailing optimism and belief in this and my other publishing projects.

Introduction: Problems of Risk in Most Trading Systems

> It is living and ceasing to live that are imaginary solutions.
> André Breton, *Manifesto of Surrealism*, 1924

Traders never stop looking for the *perfect* system, the one that creates profits in every trade and never yields the nasty surprise of loss. This perfect system is the sure thing. And even though everyone knows it doesn't exist, the search never stops.

If such a system could be found, the entire premise of the market would be destroyed as well. What drives trading, after all, is the idea that it is possible to improve the odds and overcome the typical outcome through a few attributes: improved timing of entry and exit, reversal recognition, strong confirmation, and the ability to act rationally and contrary to the emotional herd mentality of the market.

This is where swing trading comes into play.

Many names have been given to swing strategies. A related strategy, day trading, ended up with a very negative reputation due to excesses and large losses. Today, automated systems of high-frequency trading (HFT) are controversial and are blamed for market fluctuations. In this system, automated trading takes place in a matter of seconds, reaping a small benefit on millions of shares. HFT accounts for a majority of all trades each day:

> For years, high-frequency trading firms have operated in the shadows, often far from Wall Street, trading stocks at warp

speed and reaping billions while criticism rose that they were damaging markets and hurting ordinary investors. Now they are stepping into the light to buff their image with regulators, the public, and other investors.

After quietly growing to account for about 60 percent of the seven billion shares that change hands daily on United States stock markets, the firms are trying to stave off the regulators who are proposing to curb their activities.[1]

Does the practice of rapidly moving in and out of positions truly create adverse effects in the market? It's true that those large institutions applying algorithmic methods to move in and out of positions are profiting. It's also true that they exploit the system to get these profits. But the extent to which this harms retail investors is far less certain.

The fact that the practice of rapid trades does create profits doesn't have to mean someone else loses. That's not how the market works. Swing trading, for example, is a much slower version of HFT, in which an individual moves in and out of positions in three to five days (typically), using timing techniques to exploit exaggerated price movement and then exiting with small but frequent profits.

The question is whether this practice harms other, longer-term buy-and-hold positions. How does a rapid in-and-out trading system create any damage to others? In the auction market, buyers and sellers transact shares by arriving at a meeting of the minds about value. Trades occur when both sides agree on the price of shares. So whether you are in a position for three days or three years (or three seconds), the price you pay or receive is part of that auction market.

The idea that one trader's profits have to come at another trader's loss is simply unsupported. Swing trading is a system for acting on price changes. Swing traders expect large but sudden price movement to be exaggerated, which means that it will usually self-correct within three to five trading sessions. When a trade is entered into on this premise, it's a response to price movement created by other traders. So if a stock price falls four points, it means many other traders wanted to dispose of shares, and that selling demand drove the price down. If you pick up shares after the four-point drop and prices later rise, you profit. It's true that the initial sellers lose as a consequence, but they willingly sold their shares.

The market's price movements occur for good reasons. Sellers decide to sell in the belief that the current price is better than it will be later, and buyers buy in the belief that the current price is a bargain. This is a simple reality of supply and demand in the market. If a trader artificially creates the illusion of changes in value, that's cheating. So for example, a "pump and dump" is an action meant to drive up the price of a stock after buying it, hoping that shares can be sold at a profit once others respond to the hype:

> "Pump and dump" schemes, also known as "hype and dump manipulation," involve the touting of a company's stock (typically microcap companies) through false and misleading statements to the marketplace. After pumping the stock, fraudsters make huge profits by selling their cheap stock into the market.
>
> "Pump-and-dump" schemes often occur on the Internet where it is common to see messages posted that urge readers to buy a stock quickly or to sell before the price goes down, or a telemarketer will call using the same sort of pitch. Often the promoters will claim to have "inside" information about an impending development or to use an "infallible" combination of economic and stock market data to pick stocks. In reality, they may be company insiders or paid promoters who stand to gain by selling their shares after the stock price is "pumped" up by the buying frenzy they create. Once these fraudsters "dump" their shares and stop hyping the stock, the price typically falls, and investors lose their money.[2]

However, swing trading based only on observed price movement, trend reversal signals, and confirmation is an appropriate method for timing trades and by no means a manipulation of prices. The pump-and-dump technique is fraud, but there is no fraud in timing your decisions based on how other traders buy or sell shares.

Swing traders contrast the emotions of the market with a logical and calm approach. The majority of trading takes place as a gut reaction to the news or rumors of the moment. Swing trading is a contrarian approach. Trades are timed in response to sudden and exaggerated price movement. A true contrarian does not trade only to move in a direction opposite to that of the majority of the market. Rather, the basis of decisions is logic rather than emotions, and this is what makes the contrary moves occur so frequently. When the market consistently overreacts to news, prices move too far and then correct during the following one to three sessions.

For example, if the earnings announcement of a company exceeds the previous year's but misses analysts' estimates by one penny per share, the stock price might fall three or four points. This is often an exaggerated reaction to the news, and once the overall market realizes this, the price tends to return to its previous level. Swing traders simply time their trades to enter positions at or near the extent of the exaggerated move, and then they exit once the price returns to its more rational level.

This book explores the many aspects of swing trading, but with an added twist. Most swing traders use shares of long stock at the bottom of the swing, buying and waiting for the price to rise and then selling. Some, but not all, will also short stock at the top of an exaggerated swing and then buy to close at the bottom. In this transaction, the normal "buy-hold-sell" is reversed. The trader borrows stock from the broker and then sells it, waiting for the price to decline so it can be bought to close at a lower price—the sequence becomes "sell-hold-buy." However, shorting stock is expensive and carries a high risk, and therefore many swing traders work only one side of the trade, entering with long stock and then selling when prices rise.

Using options in place of stock, swing trading is safer and more flexible. Traders using long options can make bearish moves without taking on short-side risks, for example. This is only the most apparent benefit of swing trading with options. There are many more. This book explains and contrasts options with stock in a swing trading program. It demonstrates how reversal signals and confirmation are recognized. And finally, it provides a number of methods for using options in a swing trading program.

The goal of any trading program should be to maximize profits while controlling and reducing risks. Options can be very high-risk if used improperly, and anyone using options in swing trading or other strategies first must understand the varieties of risk involved with various strategies and combinations. A swing trading program, whether using stock or options, is one of many ways to improve timing of trades, but it demands study and analysis of price patterns and signals.

No system can guarantee 100% profits. That perfect system is worth pursuing, but it just doesn't exist. The best use of signals and confirmation will help, however, to improve the percentage of correct entry and exit timing and create a higher percentage of profitable trades. This is where swing trading as a strategy, and options as the vehicle, combine to make the system work at its best.

CHAPTER 1

OPTIONS: TRADING BASICS

> Simplicity is an acquired taste. Mankind, left free, instinctively complicates life.
> — Katherine F. Gerould, *Modes and Morals*, 1920

THE WORLD OF OPTIONS IS A LABYRINTH OF POORLY UNDERSTOOD rules and jargon, often characterized as high risk and exotic.

The truth: Options cover a broad range of risk, from speculative all the way to ultraconservative. There are rules and jargon, all of which cloak the truth: Options can be high risk but don't have to be, and they can be exotic or elegantly simple. It's all a question of how the option itself is applied.

In the context of a *swing trading strategy*, the use of options includes a wide range of strategies. This chapter summarizes the basics of options trading in the context of developing an options-based swing trading strategy. A few commonsense rules offer a starting point:

1. *Simple is better.* The simple option is invariably preferable over the complex strategy combining hedging features, offsetting risks, and multi-legged position design. In this book, most of the examples use single-option positions to demonstrate likely outcomes. However, you can use multiples to create higher position return and risk profiles. Simple is better, not only in how examples are provided, but also in application of strategies in a real-world trading environment.

2. *Low risk is better than high risk.* This might seem obvious, but if you look at how traders make decisions, you quickly realize that a tendency to favor high-risk positions is a flaw in thinking and a common problem. Options traders, like moths to the flame, are drawn to the more exotic and complex strategies. But the danger here is in unintentionally entering high risk positions when you intended the opposite—this is the all too common flaw in how trading is done, and it's a problem to be aware of and to avoid.
3. *It's not a question of long or short, but of risk awareness.* The options trade often is entered into with a focus on the profit potential and a completely blind eye toward the risk level that is also involved. To improve your percentage of profitable trades, you also need to know *all* of the possible outcomes, losses as well as profits.
4. *The best of all worlds is to get the benefits with as few risks as possible.* Options-based swing trading works best when designed to create more benefits than risks. This includes four primary approaches to the strategy:
   - *diversification* (lower cost per unit means you can work many different swings at the same time, compared to the capital limits of shares of stock),
   - *leverage* (one option controls 100 shares of stock, both long and short),
   - *reducing risk* (accomplished by selection of strikes and expirations meant to ensure that (a) the associated risks are manageable and (b) if and when price move s against you, it is possible to close or roll forward, further managing or removing the risk of loss), and
   - *flexibility* (options strategies come in many shapes, sizes, and combinations, and this lets you trade according to the underlying stock value, the current volatility, and your personal risk tolerance).[1]

OPTIONS: A REVIEW OF THE BASICS

Options provide specific benefits to their buyers (those who buy or go long); on the opposite side, option sellers grant those privileges to the buyer. The option is not a tangible product, but a contract, and its rights rise or fall based on changes in the price of the stock that an option relates to. The rights and characteristics of every option are called its *terms*.

There are four precise terms for every option. And these terms cannot be changed or amended. They are:

1. *Type of option.* There are two types of options, calls and puts. A *call* grants its owner the right, but not the obligation, to buy 100 shares of stock. This right can be exercised at a fixed price but must be taken before the expiration date of the option. A trader who sells a call grants these rights to the buyer.

    A *put* grants its owner the right, but not the obligation, to sell 100 shares of an identified underlying security at a fixed price. This right has to be exercised before the put expires. A trader who sells a put grants these rights to the buyer.

2. *The underlying security.* Every option is tied to a specific underlying security (the "underlying"), which may be a stock, index, or exchange-traded fund. Each option controls 100 shares of the underlying, and as the price changes, so does the value of the option.

3. *The strike price.* Options are further identified by the strike. This is the price per share at which an option can be exercised. Thus, if the underlying price moves above the call's strike, the call will become more valuable because its strike is fixed. If the underlying price moves below the strike of a put, the put becomes more valuable.

    When the underlying price is higher than a call's strike or lower than a put's strike, the option is in the money. When the underlying price is lower than a call's strike or higher than a put's strike, the option is out of the money. If the strike and underlying price are identical, the option is at the money.

    These relationships are shown in figure 1.1. The example identifies the price of $12 as the strike. Whenever the underlying price is also $12 per share, all options with that

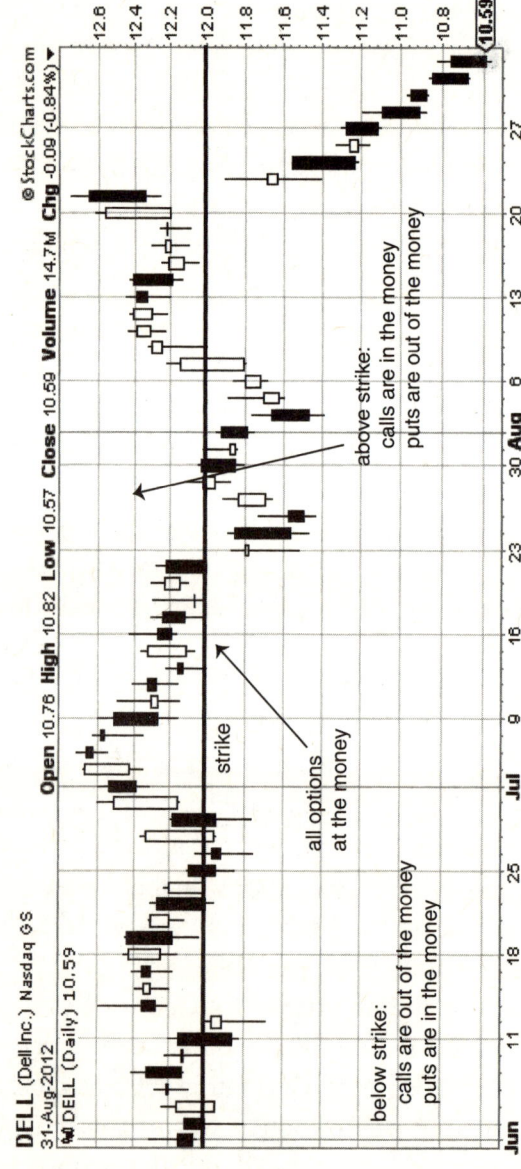

Figure 1.1 "Moneyness" of the option
Source: StockCharts.com.

strike are at the money. When the price is above $12, calls are in the money, and puts are out of the money. And when the underlying price is below $12 per share, the opposite is true: Puts are in the money, and calls are out of the money.

This status of each option, known as its "moneyness," is a key to the swing trading program. The strike price identifies not only the point at which an option can be exercised, but also the point at which the intrinsic value of the option begins to accumulate.

4. *Expiration date.* The fourth term is the expiration date. Every option expires on a predetermined date. It is the third Saturday of the expiration month (and the last trading day is the Friday just before).

On the expiration date, every outstanding option pegged to it expires and becomes worthless. On the last trading day, options in the money are exercised. If the owner of an option does not take action, *automatic exercise* takes place. The clearing company exercises every in-the-money option when the holder does not provide instructions. This applies to the majority of options on US stocks.

Long and Short Options

Swing traders using shares of stock have a serious dilemma. When the swing is at the bottom, positions are easily opened by purchasing shares. The idea is to hold until the swing turns and moves up; the shares are then sold at a profit. However, with the swing at the top of the cycle, what happens next?

The traditional system is to short shares of stock to play a bearish, downward move. This presents numerous problems. First of all, the brokerage firm probably will require a trader to sell at least 100 shares. The process is complex: To go short with stock, you have to borrow shares from your broker and then sell them. You pay interest on the margin account where the shares were borrowed. In addition, you risk an increase in share price. In that case, you have to put more capital on deposit to meet the margin call that results. The market risk is substantial because in theory at least, share value can continue to rise indefinitely.

Because of these complex costs and risks, many swing traders avoid bearish swings and only open positions at the bottom. This means they go long, wait for a price increase, and then sell. Another swing is not made until the swing once again falls and reaches a reversal signal. Under this system, only half of the swings are exploited.

A "reversal signal" tells you the direction of price movement is likely to change. Such signals appear in the form of traditional technical price patterns (double tops and bottoms, triangles, price gaps, tests of support and resistance, or head and shoulders, for example), candlestick indicators, volume spikes, or momentum oscillators, tests of the strength or weakness of a trend. A signal may be bullish (likely to reverse to the upside) or bearish (likely to reverse to the downside). When stock is used to swing trade, a bearish move consists of shorting stock.

With options, this problem of needing to short stock is eliminated. If you want to limit risk exposure, your swing trading program can consist entirely of long calls at the bottom of the swing and long puts at the top. When the cycle bottoms out and a reversal signal appears, you buy calls, wait for the price to rise, and then sell to close. When the swing has moved up to a peak, you spot reversal and buy puts. You then wait for the price to fall, and then you sell the puts. In both up and down cycles, your exposure is limited to the cost of the option.

A long position (opened with the sequence buy-hold-sell) is the best known among traders. A short position (sell-hold-buy) is not as well-known, but it represents the opposite kind of move. Options are quite flexible so you can open either long or short positions for swing trading. The order sequence is:

For long positions
   1. Buy to open
   2. (Hold)
   3. Sell to close

For short positions
1. Sell to open
2. (Hold)
3. Buy to close

When you sell to open a position, you are paid a premium. When you close the short position, you have to fund the buy to close the order. A short position is further distinguished by being either covered or uncovered.

A *covered call* combines 100 shares of stock with one short call. If the underlying price rises above the call's strike, those 100 shares are called away by exercise of the call. So it makes sense to pick a strike above the original basis in stock, so that exercising the call creates a capital gain rather than a capital loss.

An *uncovered call* (also called a naked call) is created by selling the call without the coverage of 100 shares of stock. In the event of exercising the option, the call seller will have to pay the difference between the current value of stock and the strike price. This difference, minus the premium received for selling the call, may be a loss that will be greater if the underlying price rises well above strike. For example, you sell a 35 call (meaning the strike price is $35 per share—options parlance is to express strikes without dollar signs) and receive a premium of 3 ($300). (In options parlance, the dollar amount is reduced to the dollar value per share and expressed without dollar signs; thus, "3" means $300). The stock price rises to $42 per share and the 35 call is exercised. Your net loss is 4 ($400) before calculating transaction costs:

Current price of 100 shares of stock	$4,200
Less: Strike price value	3,500
Net difference	$ 700
Minus: short-call premium	300
Net loss before transaction costs	$ 400

A *covered put* is created by selling one put when you also have shorted 100 shares of stock. In the event of a rise in the underlying price, premium from the covered put provides a degree of safety;

however, if the underlying price rises beyond the level of this discount, a loss will occur. In that respect, a put cannot truly be covered as a call can be. For example, you have shorted 100 shares of stock at the initial price of $35 per share. If the stock price declines, you profit by $100 for each point of decline. However, you also sell a covered put for 4 ($400). If the stock price rises to $4,200, you lose 3 ($300):

Current price of 100 shares of stock	$4,200
Less: original value of shorted stock	3,500
Net difference	$ 700
Minus: short-put premium	400
Net loss before transaction costs	$ 300

The covered put is not the opposite of a covered call because a loss can be realized. With a covered call, the "cover" is complete. The only loss is the opportunity loss incurred. In other words, if you had not written a covered call, you could have made a higher profit by holding stock. In the case of a covered put, that cover is limited to the amount of premium received.

An *uncovered put* (also called a naked put) involves selling a put and receiving a premium. It can be closed, rolled forward, allowed to expire, or it can be exercised. In that case, you will have 100 shares put to you at the strike, meaning you are required to buy 100 shares at that fixed strike. So if the stock value declines to $31 per share and you have sold an uncovered put with a 35 strike, your loss on the exercised put is four points, or $400. This loss is reduced by the amount of premium you received when you sold the put.

TYPES OF VALUE IN THE OPTION PREMIUM

Option premium consists of three distinct and different kinds of value: Intrinsic, extrinsic (or implied volatility value), and time value.

Intrinsic value exists only when an option is in the money (underlying price higher than the call strike or lower than the put strike). Intrinsic value is easily computed as equal to the number of points in the money. For example, if a call's strike is 12 and the current value per share of the underlying is $12.50, the call is 0.50 in the money. If the put's strike is 12 and the current value per share is $11.00, the put has one point (1.00 or $100) of intrinsic value.

Extrinsic value (implied volatility value) is the most complex portion of the option premium. It reflects changes in volatility; that is, when risk is greater, volatility rises and increases the premium on options. When volatility falls, so does option premium. Extrinsic value is most often lumped together with time value (below), and the reasons for or against this combination are debatable.

The argument favoring combination of these two is based on the idea that volatility directly affects time value and may increase or decrease it. The argument against inclusion is based on the belief that time value is unchanging and that any variation in premium beyond the predictable time decay every option experiences is attributable to volatility.

As a swing trader, you do not have to be especially concerned with the debate over extrinsic and time value. The strategy, as explained in coming chapters, is going to work best when options are due to expire within a month or less. At this point in the option cycle, time value is close to zero, so an at-the-money or in-the-money position is most likely to respond to changes in the underlying point for point. That is exactly what you hope to see when using options for swing trading.

Time value, whether treated as a stand-alone form of premium or lumped in with volatility, is going to decline over time. This effect, time decay, speeds up so that during the last two months of the option cycle, time value is decelerating rapidly. During the last few weeks of the cycle, time value falls at its fastest rate, finally reaching zero at expiration.

Time value falls on a trajectory similar to the decline in the balance on a home mortgage. Amortized over 30 years, the mortgage is only one-half paid off at about year 24 or 25. The rest gets paid down during the remaining five years. Time value appears to decay at the same slow rate for options far from expiration and then speeds up as shown in figure 1.2.

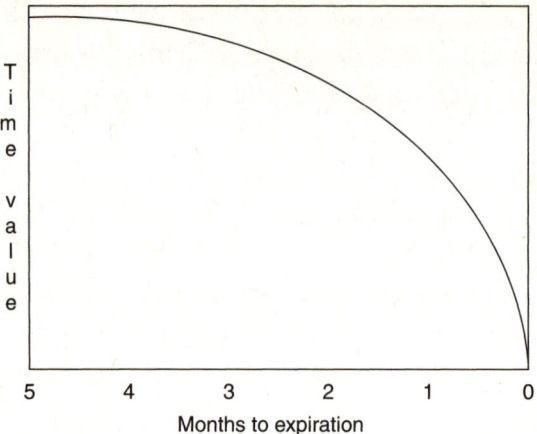

Figure 1.2 Time value and time decay
Source: Figure created by author.

The three types of premium—intrinsic, extrinsic, and time value—make up the total premium value of every option. The important fact about accelerated time decay is that it may offset the increase in intrinsic value as expiration approaches.

For example, a long option was purchased for 5 ($500) and as expiration is nearing, premium value fell to 3. However, the option was at the money. Over a one-month period, the option moved 1.5 points in the money, but the overall premium value declined by 2 points. This was due to time decay.

This illustrates why swing trading relies on the use of very short-term options at the money or in the money. If positive underlying movement were offset by time decay, even a well-timed move could end up losing money. If you use options expiring in less than one month, very little time value remains in the premium. This makes profitable outcomes more likely. Even so, you will struggle against time value whenever you are using long options and even when close to expiration. With this in mind, some swing trading strategies are based on using short options or combinations of options.

Most options strategies involving long positions are a balance between time and cost. The longer the time left until expiration, the higher the cost. So traders usually want the longest possible time for the least possible cost. Swing trading is an exception to this rule. Because the typical swing lasts between three and five days, using soon-to-expire contracts makes the most sense for three reasons:

1. *Short-term options are very cheap.* With most or all of the time value gone, short-term options are going to be very cheap. In fact, they represent the best form of leverage for that very reason. For example, an at-the-money (ATM) option expiring in two weeks and costing 0.50 ($50) on a $40 stock is a great value. For only $50, you are able to control 100 shares of stock by owning the option. And because it is ATM, this option is going to track movement in the money (ITM) as close as possible to a point-for-point change—because the premium will consist mostly of intrinsic value. When the option is ITM, it means the stock price is above the call's strike (or below the put's strike). The moneyness of the option is crucial for appreciating how intrinsic value changes:

   Call
   At the money: underlying is identical to the strike
   Out of the money: underlying is lower than the strike
   In the money: underlying is higher than the strike.

   Put
   At the money: underlying is identical to the strike
   Out of the money: underlying is higher than the strike
   In the money: underlying is lower than the strike.

   Can the premium ever be 100% intrinsic? Probably not. There will always be some remnant of time value up to the day of expiration, and extrinsic value (volatility) may still be a factor in the overall valuation of the option. However, this moment in the option's lifespan—the last two to four weeks before expiration—is the most reactive time between the option premium and the underlying price . This makes these options ideal for swing trading.

2. *Properly selected, these options tend to respond point-for-point to movement of the underlying security.* The properly selected

option is the best for swing trading. A properly selected option is one ATM or very slightly ITM. As the underlying moves in the direction of placing the option ITM (upward for long calls, downward for long puts), the increased value of that option is going to be realized immediately.

The combination of time and proximity makes options-based swing trading a potentially profitable strategy. The time has to be very short in order to minimize time value, and proximity means the option's strike has to be as close as possible to the current value of the underlying. As long as you develop a reliable method for spotting likely reversal patterns and confirmation in the underlying price, the option is more likely than average to become profitable very rapidly. You will not time trades perfectly, of course, but using these options along with smart analytical charting and confirmation tools, you will improve the rate of well-timed entry and exit decisions.

3. *The lack of time value means little adjustment will be made to premium value.* The problem with options expiring more than two months from now is that their premium is not always responsive to movement of the underlying. Thus, many holders of long options have observed that the underlying price may move ITM by two or three points with little or no change in the option value. Why is this? The theory of intrinsic value states that the option is supposed to change point for point when it is ITM.

What actually occurs is an offset. When the option has more than two months until expiration, even intrinsic price movement is not a guarantee of ITM status by expiration. As a consequence, increased intrinsic value may be offset by decreased extrinsic value (volatility). Some analysts lump this in with time value, but it is not logical to conclude that time value changes due to movement of the underlying. Time value is affected by only one thing, and that is the passage of time. Volatility, however, reflects changes in the perception of future value; that is, when an option expires more than two months in the future, ITM movement adds risk rather than reducing it. Thus, when intrinsic value rises, premium value reacts to a lesser degree because extrinsic value falls. This is a reflection of the added uncertainty of ITM status that far in the future.

For swing trading purposes, once the option is inside of the two-month zone, this offset between intrinsic and extrinsic value is much less of a factor; once inside the one-month zone, it is barely a factor at all for ATM or ITM contracts. That is why selecting these short-term options makes sense, especially since the swing itself is not expected to last more than three to five days.

These observations explain why using soon-to-expire long options for swing trading is preferable over longer-term options. However, considerations of time affect the use of shorted options as well. When you have shorted an option, the rapid decline in time value is just as much a benefit as it is a problem for long positions. The more decline you experience, the more profitable an open short position becomes. This opens up a broad range of possible swing trading strategies using short options.

Rolling Techniques

Whenever you have opened a short position, rolling is one of the possibilities. Short positions include covered or uncovered calls or puts. On any of these, if the option moves in the money, it creates exercise risk. While some strategies are designed to accept exercise (covered calls, for example, might be designed to generate exercise and a resulting capital gain on the underlying), not all short positions are set up for this outcome.

The possibilities include the following:

- *Exercise*, in which case 100 shares of stock will be called away (exercise of a short call) or 100 shares of stock will be put to you (exercise of a short put). When a call is exercised, the current value of the underlying will be higher than the strike. And when a put is exercised, you acquire shares above current value. With these points in mind, accepting exercise is not always desirable.

- *Expiration*, at which point the option becomes worthless and all premium received represents profit. Many options, when deep out of the money, are simply allowed to expire because there is only a remote possibility of movement in the money. However, when proximity of strike to current price is not deep, it may be prudent to close the position and take a small profit rather than risk adverse price movement and exercise.
- *Closing* is the taking of a profit or a small loss in order to avoid the possibility of exercise. Closing also frees up capital and margin so that subsequent positions may be opened. Closing makes sense as a means of mitigating or avoiding the risk of exercise or just for taking profits because they are available.
- *Covering* is an action taken to reduce the threat of exercise of an originally uncovered position. Covering is accomplished for a call by buying shares of stock or, for either option, by opening a long position. The long position may be used to address exercise if the original short option ends up in the money. The problem with cover via a long option is that it costs money, often more money than the original income from opening the short position. Cover may involve positions expiring later or expiring at the same time but with different strikes. For example, if one-point increments are available, opening a long position one point from the original short caps exercise loss at one point but also requires payment of premium for the new option. This is not desirable in either case because it translates into accepting a loss.

All of these potential outcomes contain flaws in one form or another. Unless you want a covered call to be exercised and stock called away, it is almost always desirable to avoid exercise. Once an option has moved in the money and exercise is a probable outcome, it also means that greater profits are possible if exercise is avoided.

If a call is in the money, it means the current price per share is higher than the strike. By avoiding exercise, you may be able to increase profits upon later exercise or at least to defer exercise for the moment. If a put is in the money, exercise results in your acquiring shares above current market value. The only ways out of this situation are to (a) wait for the underlying to rebound, (b) write covered calls against the underlying, or (c) avoid exercise to create future profits or defer the loss.

Loss avoidance or elimination is accomplished by yet another choice open to you if you have shorted an option, namely:

Rolling consists of closing the current short position (entering a buy to close order) and then opening a later-expiring position (entering a new sell to open order). This takes the current position out of exercise range in most cases. Most short options are exercised on the last trading day, the third Friday of exercise month. However, many are also exercised immediately prior to ex-dividend date for the dividend month. (This points out the strategic importance of avoiding the exercise month for short-call positions if you don't want to get exercised.)

Not all short calls are subject to exercise right before ex-dividend date even if they are in the money. A holder of long calls will exercise only if the net cost of buying the call will be greater than the in-the-money value adjusted by the dividend dollar value. This eliminates many long-call holders and also explains why not all open positions get exercised at this point.

Rolling for any short position can take several forms. These include:

Rolling forward to the same strike—when you replace a current month position with a later-expiring one at the same strike, this creates a net credit because there will be more time value in the later position. Thus, the forward roll appears to be a sensible exercise-avoidance strategy that also generates more income. However, there are three problems with this type of forward roll. First, it delays the period during which you remain exposed not only to exercise but also to the requirements to maintain margin. Second, you might roll forward into an ex-dividend month, thus increasing your risk of early exercise. Third, if the underlying has moved upward, rolling to the same strike might convert a qualified call into an unqualified call. If you have owned the underlying less than a year, this means the count toward long-term capital gains is tolled until the option is closed; meanwhile, if exercise does occur, your underlying profit will be short-term even if by that time you have owned the stock for more than a year.

Rolling a call forward to a higher strike or rolling a put forward to a lower strike—a forward roll may also consist of replacing a current strike and expiration with a higher strike (for a call) or a lower strike (for a put), also with later expiration. This not only defers the threat of expiration, but it sets up a higher profit or reduced loss if the later position is eventually exercised. This forward-and-up or forward-and-down approach may be possible at a net breakeven or small credit, but it is more likely to create a net debit. Traders may rationalize this by comparing the net debit to the improved outcome scenario. For example, if a call's strike is increased by 2.5 points and the net debt is one point, the outcome is positive by 1.5 points, assuming exercise does occur later. You need to adjust your overall net basis in order to identify an adjusted break-even point when offsetting changed strikes for rolling debits so you can avoid creating an overall net loss in this forward roll.

Rolling a call to a higher strike, or rolling a put to a lower strike, with the same expiration–this form of rolling keeps the expiration at the same level and creates a net debit. It is advantageous only when the difference in the premium levels (net debit) is smaller than the changed exercise value (smaller loss or larger profit). This is difficult to accomplish, however, due to the offsetting extrinsic value likely to be found in options of the same expiration but with varying strikes.

BASIC STRATEGIES

Options strategies come in dozens of variations, some are high risk and others are very conservative. Some strategies are direction neutral; that is, profits are achieved with underlying movement in either direction but require a minimum number of points.

The basic long positions or short positions are only starting points for the development of dozens of other strategies. Swing trading strategies can be based on many of these variations, including:

- long calls and long puts,
- long calls and short uncovered calls,
- long calls and short covered calls,
- long and short covered calls employing ratio writes,
- long and short puts,
- short calls and puts,
- synthetic options positions, and
- multiple contract and weighting in ratio calendar spreads.

These eight swing trading strategies all employ options in different configurations. They may be used in combination or as primary emphasis within the swing trading program. The key in selecting one strategy over another is to base the decision on risk levels as well as on the current price pattern and likelihood of reversal of the underlying price.

Basic options strategies beyond the use of long or short options by themselves include:

Spreads, the simultaneous opening of positions with the same strike and different expiration (horizontal spreads), the same expiration and different strikes (vertical spreads), or different expirations and strikes (diagonal spreads). These are further distinguished by selection of either long or short contracts and by the use of either calls or puts. Expanded variations include combinations of bullish and bearish in the same strategy or long and short in the same strategy. Spreads can be configured in dozens of ways.

Straddles, the combination of option positions with the same strike and expiration. These may consist of calls and puts, either long or short. The straddle generally creates either a limited loss zone with profit zones above and below or a limited profit zone with loss zones above and below. As with all combination strategies, the selection of long or short straddles should be based on accurate perceptions of risk and reward and a willingness to accept those risks. Within a swing trading program, a straddle is appropriate only if it is perceived as likely to generate short-term profits for acceptable risks. Straddles often are not closed all at once; one side or the other may be closed upon becoming profitable, with the other side left open until it is later closed or allowed to expire. However, one danger in the closing of part of a position is that a relatively safe short position may end up exposed as an uncovered position due to closing part of the position. You need to be aware of the benefits and consequences of closing positions at different times.

THE LEVERAGE ADVANTAGE OF OPTIONS

The strategic distinctions between single options and combinations of option positions define levels of risk and hedging that are possible in an options-based swing trading strategy. Options can be used to hedge risk, control and create profits, or leverage capital. Leverage is the attribute making options ideal for swing trading.

For a small percentage of the cost of 100 shares (approximately 5%) you can control those 100 shares by buying options in place of stock. This means that market risk is lower because the most you can lose is the cost of the option itself. One way to look at this is that options keep your maximum loss at 5% of the value of 100 shares. But there is more to this than just risk control. Options also enable you to swing trade with greater flexibility.

If you are working with a capital base of $20,000, you can swing trade with 100 shares of a $200 stock or 100 shares of two $100 stocks, for example. But with options, you can diversify among many more issues than you can with shares of stock. So with lower risk and greater flexibility, you need less movement in the underlying for the swing trade to become profitable.

An offsetting factor is the margin requirement. You cannot just trade options to the maximum of your capital base because margin requirements limit how much exposure you can accept. This means that you have limitations on the scope of swing trading, just as you do if you use shares of stock. It is not the leverage by itself that makes options attractive, but the reduced risk and greater flexibility you gain. An ATM or ITM option is likely to become profitable with very little movement in the underlying, which means that swing trades can turn into profitable trades within one or two days or even within one trading session. This is less likely when you are trading with shares of stock.

For example, if your goal is to close a position if it doubles in value or when it loses half its value, consider how differently stock and options work. With a $40 stock, you would need the price to move to either $80 or $20 before acting on this goal. So for stock, it is more likely that you would set a dollar-based goal and bailout level. However, if you can buy an option for $200 on that same stock, you can reach the double or half goal with only a couple of points of intrinsic value movement. Option flexibility is attractive for swing trading because you can reach either percentage-based or dollar-based goals very rapidly.

A $40 stock rising to $42 is a 5% gain. But a $200 option on the same issue doubling in value after a two-point underlying price move is a 100% profit.

All options strategies should be evaluated as potential vehicles for swing trading based on their cost or benefit, risk levels, and potential profit or loss. Analysis of options strategies is most accurate when all outcomes are considered. If a loss is among the possibilities, how much of a loss is likely? How can that loss be mitigated or avoided? And does the risk of loss match your personal risk tolerance?

Swing trading, like all strategies, will work for you only if the appropriate options strategies are used. A strategy is appropriate only if it is fully understood (including potential profit as well as potential loss) and only if those levels are suitable.

Suitability involves not only your tolerance for risk but also your experience and knowledge about options, an appreciation for the likely range of outcomes, and your ability to set and follow your own rules or "self-discipline risk." Most options traders understand from experience that setting rules is easy, but following them is much harder. Success in trading options within a swing trading program requires development of a clear series of goals (relating to profit as well as loss levels) and the ability to follow those rules once you set them.

Options form a good basis for swing trading. The next chapter introduces a review of the basics of swing trading and shows how options are a good match within a swing trading strategy.

CHAPTER 2

SWING TRADING: THE BASICS

> No endeavor that is worthwhile is simple in prospect; if it is right, it will be simple in retrospect.
> Edward Teller, *The Pursuit of Simplicity*, 1980

YOU HAVE A GREAT ADVANTAGE IN THE MARKET.

Individual investors can move quickly in and out of positions without having to worry about the effect of their decisions on broader market prices. This is no small point in the evaluation of swing trading strategies. Institutions cannot swing trade effectively due to their size in terms of dollar value and shares owned.

Large institutional traders transact billions of dollars each day, which means that they have maximum influence over the market as a whole in terms of trading activity. Institutional trades account for about 70% of all trades in the market, so their influence cannot be ignored. However, do institutional trades distort or control stock prices? Evidence suggests that they do not.

Two theories about institutional influence are worth understanding. First is the effect of *herding*, a belief that institutional demand destabilizes stock prices. Herding is a practice among institutional investors in which managers follow one another in and out of the same issues. This crowd mentality, in fact, is witnessed not only among institutional investors, but also among individuals ("retail investors").

The second theory is that institutions tend to *not* make decisions based on fundamentals, in spite of widespread belief that they do. The belief is that because fundamental strategies take too long to create profits, institutional money managers tend to follow technical and short-term strategies. In other words, institutional managers may acknowledge the advantages of short-term trading strategies such as swing trading. The big question is: do such practices affect prices in the broad market?

An extensive study of this question included price analysis of hundreds of stocks traded by institutions. That study concluded that there is

> no consistent evidence of a significant positive correlation between changes in institutional holdings and contemporaneous excess returns.... We conclude that there is no solid evidence in our data that institutional investors destabilize prices of individual stocks. Instead, the emerging image is that institutions follow a broad range of styles and strategies and that their trades offset each other without having a large impact on prices.[1]

It appears that the belief in institutional power to control prices is not well founded. In fact, it seems more likely that individuals have a great advantage in exploiting short-term price trends because they do not have to figure out how to transact thousands of shares at the same time.

This is the essence of swing trading.

The conclusion of the study that institutional managers do not necessarily follow fundamental principals is startling and will surprise many conservative mutual fund investors, shareholders in insurance companies, and beneficiaries of pension plans, all of whom take comfort in the fundamental and conservative investing objectives so often stated by institutions. In fact, those money managers see the same things that swing traders see, momentary advantages in price trends that can be acted upon to create small but consistent profits.

Swing trading is a contrarian approach to extremely short-term price movement. Anyone who tracks the market has observed that in specific conditions stock prices tend to move to an exaggerated degree, but correct within a few sessions. For example, an earnings report misses estimates by a few cents, and the stock plummets four points. Within two days, the entire drop (or most of it) has been recovered, and prices stabilize within the previously established trading range.

Why does this happen? The tendency of the market is to be extremely chaotic in the short-term trading cycle due to the attributes controlling the market. The crowd, that nameless, faceless majority, tends to act and react emotionally. The two prevailing emotions in the market are greed (seen when prices rise or when good news appears) and panic (seen when prices fall or bad news appears). The consequence is that price movement is exaggerated.

The swing trader acknowledges this irrational attribute of the market and resists the temptation to follow greed and panic reactions. Taking a contrarian approach, the swing trader recognizes these overreactions and does the opposite of the crowd. When prices jump suddenly in an exaggerated reaction to good news, the majority tends to want to jump on board and get in on the action. This means a majority of buy orders show up right at the top of the swing. The swing trader looks for this irrationally exuberant timing and takes a bearish position, knowing that the exaggerated jump in price is likely to retreat.

The same is true with bad news. A majority of traders sell when bad news is announced, driving prices down and creating panic among even more traders. This is why a small negative earnings report might cause a drop of several points in prices. The swing trader recognizes the panic moment and takes up a bullish position, knowing that prices will be likely to recover these losses.

Swing trading is contrarian, not because timing of entry and exit are the opposite of those chosen by the majority of traders at such times, but because the decision is rational rather than emotional. This is essentially the key to contrarian investing—following the logic of market movement rather than following the emotional overreaction of the majority.

IT'S ALL ABOUT TIMING

Swing trading sounds easy, and the underlying premise is straightforward. But timing is never easy. With this in mind, the premise behind swing trading is not that you are going to be right 100% of the time, but that applying a few logical principles will improve the frequency of profits.

Every trader understands the distinction between misreading a chart and timing a chart. If you misread, it means you expect the price to move in one direction but instead it moves in the opposite direction. As common an error as this is, an equally frustrating one is that of incorrectly timing entry or exit of trades. You might be entirely right in your expectations of a trend's direction and duration, but when do you enter a position and when do you exit?

Every trend (including the very short-term trend) is different and will perform in its own way. Some reversals, for example, occur quickly and turn sharply. Others provide a signal but experience a delay, and during this lag time leftover momentum keeps the price moving in the established direction before it turns. Other reversal signals are followed by a period of sideways movement before the trend reverses. And, of course, some reversal signals are quite strong and are accompanied by equally strong confirmation, but even so they turn out to be false signals.

Timing is the key to improving your entry and exit success. However, you cannot expect 100% accuracy in entry or exit, and in some cases the outcome will mislead you. So the goal has to be to improve your timing, not to remove all risk. Here are some guidelines:

1. *Diversify your trading risks.* Traders fall into patterns, and one of the most destructive is to follow up a successful trade by doubling down, putting even more money at risk hoping for more profits. Remember that you can never achieve

100% perfect timing, and putting too much into a single trade eventually will create a very large loss. For this reason, your trade increments should be divided up so that a single loss will not be devastating.
2. *Always act with confirmation.* No trade should be entered or exited based on a single indicator. A basic premise underlying all technical analysis is especially applicable to swing trading: In a timing move, always require signal and confirmation before you act.
3. *Rate signals based on strength and reliability.* Some signals are exceptionally strong, whereas others have only about a 50% chance of being correct and cannot be used reliably. For example, a short list of candlestick reversal signals of exceptional reliability should include the engulfing pattern, three white soldiers, and three black crows. All of these occur often and are extremely reliable. Signals with closer to 50% reliability (harami and doji, for example) can be dismissed as leading signals, but when used to confirm other reversal signals they may have greater value.[2]
4. *There is nothing wrong with taking profits.* It is easy to overlook the simple truth of this statement. Swing traders may easily become focused on the need to find a signal before they act. However, there is a distinction between a swing trade and a profit trade, for lack of better terms. In a swing trade, you expect timing to guide your judgment. In a profit trade, profits are taken when they materialize, even if the swing signal is not present. Thus, taking profits is a perfectly acceptable strategy even if it means timing was poor because greater profits could have been earned by waiting.
5. *Once you see that timing was off, close the position.* No strategic analysis will produce 100% perfect timing, and some portion of your trades will move in the wrong direction, often right after you commit capital. The purpose to a timing strategy is to improve the frequency of well-timed trades, but how do you manage trades that are not working? Avoid the tendency to stubbornly hold on even when you can see that the price is contradicting the signals. Cut your losses and close down the

trade immediately and try again in different circumstances. That is the smart swing trading move.

Short-Term Price Cycles

Swing traders are visual analysts. They study charts looking for predictable price cycles and patterns. Some very clear and repetitive patterns can be found, and their meaning in terms of future price movement is a powerful tool for timing trades.

Among these patterns are the exceptionally strong candlestick short-term trend reversal indicators (notably the engulfing pattern, three white crows, and three black soldiers, all of which occur often), and in Western technical analysis, there are well-known patterns such as triangles and wedges, double tops and bottoms, and price gaps.

Because charting is widespread and instant charts are available online free of charge, more people today consider themselves "chartists" than ever before. With this free access, thanks to the power of the Internet, the world of technical analysis no longer belongs only to a small number of insiders of those willing to pay thousands to a charting service. This free access has vastly expanded the population of technicians.

Swing traders who also are serious students of technical analysis are aware, however, that this larger population of chart watchers does not have an increased level of expertise. It only increases the number of participants, including those whose knowledge and interpretive skills are as limited as they were before free access to charts. The truth is, many traders do not want to put in the time to learn charting skills; this population of chart watchers includes many who believe that solely because they have free charts, they understand how to interpret the signals on those charts.

Increased availability of charts might cheapen the perceived importance of study and acquisition of knowledge, and a broader population of chart watchers is less likely to be skilled than a smaller core of chartists. This is a great advantage for swing traders. Just as swing traders exploit the emotional gut reactions of greed and panic, they may also exploit the tendency of a majority of technical analysts to misread the signs or to place too much weight on unconfirmed reversal signals.

One symptom of this is a widespread belief among technical investors in a skill set based solely on analysis of charts, but without any serious acquisition of analytical abilities. A truly skilled chartist knows that the first step in seeking reversal is to look for repetitive patterns that have proven reliable in the past. The less skilled technicians want a broader, more esoteric and complex series of signaling methods and ignore the possibility that the signals these produce might be far less reliable. In other words, finding a reversal signal does not mean action is demanded in response. Experience tells the skilled chartist that skill is required in recognizing false signals as well as reliable ones, in relying on trusted confirmation, and in avoiding self-fulfilling prophecies (if you think a stock's price "should" rise because you own shares, you are likely to notice only bullish signals and fail to see bearish ones).

Price cycles do occur, according not only to the Dow Theory and its three trend types but also according to swing traders and their extremely short-term focus. Prices move through price cycles of varying duration, but those price cycles repeat. Beyond the cyclical realities of trading ranges, tops and bottoms, and sideways movement (congestion), swing traders can exploit great opportunities not so much by seeing these patterns but by seeing how a price *departs* from them due to the common overreactions based on greed and panic.

As prices rise, the greed reaction is a form of addiction, a thrill that traders experience as they acquire shares to take part in coming riches or continue to hold even in the face of reduced upward momentum. What many fail to realize, however, is that the downtrend causes just as much addictive behavior, just in the opposite direction. The uptrend prompts greed and the euphoria that goes with it, whereas the downtrend prompts panic and the dread it creates. Both of these reactions are irrational, and swing traders place themselves in a position to recognize that uptrends and downtrends of short duration are simply price cycles of the moment and not causes for greed/euphoria or panic/dread.

Traders subject to the emotional irrationality of the market make the mistake of not recognizing the role of price patterns. . And so an uptrend and its promise of fast profits is interpreted as a reward for being a smart trader, and a downtrend is seen as a punishment, betrayal, or broken promise. None of these emotional responses are valid, of course, because the market does not have a consciousness. It simply moves in response to the underlying causes, and price patterns are the outcomes—impersonal, unintentional, unconscious, and *natural* in the auction marketplace.

Swing traders further realize that price cycles are not continuous. A sudden move above or below rational trading levels is an opportunity, not because it represents a price pattern, but because it is a departure from that pattern. Most of the time, prices are likely to move within a predictable pattern, and swing trading opportunities occur as exceptions. Most traders are impatient, addicted to the thrill of the trend, and unaware of their flaws in how they observe and react when prices do move. Swing traders tend to be those off to the side, observing price but, equally important, also observing the behavior of other traders.

KEY ASPECTS OF THE CHART: RESISTANCE AND SUPPORT

Great attention has to be paid to the concept of the trading range. Technical analysis is based on the study of relationships between price and how it moves toward (or beyond) resistance and support levels.

Resistance and support represent the borders of the trading range, so any important reversal signals found at or near these levels is going to have more meaning than the same signals appearing at midrange. If price moves above resistance or below support, reversal is highly likely as well. At these points in the price trend, resistance and support levels are tested. Will price retreat, reaffirming the current trading range? Or will it continue above or below, setting a new trading range for the underlying security?

Swing traders especially are aware of some facts concerning resistance and support, such as the following:

1. *Reversal is more likely at the trading range borders than anywhere else.* The resistance and support price levels—whether horizontal or dynamic—are the true tests of trend strength and momentum. The appearance of a reversal signal gains power and importance when it shows up at these levels.
2. *Gapping price movement through resistance or support adds to the likelihood of reversal.* Confirming a reversal signal, gapping price action adds to a likely reversal. This is especially the case when the gap takes price above resistance or below support; price is then likely to reverse and fill the gap, but if it does not, then the newly set trading range is even stronger. Another condition worth watching is the runaway gap, a series of price gaps over several sessions moving through resistance or support. This demonstrates strong momentum and adds to the likelihood that the breakout will hold.
3. *These price levels are guidelines only, but they are important.* Swing traders do not care whether prices move higher or lower; they only want to be positioned to exploit that direction and to recognize reversal when it occurs. Resistance and support are the "red zones" of reversal where price direction and momentum matter the most.

Reversal and support come in several shapes and sizes. They are crucial to effective swing trading, so six different types are illustrated below.

HORIZONTAL RANGE

First is the standard horizontal trading range, in which both resistance and support remain at the same level with prices ranging in between. For example, Wells Fargo's chart in figure 2.1 displays a horizontal trading range for six weeks before prices broke out above resistance. Notice how price levels tested resistance briefly but never closed above it and how support was tested three times. All of these tests were in the form of upper and lower shadows, but no opening or closing price levels violated the trading range.

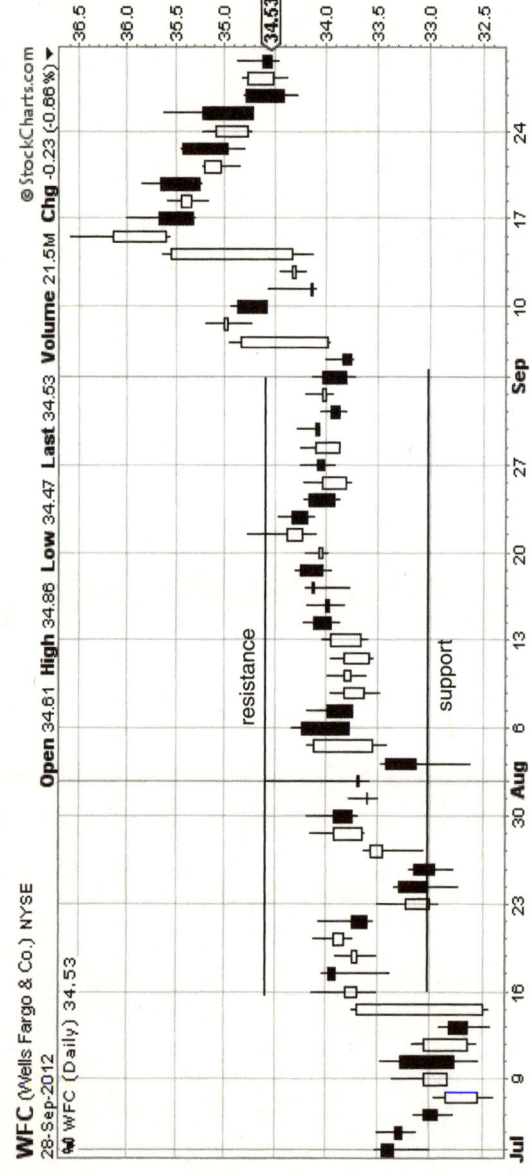

Figure 2.1 Horizontal resistance and support
Source: StockCharts.com.

Triangle Continuation

The second type of trading range pattern is the triangle. In this format, one side or the other remains flat while the other side narrows and moves toward the first. This creates a triangle, which is a continuation pattern. For example, the chart of 3M in figure 2.2 consists of flat resistance and rising support. As a continuation would be expected to behave, once the triangle narrowed, price levels broke through and moved above resistance.

Wedge Reversal

The wedge is similar to the triangle, but this is a reversal formation. In the wedge, both resistance and support move in the same direction, but the range narrows. This is an exceptionally strong reversal signal. For example, in figure 2.3 Yahoo! has two different wedges, a bearish reversal and then a bullish reversal. At the conclusion of the first (bearish) wedge, a large downward gap confirmed the bearish change of direction. However, even as price levels continued to decline, a bullish wedge formed, predicting a reversal to the upside. In fact, by the end of the period the price level had returned to its starting point.

Rising Range

Some trading ranges remain consistent in terms of breadth of trading between resistance and support, even as price levels rise. This rising range provides a degree of certainty, especially if the breadth remains consistent over an extended period of time. For example, in figure 2.4 Exxon Mobil rose consistently over a three-month period, but the trading range remained within 2.5 points. A single decline below support quickly reversed back into range.

Falling Range

The range may also decline over time, and the tendency described above may be observed. The breadth of the range remains a constant even when overall price levels fall. For example, on the chart of Potash Corp. in figure 2.5, a sharp decline over five weeks occurred, but the breadth remained within 2.5 points. Some momentary moves both above resistance and below support were corrected immediately.

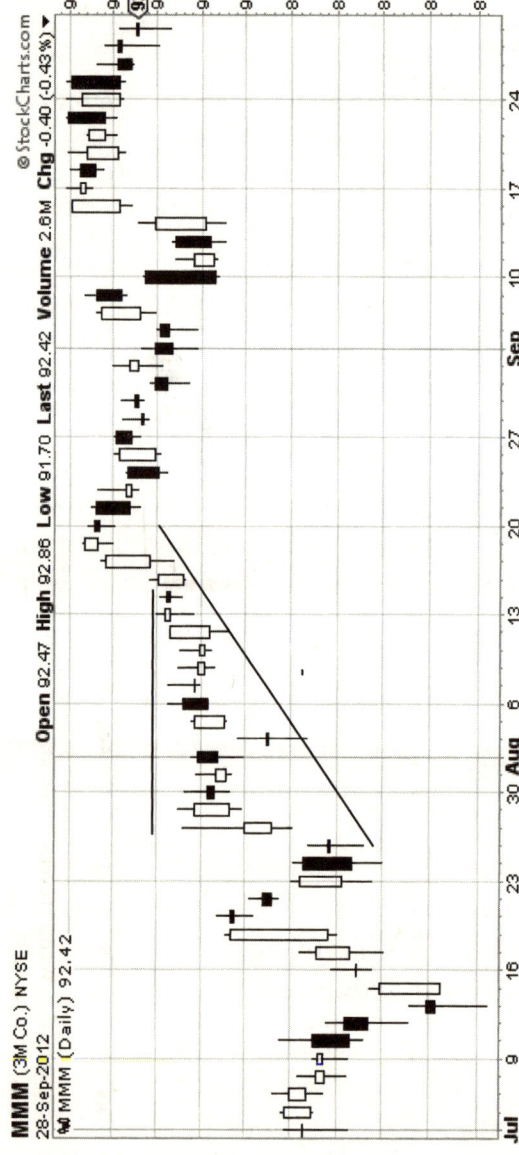

Figure 2.2 Triangle continuation resistance and support
Source: StockCharts.com.

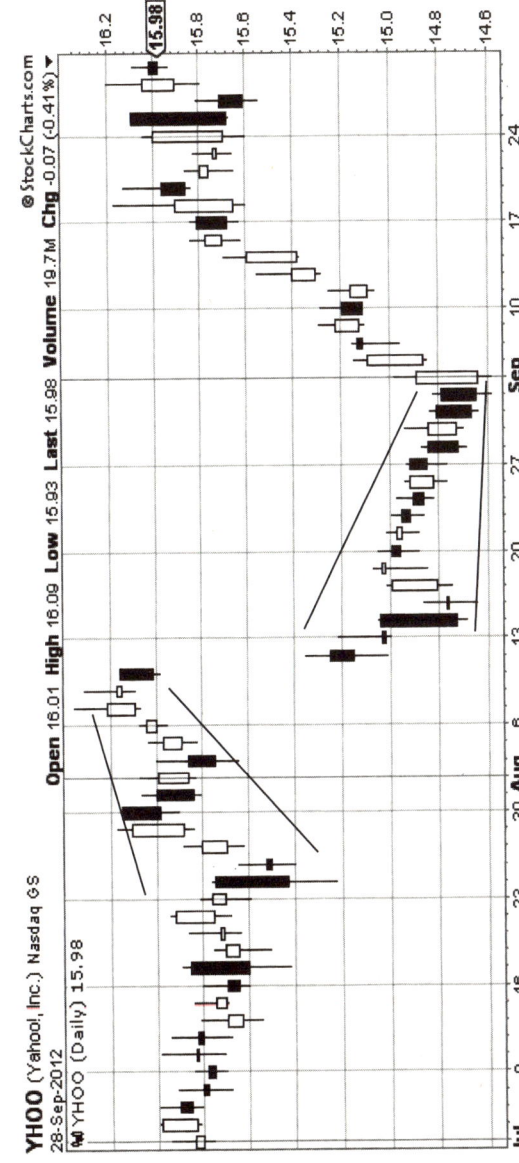

Figure 2.3 Wedge reversal resistance and support
Source: StockCharts.com.

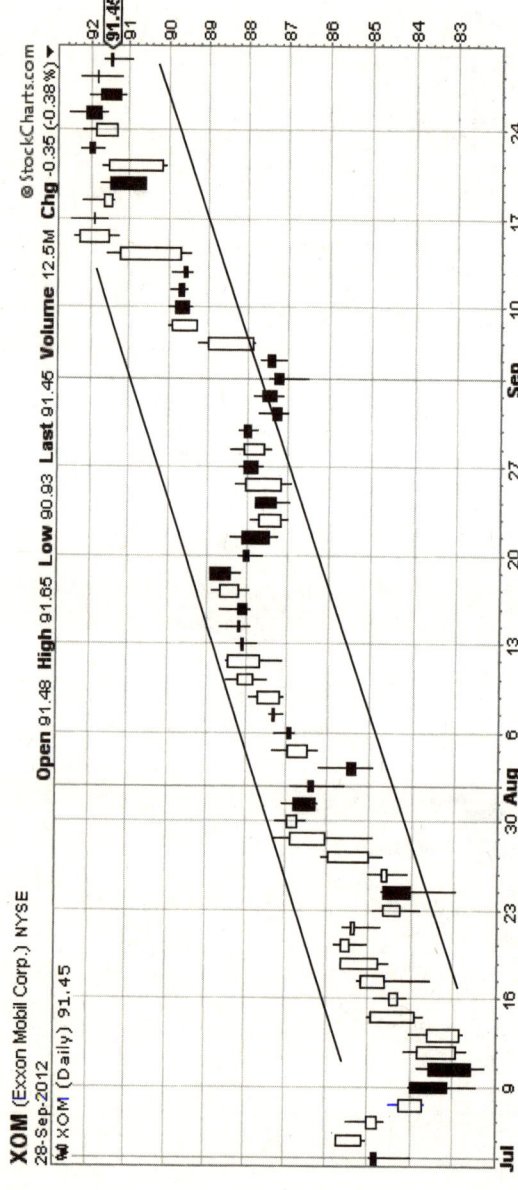

Figure 2.4 Rising resistance and support
Source: StockCharts.com.

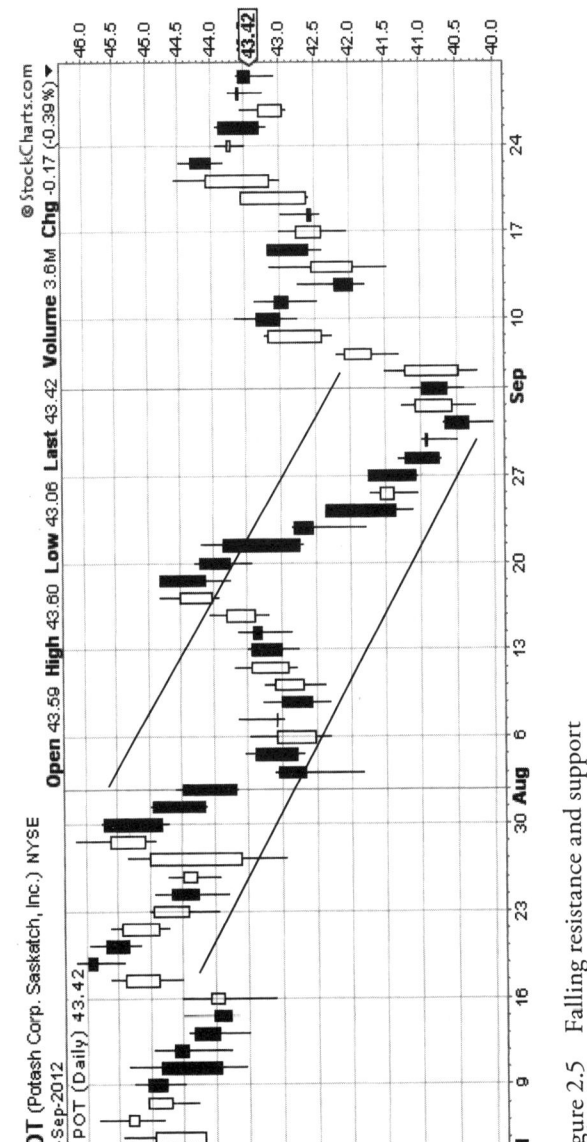

Figure 2.5 Falling resistance and support
Source: StockCharts.com.

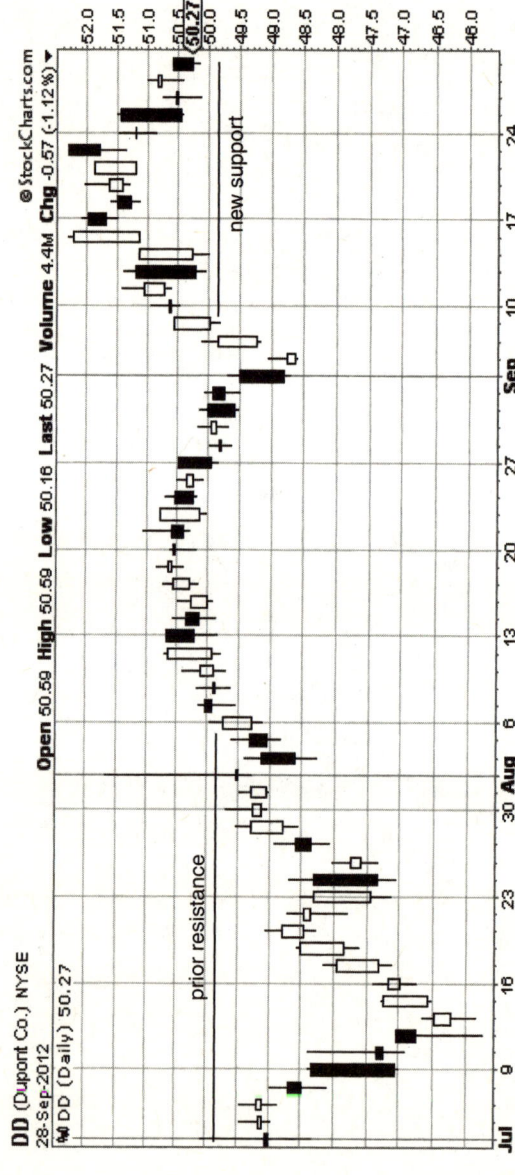

Figure 2.6 Resistance or support flip
Source: StockCharts.com.

Trading Range Flip
A final pattern worth noting is the so-called flip. When prices move through resistance and remain there, the previous resistance level often becomes the new support level. When prices break out below support, the prior support becomes new resistance. The flip is useful in determining whether or not the breakout is going to hold. As the newly set borders are tested and hold, the likely establishment of a new trading range is confirmed. For example, as shown in figure 2.6, DuPont experienced an uncertain rise above resistance, then a retreat and a second try. The indicated new support became the test price; as long as price does not fall below that level (prior resistance), it means the new support is likely to hold.

SWING TRADING BASICS

The study of price patterns and momentum is essential to the improved timing of entry and exit. That's the goal of swing trading: improving the timing. No one can promise a system to deliver 100% perfect timing. However, spotting reversal relies on pattern analysis and confirmation.

Swing trading in its most basic form depends on three types of reversal signals. These are:

1. *Narrow-range day (NRD).* The NRD, known among candlestick chartists as the doji, is a session in which the opening and closing prices are identical or very close. Such a day may have trading ranges both above and below, but the fact that price opens and closes at the same level is viewed by swing traders as very significant and as a likely signal of reversal.
2. *Reversal day.* A short-term trend, by definition, consists of three or more sessions moving in the same direction. Second, each session in an uptrend should open higher than the previous session and should also close higher. In a downtrend, each session should open lower and also close lower than on the previous day. Given these definitions, a reversal day is

a session moving in a direction opposite to the short-term trend. This often marks the end of the trend and is the first sign of a reversal.
3. *Volume spike.* In addition to the all-important NRD and reversal days, swing traders place importance on volume spikes. These are sudden exceptionally high-volume days in comparison to preceding sessions; by definition, a spike requires that volumes return to previous levels. High volume indicates higher than average interest among traders, and when that high volume shows up at the same time as other reversal signs, it increases the likelihood that a reversal is about to occur.

These basic signals are only the starting points for swing trade analysis. Beyond these, it makes sense to rely on traditional charting analysis. . Traditionally, stock-based technical analysis focused mainly on chart reading, and options-based technical analysis focused exclusively on implied volatility (usually through study of changes in delta, gamma, and the other "Greeks").

In the chart-based approach to using options in swing trading, both of these are combined. Charts are studied using four primary methods: price analysis through candlesticks, price patterns found in Western technical analysis, volume indicators, and momentum oscillators. All four add insight to trends and help to spot reversals; however, when these are used to spot and confirm reversals as part of timing for options positions, timing will be improved and as a result the swing trade success rate will increase.

TECHNICAL ANALYSIS SIGNAL BASICS

Reversals occur both in traditional price formations and in candlestick indicators. Traditional reversals often occur at or close to resistance and support and may be found in many forms. There are many, but four are especially strong:

1. *Head and shoulders.* This pattern has three parts. All are tops. The first and third are the shoulders, and the middle, higher

top is the head. After the pattern shows up, price is expected to retreat. The shoulders may approach or even touch resistance, and the head may break through. This is a very strong bearish reversal signal.

An example is shown in the chart of Altria (MO) in figure 2.7. In the first month, the chart shows a weakening uptrend, clearly marked with the shoulders and the head, and then a reversal occurred and led to an extended downtrend.

The opposite is called the inverse head and shoulders. In this pattern, bottoms replace the tops, and the head may break through support. When this occurs, it is a strong bullish signal. For example, as shown in figure 2.8, Apple (AAPL) ended its downtrend with an inverse head and shoulders and then immediately reversed into an uptrend.

2. *Double bottom or top.* Double tests of support (double bottom) or resistance (double top) are very common and also may represent a momentary breakthrough and retreat. Once the double test fails, price tends to move in the opposite direction. Dell provided an example of both (fig. 2.9). The double bottom marked the conclusion of the downtrend and was followed by a brief uptrend. The double top was prominent with consecutive violations of resistance, a downward gap, and then a strong reversal and downtrend.

3. *Price gaps.* Technicians know that gaps occur often, so distinguishing between common gaps (with no special signaling value) and meaningful gaps (runaway, breakout, and exhaustion) requires careful study and confirmation. The chart of JC Penney (JCP) in figure 2.10 includes examples of several gapping price patterns. The first three could be interpreted as runaway gaps as the uptrend began. However, prices declined briefly before resuming. In this pattern, the fourth gap— which was a strong move—may have provided confirmation of the uptrend's continuation. The last gap followed a doji session with an unusually long upper shadow, a strong sign that buyer momentum was gone. This exhaustion gap marked the end of the uptrend and the beginning of a reversal.

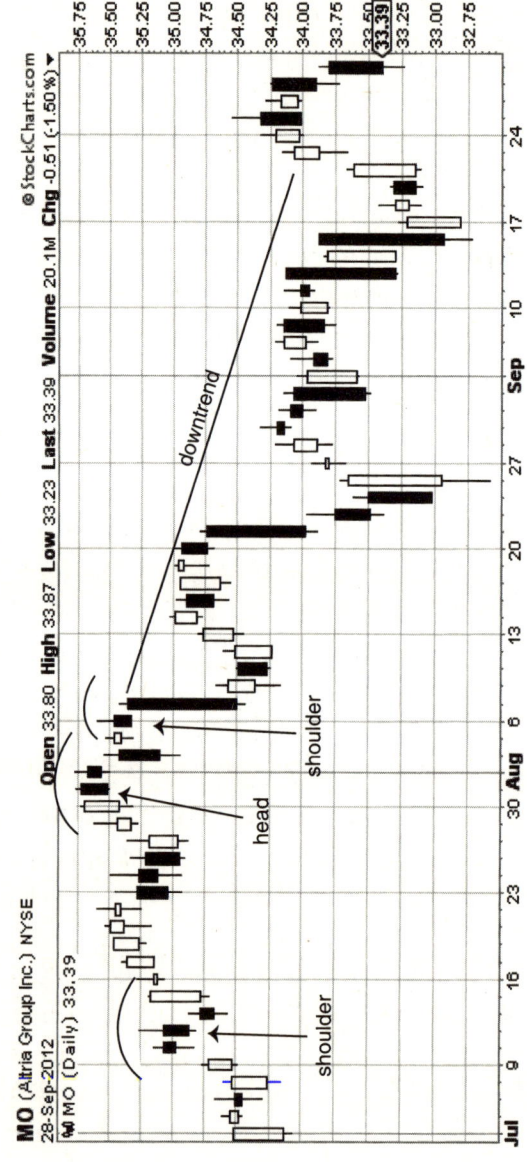

Figure 2.7 Head and shoulders
Source: StockCharts.com.

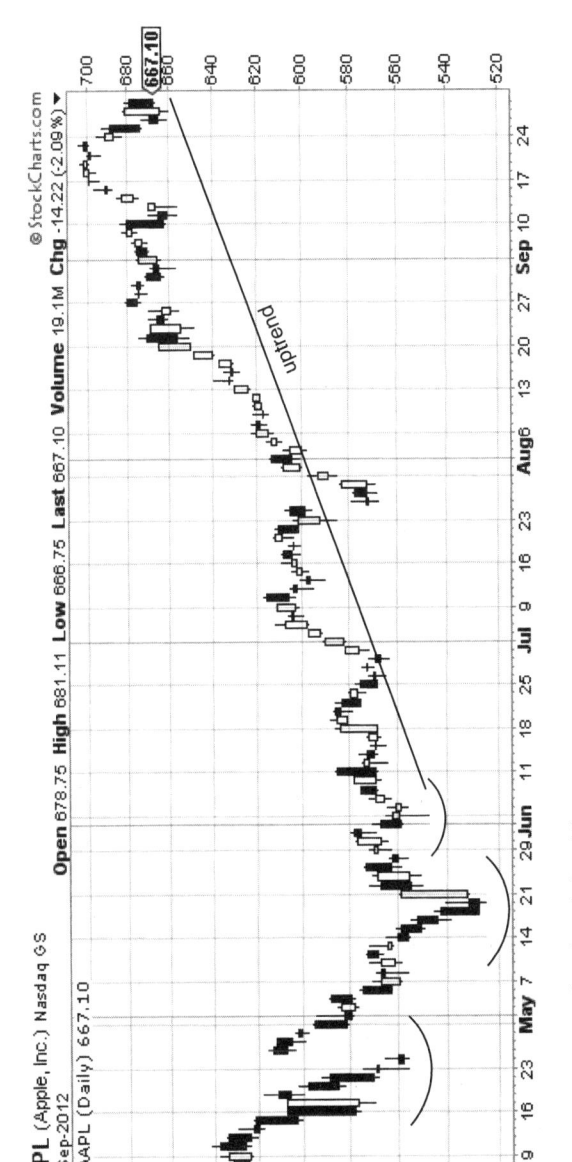

Figure 2.8 Inverse head and shoulders
Source: StockCharts.com.

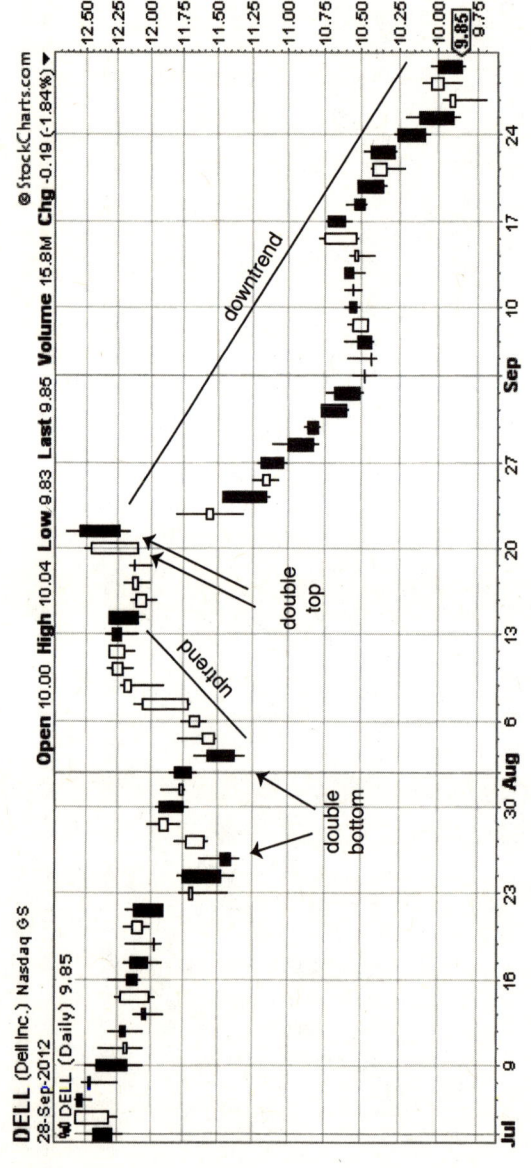

Figure 2.9 Double bottom and double top
Source: StockCharts.com.

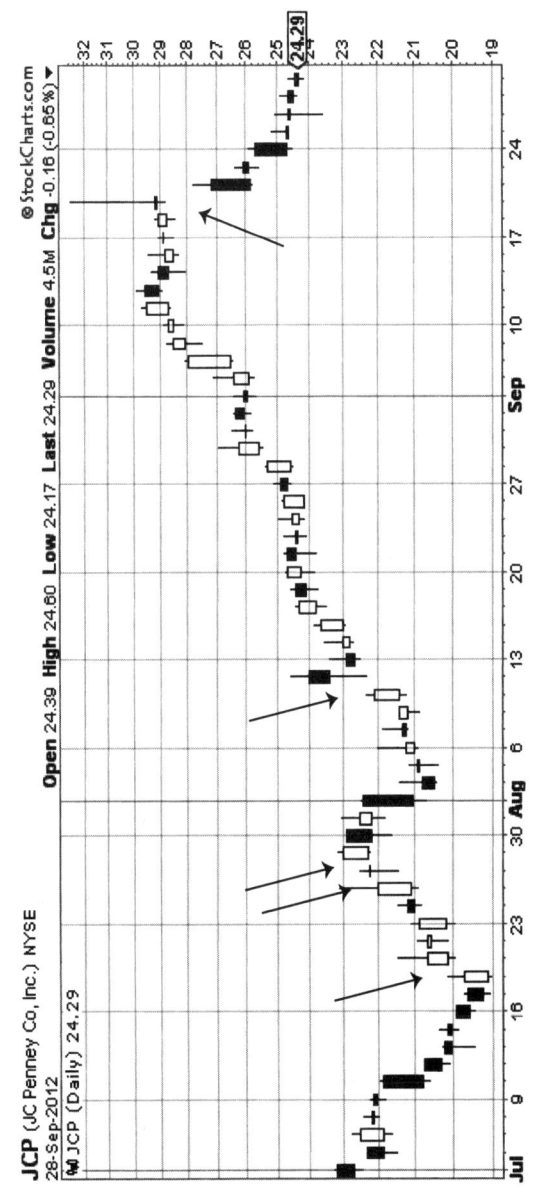

Figure 2.10 Price gaps
Source: StockCharts.com.

4. *Triangles.* Figure 2.2 provided an example of the rising triangle form of reversal, in this case for 3M. Two additional types of triangles are also found in charts. The falling triangle is a bullish reversal, and an example is found in the chart of Coca-Cola (KO) in figure 2.11. The brief but strong uptrend evolved into sideways movement, but the falling triangle was strong evidence that prices would reverse and move down, which is what they did.

The symmetrical triangle (also called a coil) is characterized by a falling resistance and rising support at the same time. As the triangle narrows, a new trend (or resumption of a previous trend) follows. The symmetrical triangle is the most difficult to interpret because it can indicate either continuation or reversal. For example, as shown in figure 2.12, McDonald's (MCD) began with an uptrend and then moved into the symmetrical pattern. Because price gapped lower after conclusion of the triangle, the initial indication was of a downtrend. However, the price moved upward in a delayed resumption of the previous uptrend.

For swing traders, these many different technical signals are valuable in determining the timing for entry and exit. In addition to the price-specific indicators, another area worth tracking is volume. Besides the volume spike, you should also look for popular volume indicators including on-balance volume (OBV) and accumulation/distribution (A/D), both of which measure the dominance of either buyers or sellers as trends evolve.

A final type of traditional analysis is the use of momentum oscillators. These are calculated measurements of the direction of a trend as well as of its speed and strength. As trends come to their end, momentum tends to fall, often anticipating price reversal. Momentum is a powerful form of confirmation, and examples in coming chapters demonstrate how timing based on oscillators can be fine-tuned effectively.

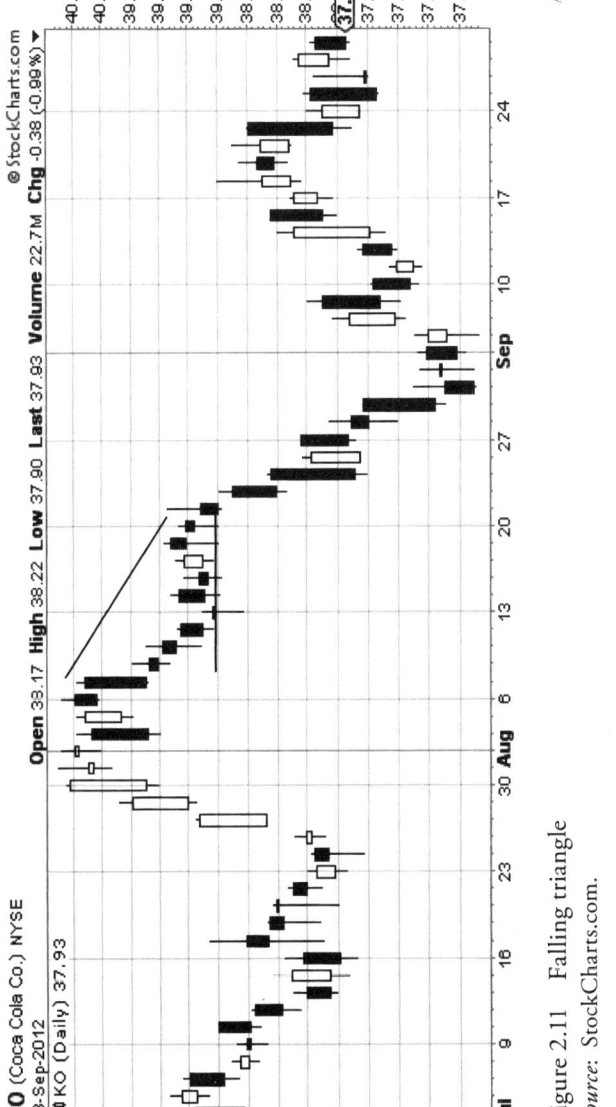

Figure 2.11   Falling triangle
Source: StockCharts.com.

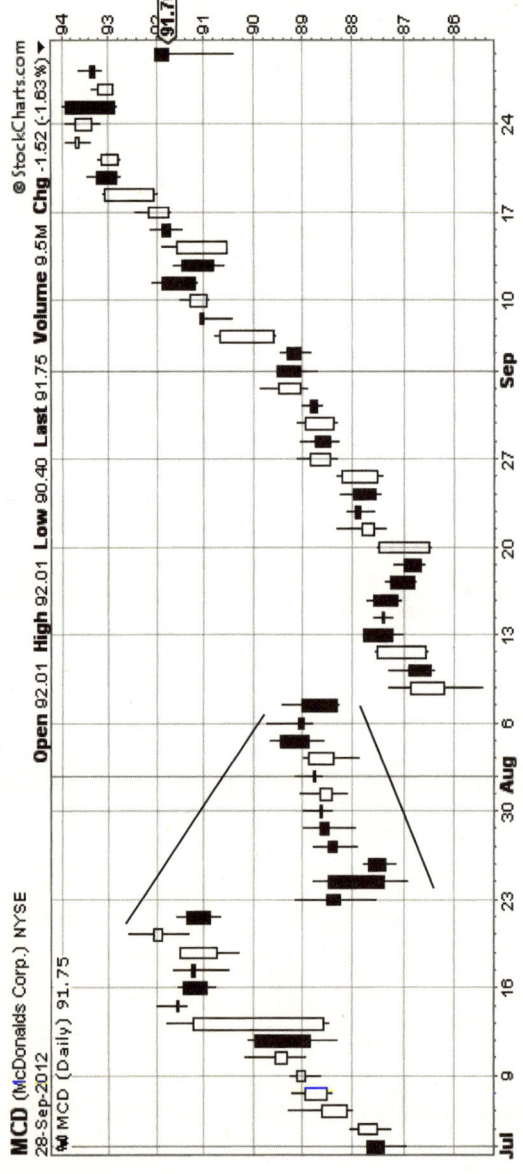

Figure 2.12 Symmetrical triangle
Source: StockCharts.com.

CANDLESTICK BASICS

Technical indicators come in many forms and provide insight into price behavior. Candlestick reversals are equally varied and consist of many signals that are reliable and that also appear often. There are literally dozens of different one-session, two-session, and three-session candlestick types, and this is an area deserving of in-depth study and mastery. Swing traders relying on candlesticks know that reliable reversal can appear in many forms. The focus here is on a short list of highly reliable indicators: the engulfing pattern, three white soldiers, and three black crows.

Like all signals, these are highly reliable reversal patterns, but in order to act as reversals, they have to show up at the top of an uptrend or at the bottom of a downtrend. When they do not, they may act as continuation signals, and in this way give you equally valuable insight into the trend.

These candlestick indicators are summarized on the chart. The engulfing pattern can be bullish or bearish and consists of two consecutive days. The three white soldiers pattern is a bullish three-day indicator. And the three black crows pattern has three consecutive sessions and is bearish.

An example of the bullish engulfing pattern was found on the three-month chart of General Mills shown in figure 2.13. In fact, two bullish engulfing indicators appeared in close proximity, the second one confirming the first. Following these, prices trended upward as expected.

The bearish variety showed up on the chart of Microsoft in figure 2.14. This was an interesting occurrence since it was immediately followed by a large downside gap. A chartist could have entered a trade during the second session once it became apparent that the bearish engulfing pattern was forming. The downtrend continued for four additional sessions and ended with an upside gap and reversal day.

In the chart shown in figure 2.15, the three white soldiers pattern appeared three times, and each had a different meaning. The first was a reversal signal. Soon after, a second three white

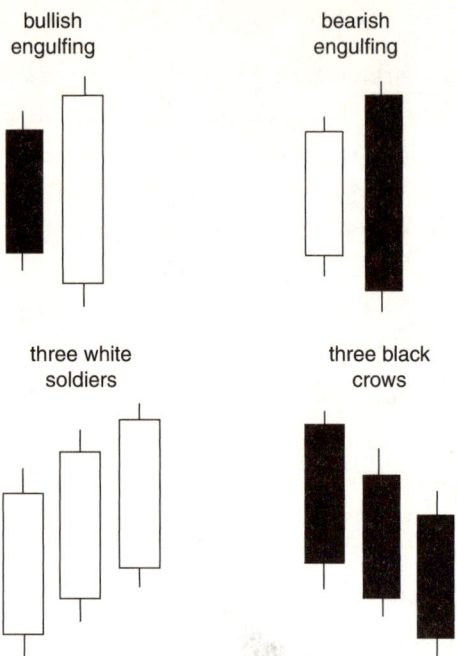

Figure 2.13   Highly reliable candlestick reversal indicators
Source: Figure created by author.

soldiers pattern appears that served as a continuation pattern for the uptrend and also confirmed the first signal. The third three white soldiers pattern was also a continuation of the established uptrend.

The charts of Chevron shown in Figure 2.16 and Research in Motion (now Blackberry) in Figure 2.17 show reversal and continuation patterns based on three white soldiers and three black crows. These reversals and confirmation patterns were strong on both charts.

Types of Confirmation

In addition to finding reliable reversal signals, you will need confirmation. No signal should be acted upon for either entry or exit until it has been confirmed independently.

Swing trading reversals can show up in the form of Western signals (double tops and bottoms, head and shoulders, price gaps,

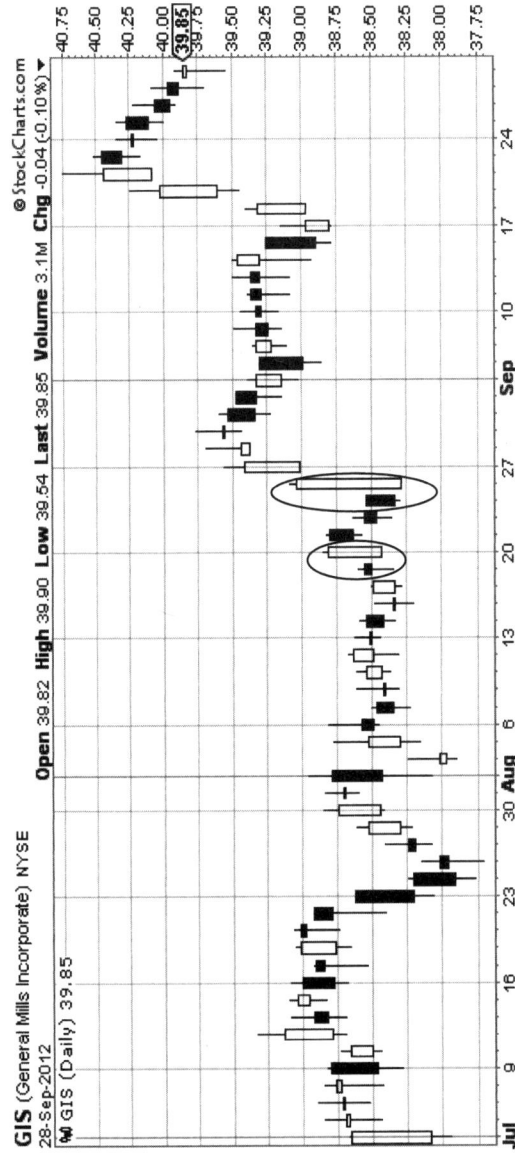

Figure 2.14 Bullish engulfing
Source: StockCharts.com.

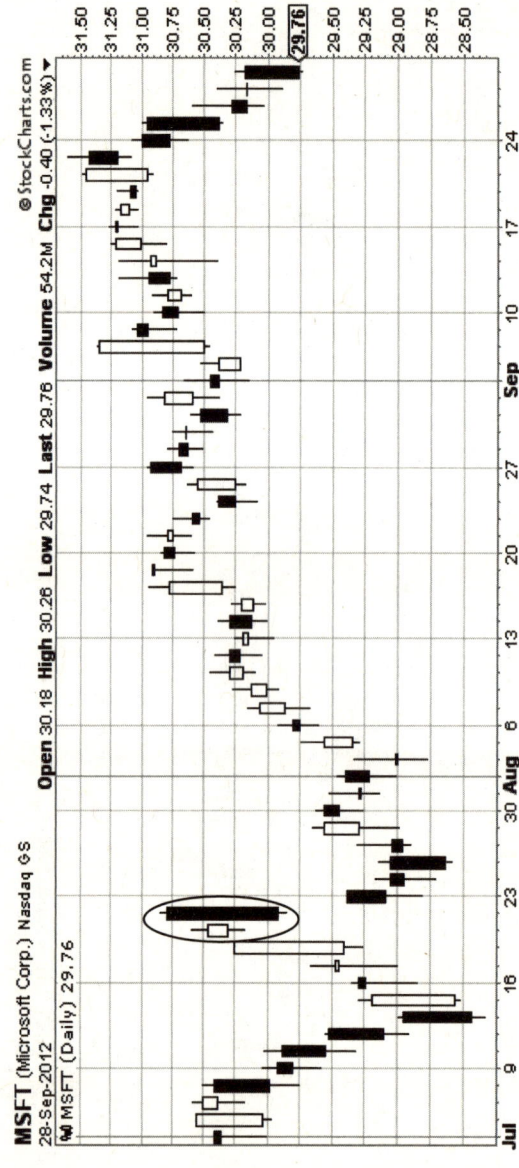

Figure 2.15 Bearish engulfing
Source: StockCharts.com.

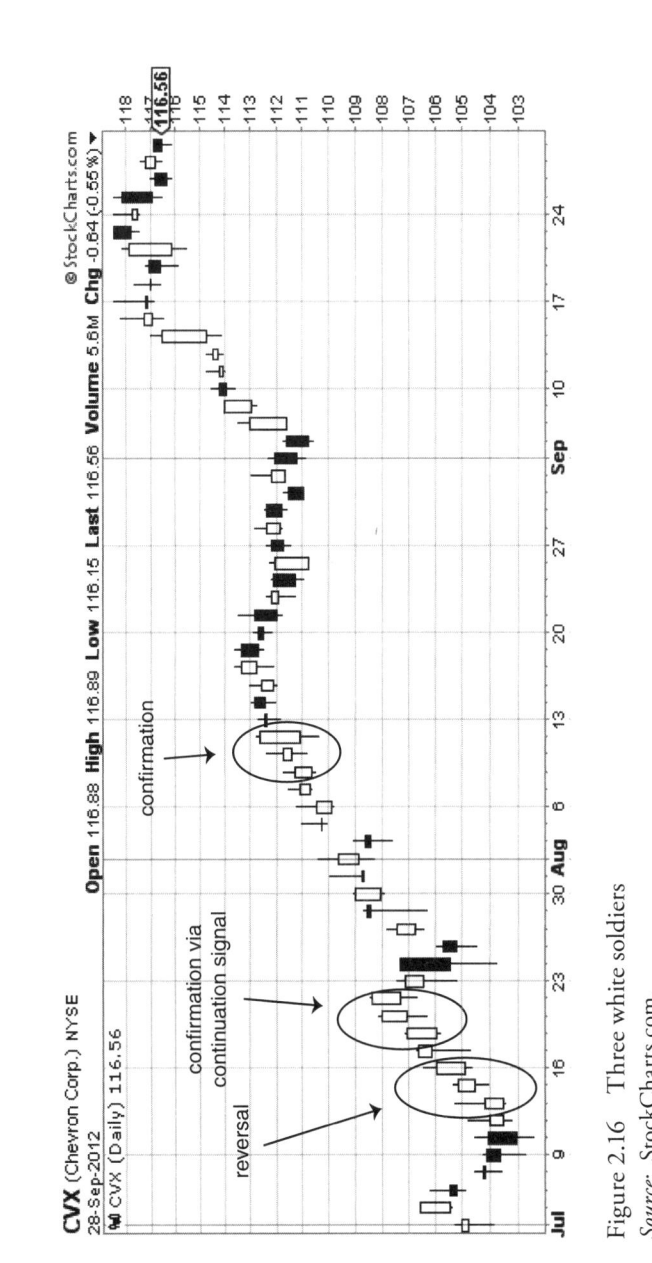

Figure 2.16 Three white soldiers
Source: StockCharts.com.

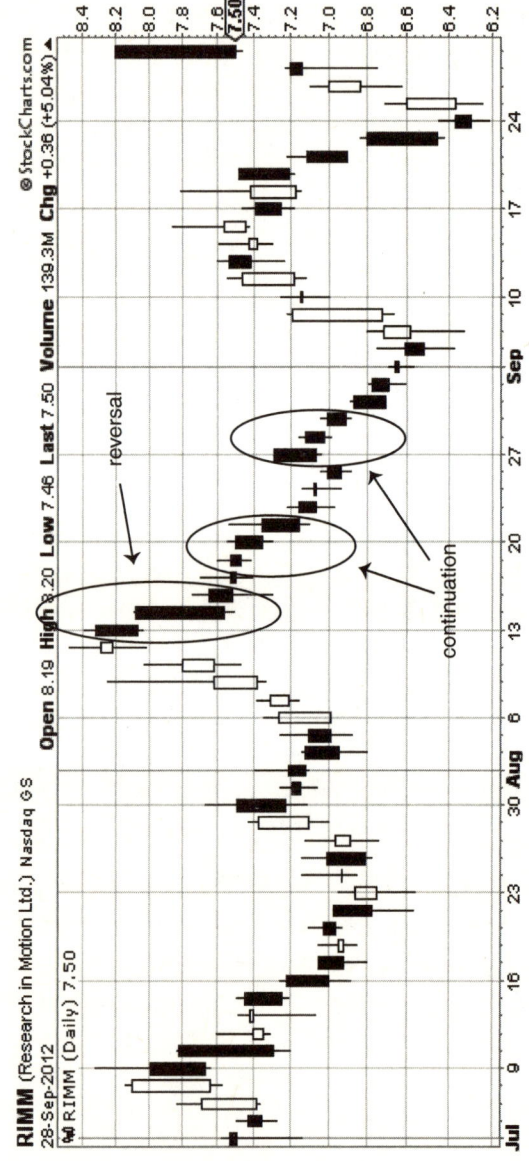

Figure 2.17 Three black crows
Source: StockCharts.com.

failed breakouts) or by way of candlestick signals. Any initial reversal signal can be confirmed by a number of independent signals. These will include:

1. *Candlestick indicators.* Any reversal signal, including candlesticks, can be confirmed by other candlestick signals. In fact, this is quite common and provides one of the strongest forms of confirmation.
2. *Western technical patterns.* Confirmation also is found among the double tops and bottoms, gapping price patterns, head and shoulders, wedges, and triangles, to name a few of the most reliable price patterns
3. *Volume indicators.* In addition to the easily spotted volume spike, many additional indicators have been devised to track strength or weakness in volume trends. Among these, On Balance Volume (OBV), Chaikin Money Flow (CMF), and Accumulation Distribution (A/D) are popular and used most often.
4. *Momentum oscillators.* Momentum is a measurement of price direction and speed. As a trend approaches its end, momentum tends to slow down. These include Relative Strength Index (RSI), Moving Average Convergence/Divergence (MACD), Bollinger Bands, and the Stochastic Oscillator.

The combination of many different methods for judging price, volume, and momentum are used together to help improve timing of entry and exit. Swing traders can use all of these types of indicators effectively. Even so, swing trading involves specific types of market risks, so as with any strategic approach to trading, swing traders need to build risk reduction and avoidance policies into their strategies. This is the topic of the next chapter.

CHAPTER 3

DANGEROUS WATERS: RISK INHERENT IN COMPREHENSIVE SWING-BASED STRATEGIES

> There can be no real freedom without the freedom to fail.
> Eric Hoffer, *The Ordeal of Change*, 1964

OPTIONS AND RISK

By their nature, options are perceived as carrying high risk and properly so if used in a risky manner. These contracts can be very risky and speculative, but they can also be quite conservative, income-generating, and risk-reducing. It all depends on how strategies are selected and applied. Swing trading is perfectly suited to the use of options, and market risks are effectively managed with options in place of stock.

When well-known option risks (pending expiration and time decay, for example) are coupled with the risk of short-term price movement of strategies such as swing trading, risks can be even greater. However, when properly selected, options can also present lower risks in a swing trading program than using shares of stock would.

All options traders face a range of risks and have to be especially aware of the context of those risks as part of their swing trading strategies. A comprehensive strategy—one based on the exclusive use of options in place of stock for swing trading—includes the range of options risks as well as risks specific to swing trading.

Information and Knowledge Risks

A great challenge for any level of options trading is the combination of information risk and knowledge risk. A great universe of information may be found online and in publications, but a lot of it is biased and even wrong. However, as most experienced traders have learned, you cannot rely on information by itself to learn to manage other risks or to know how to structure your trades. When you add the risks of swing trading to the options-based information and knowledge risk, you have a daunting challenge to overcome.

Information is acquired through study and analysis, not just of terms and rules, but of actual trades. This means you need to trade in options and in swing trades, either using real money or through a paper trading function. To learn all about how options trading works without risking real money, check the virtual trading function, offered free by the Chicago Board Options Exchange (CBOE) on its website (www.cboe.com / tools / virtual trade). The advantage to starting here is that your trades will be based on current values, and margin requirements are applied against your virtual portfolio.

This starting point for gaining information is not enough, however. Gaining knowledge about options and swing trading requires experience in trading as well. This demands that you study not only options and the basics of swing trading but also a range of technical indicators. Swing trading will not work in isolation, but it has to be a part of a knowledge base that includes many technical price, volume, and momentum signals, charting patterns, and awareness of broader market risks.

Goal-Setting and Self-Discipline Risks

Once you have acquired information and knowledge (assuming this means that you have enough insight to understand the risk challenges of options and of swing trading), the next step is to know how to set and follow goals for yourself.

This sounds easy. But as every trader has probably learned through losing money in trades, it is easy to set goals but much more difficult to follow those rules once a trade begins to develop. Every experienced options trader has gone through the rationalization of why a goal will not be kept. For example, if you buy a long option, you might set a simple goal: "I will sell and take profits if the value doubles. I will sell and cut losses if I lose 50% of the value."

This goal is reasonable. You either double your money or lose half. But what happens as the trade develops? If the price does double, the tendency is to listen to the inner voice telling you, "I should hold on a while longer. I might make an even bigger profit." But if the price declines then, you set a new goal for yourself, namely, that you *must* get back to that double-up point. Instead, you end up riding the trade down all the way to worthless expiration.

If the trade loses, that same voice tells you to not cut your losses: "I don't want to lose money on this trade, so I'm going to hold on for a little while longer, hoping the value returns to my entry point." Once again, you end up riding the trade down to zero value on expiration date.

In either of these scenarios, you have to ask yourself when you can close the position. There When can you honor your goal and either take profits or cut losses?. The problem of goal-setting and self-discipline risk is that if you don't exercise it, you have to expect losses. They become inevitable.

Here is a suggestion: Focus on self-discipline to succeed as a swing trader, especially when using options. The plan is so sensible and potentially profitable that the primary reason why it might fail is a lack of self-discipline, and therefore this "discipline risk" is worth overcoming. Just as swing traders need to be self-disciplined to act as contrarians (buying when most traders are panicking and selling when most are riding prices upward), it is an equal requirement to act as a contrarian within your own mind. Disciplined traders are able to argue against following preestablished rules of entry and exit because they recognize that this singular attribute—following smart rules—defines success in swing trading.

MARGIN RISKS

Many traders, especially those who are intent on learning all about options, overlook the substantial risk of margin requirements. Every options trader needs to download and study the CBOE *Margin Manual* at http://www.cboe.com/LearnCenter/pdf/margin2-00.pdf to discover how margin works, both initial margin and maintenance, for a variety of different options trades.

Easily overlooked is the change in margin requirements when prices move against the trade. For example, a short position is opened, but the underlying moves in the wrong direction, increasing the risk of exercise. Will you be required to put up more equity or cash on margin? Can you afford to? What are the margin requirements for complex multicontract strategies? The simple theory of a strategy looks good on paper until you realize that the initial margin and further margin requirements are beyond your capital resources. Margin risks are especially serious when you have opened uncovered short positions. In these positions, margin is going to be based on exercise value and not only on the initial value of the option.

LOST OPPORTUNITY RISKS

Options are all about creating opportunities you do not have when you hold stock (for example, leveraging stock to increase income or reducing risk with protective puts). The market is also about *lost* opportunity, however.

This is especially true in any situation in which having an option open places a ceiling on potentially higher income in exchange for the certainty of lower, consistent, and low-risk income. The covered call is a perfect example. In this strategy, you use 100 shares of stock to eliminate the risk of selling a call. You receive income when you open the call; if properly structured, that will yield double digits on an annualized basis. However, you also create the risk of lost opportunity by entering into this strategy.

The lost opportunity is represented by the profit you might realize by just owning shares of stock. Without the encumbrance of a short call, your stock's market value might rise indefinitely and create a very high level of profit. However, every stockholder knows that the risk of loss is equal in the sense that share value might also fall. In order to accept the covered call strategy, you have to be willing to accept the occasional lost opportunity in exchange for a consistent level of profits.

How often does a stock's price rise in this manner? For some it happens often enough to reject covered call writing. For others, exercise as the price for safety and certainty of profits justify the strategy. For these traders, the lost opportunity is worth living with.

For example, if you own a $50 stock and you can sell a covered call expiring in two months for 2.50 ($250), that's a 5% yield (based on a 50 strike). Annualized, that works out to 30%—5% in two months: (5% ÷ 2 x 12 = 30%).

This version of lost opportunity demonstrates the trade-off for options strategies. If you can create a consistent double-digit return from options that is safer than just owning stock, then the lost opportunity is not as severe as it would be if net return were lower. Why is covered call writing safer than just owning stock? If you buy the $50 stock without the option aspect, you are at risk for your basis of $50 per share. But if you sell a call and get a premium of 2.50 ($250) for it, this reduces your net basis to $47.50 per share. This discount in your basis builds a cushion so that as long as the stock price remains at or above $47.50, you have not lost any net value in the position.

The lost opportunity risk has an offsetting benefit in this discounted basis. Even so, many investors avoid covered call writing because they do not want to place a ceiling on their earnings from the stock positions, even if that ceiling is in the double digits.

Tax Risks

Options traders, like all investors, have to contend with a daunting and complex series of federal, state, and local tax rules. On the federal level, dividend and capital gains rates are forever in doubt because these rates are raised and lowered for political reasons, rather than for the economic value of a specific rate.

One tax risk faced by options traders is this uncertainty. If you don't know what next year's rates will be, how does that affect your behavior today? If investors believe that the capital gains rates are going to rise, that creates an incentive to sell shares before year-end. As a direct consequence, prices will fall, perhaps significantly. Investors wanting to avoid a higher rate can impact the values of stock and options by acting rationally in the face of uncertainty.

A second tax risk is the degree to which taxes reduce net profits, perhaps below your breakeven point. The higher your effective tax rate, the higher the rate you need to earn just to keep up with inflation. Traders need to be aware of their after-tax net return and breakeven point. Some options trades are so marginal that they make the yield too small for the risk involved. If both your tax rate (federal, state, and local combined) and inflation rate move higher, you need to earn a higher yield just to keep up. This means having to either take greater risks or settling for deterioration in your capital's net purchasing power.

To find your after-tax and post-inflation breakeven point, divide the current inflation rate by your net income after taxes (taxable income less tax liability). The result is the percentage you must earn just to break even. For example, if your combined federal and state income tax rate is 45% and you assume 3% inflation, your breakeven requirement is:

$$3\% \div (100 - 45) = 5.5\%$$

In this example, if you earn less than 5.5% net on your combined investments, you are losing after taxes and inflation. This is a difficult rate to beat. Some investors will look for higher than average dividend yields as a result. However, uncertainty affects this decision as well. If future dividends are going to be taxed at ordinary rates (the rate on earned income) rather than the favorable rates of the past, then the higher dividend yields are affected, requiring you to earn even more to reach breakeven.

Federal (and state) tax policy affects the tax risk for all stock and option trading, requiring you to accept lost purchasing power or take on higher risks than you can afford. This is where wise and profitable options strategies may help overcome the problem of tax risk. If swing trading with options is executed based on sound timing principles ensuring improvement in identifying reversal points, a series of small short-term gains may offset the double risk of high taxes and high inflation.

LEVERAGE, DIVERSIFICATION, AND STOCK SHORTING RISKS

Investors and traders face specific risks associated with the use of capital and how to reduce exposure. These are the risks of leverage, diversification, and shorting stock.

Leverage—the use of a small amount of capital to control a larger amount—is an especially severe potential risk. Every trader using margin to trade should be aware of how margin requirements accelerate market risk in the event of loss. For example, if margin maintenance is 50% and you have bought $20,000 worth of stock, the investment consists of two parts: $10,000 in cash and $10,000 borrowed—leveraged—from the brokerage firm. If the value of the underlying investment declines, you are required to place additional cash and securities at risk to maintain the margin relationship. This is a problem faced by every investor using the margin account, and using it to the maximum makes the risk more severe. It's true that if the underlying securities increase in value, the overall benefits are doubled with a 50% margin. However, if the value falls, you are required to put up more cash to maintain that 50% relationship.

In a swing trading strategy using margin to expand capital using stock, leverage risk is constantly present, and because swing trading does not ever provide certainty, a one-time large decline in value could place the entire plan at risk.

The diversification problem is equally severe. Using a limited capital base, how many different stocks can you trade to make a swing trading program effective? Many swing traders have to buy a small number of shares to accomplish diversification or, alternatively, decide to abandon diversification altogether and place funds into swing trades on one stock.

Both of these choices present problems. By forcing diversification with limited capital, the limit in the number of shares traded translates to a smaller dollar amount of potential profits. At the same time, the margin risk does not disappear either. A market-wide move affecting several different stocks adversely can further damage the liquidity of a swing trading strategy. Even a diversified strategic approach does not ensure that such a broad-based valuation change will not occur. In that case, the margin call may come at the worst possible time, when funds are depleted. As a consequence, a trader may have to liquidate some holdings at the very moment when it makes sense to wait out the swing.

Stock-based swing traders have to decide how to contend with the special risks of shorting stock. In the "perfect" swing trading strategy, you buy shares at the bottom of the swing and then sell at the top, *and* you then short stock at the top of the swing and buy to close at the bottom.

Realistically, this perfect approach is not always possible. Most stock traders are not willing to go short due to the high cost and the higher risks involved. Shorting stock is a complicated strategy. First, you have to borrow shares from your brokerage firm. Next, you sell those shares. During the time the trade remains open, you have to pay interest on the borrowed shares. You hope the share price declines so you can buy to close at a lower price and earn a profit. However, if the price of shorted stock remains range-bound, you have to pay interest for a longer period than you had hoped. If the share price rises, you have to increase your margin and pay more interest, and you might end up having to close the position at a loss.

Because of the high risk of shorting stock, swing traders are prone to trade only the long side or the bottom of the swing. When prices rise, the long positions are closed. Then the trader waits out the trend until it declines once more. This approach limits your potential to half the swings available.

SWING TRADING RISK ISSUES AND SOLUTIONS

Swing trading with options solves the leverage, diversification, and short-selling problems faced by stock-based traders.

Options provide the most effective and low-risk form of leverage possible. Most leverage consists of borrowing money. For example, using margin is the leverage most traders use on a daily basis. However, this increases risks significantly, especially for short-term trading. If your margin account is maxed out and prices move against you, a margin call has an immediate and destructive consequence. If you are not able to add additional cash into the account, the brokerage firm will sell enough of your equity holdings to satisfy that margin requirement. If prices continue to move in an unfavorable direction, your portfolio could be devastated. This leverage risk is precisely the reason traders avoid shorting stock.

If instead of using long and short stock to swing trade, you use long options, the leverage risk is solved. Each option moves in relation to price changes in 100 shares, and this works whether prices rise or fall. Even so, you can restrict swing trading to long positions only. When playing a short-term bullish trend, you buy calls and then sell them when the uptrend is done. When playing a short-term bearish trend, you buy puts and then sell them when the downtrend is done.

Options provide three risk-reducing attributes: leverage, diversification, and avoiding the need short stock.

First, options are a type of leverage not based on borrowing on margin. The cost of an option is typically less than 5% of the price of 100 shares of stock (based on expiration in one to two months for at-the-money contracts). The ability to leverage capital without borrowing is a tremendous advantage. Because options are cheap compared to the cost of going long or short on 100 shares of stock, the leverage risk is reduced to only the cost of each option.

Second, options solve the problems of diversification in a swing trading program. For swing traders with limited capital resources, it is difficult to effectively diversify a swing trading portfolio. If you want to trade in 100-share lots, for example, how many different stocks can you swing trade at the same time? Capital limitations also determine the price per share you can afford to swing trade—this means that capital limitations rather than actual swing opportunities determine issues you trade. If you limit your activity to dollar amounts, you have to use smaller numbers of shares per trade for higher-priced stocks. For example, if you will swing trade about $2,000 per trade, this limits exposure in terms of stock market risk. However, you can only trade 100 shares at $20 per share or 10 shares at $200 per share. This is not a specific problem, however, if your goal is to limit stock-based market risk to $2,000 per swing trade.

In this case, you are risking $2,000 per swing trade, and if the stock price moves in the direction opposite of what you expect, your stock value will decline, and all or part of the $2,000 is going to be at risk. In comparison, if you want to control 100 shares of stock for a fraction of the cost of stock, every option provides you with control over 100 shares of stock. A $20 stock is likely to offer soon-to-expire and at-the-money or slightly in-the-money options for $100 or less. The same option on a $200 stock will cost close to $1,000 given the same expiration status and moneyness.

Some traders may continue to prefer stock at lower prices for swing trading if only to reduce the cost of the options they use. For example, limiting your trades to single options on stocks priced between $20 and $40 per share will also limit your average cost per option to $100 to $200 (or less). This diversifies the market risk in terms of exposure per trade. It diversifies the risk in the sense that at $100 to $200 per trade, you can expand to many more issues than you can if you use shares of stock.

Swing trading presents short-term opportunities based on earnings surprises, rumors, or changes in guidance for future profits, to name a few examples of causes. By limiting your exposure to lower-priced stock, you are going to miss out on some swing trading opportunities. And so you will look for surprises on Microsoft and Dell while passing up similar situations for Apple, IBM, or Google. There is nothing wrong with avoiding these much higher-priced options as part of a swing trading strategy; it is only important to be aware of the limits this imposes on swing trading opportunities. These limits refer to the dollar amount at risk with options, not to the percentage cost of options compared to price per share.

For example, table 3.1 shows the options expiring in October that were available on several issues on October 21, 2012.

Although there is considerable variation for slightly ITM options expiring in a matter of weeks—from a low of 1.6% to a high of 9.4%—the comparison between dollar value and percentage of strike makes the point that an evaluation with risk in mind reveals that options create diversification on three levels: dollar cost, percentage cost, and volatility level.

Table 3.1 Option expiration, comparison of premium levels

Name	Share Price	Option	Premium	Percentage of Strike
Microsoft (MSFT)	$ 29.61	29 call	0.86	3.0%
		30 put	0.74	2.5
Dell (DELL)	$ 9.67	9 call	0.85	9.4%
		10 put	0.40	4.0
Apple (AAPL)	$637.34	635 call	15.52	2.4%
		640 put	15.58	24
IBM (IBM)	$210.60	210 call	4.00	1.9%
		210 put	3.45	1.6
Google	$759.54	760 call	22.50	3.0%
		760 put	22.00	2.9

Source: Stock listings, Charles Schwab & Company, at www.schwab.com.

Third, the risk of short-selling is overcome with options, since long puts provide the same bearish strategy as shorted stock, but with much lower risk or cost. Stock-based swing trading involves one of two strategies. The complete system calls for long stock positions opened at the bottom of the swing and closed at the top and short stock positions opened at the top and closed at the bottom. The partial system involves only the long side. The use of short stock carries considerably higher risk, which is why swing traders are likely to enter only one-half of all opportunities, those based on price declines and the expectation of rebound. The great risk in this approach is that when fully committed in long stock at the beginning of an extended primary bear market, substantial equity loss is likely. The risk is mitigated with options due to their smaller cost per option contract.

With the use of long options, there is no need to go short. Long calls are used in place of long stock, and market risk is reduced because a single call controls 100 shares but 5% or less of the cost of those shares. Long puts are used in place of short stock at the top price level and in expectation of a retreat. In the event prices continue to rise, the market risk is again limited to the relatively small cost per option. That is, with options the market risk is significantly smaller than for 100 shares of long or short stock; however, using ATM or ITM contracts expiring in one month or less, the same opportunity exposure exists as for 100 shares of stock.

EXPIRATION AND TIME DECAY RISK

The typical problem faced by any trader buying options is the conflict between expiration and time. The shorter the time until expiration, the cheaper the option, but the more difficult it becomes for that option to become profitable. And the longer the time until expiration, the greater the chances for price appreciation but the higher the cost.

Both of these conflicting problems are solved with the use of short-term options. Swing trading is one of the few strategies for which options expiring within one month are advantageous. The short time to expiration means the cost is quite low, and extrinsic value (volatility and its effect on premium) is minimal or nonexistent. And using options that are ATM or slightly ITM means the option mirroring of price movement ITM is going to be close to point for point. Longer-term options, even ATM or ITM, tend to be less reactive due to the extrinsic value effect with more time. So when an option moves ITM, it does not act point for point with underlying price movement. The extrinsic value offsets intrinsic price change to a degree, and as a result the longer the time until expiration, the less responsive option value will be to changes in the underlying, even when ITM.

When options are going to expire within one month or less and are opened ATM or ITM, the swing trading strategy is maximized. Because swing trades tend to last from three to five days, the use of short-term options is both appropriate and advantageous. Options traders may not adopt this point of view at first glance. It makes more sense in a majority of strategies involving long options to allow more time rather than less time, and the suggestion of using long options with less than a month before expiration will not be understood at first.

The distinction between strategies is found in the nature of the swing trade itself. The swing trade is entered because of a price aberration, and in the majority of cases this will be temporary. The swing trader takes advantage of the price swing because it is a consequence of overreaction by a majority of traders to price movement. . So a buyout offer at $43 per share causes the price to jump from $40 up to $47 or four points higher than the offer price. This is obviously irrational, but it is caused by a high level of demand that drives up the price. Swing traders see this and realize that the price is going to fall back to the level of the $43 offer price within one to three days. It is time to enter a position.

The opposite is also true. When earnings are reported two cents below expectation, the price may fall three or four points in the session. But swing traders realize that the selling activity drove the price down unreasonably and that price is likely to rebound within one to three days.

In both instances, the majority has acted emotionally. The greed and panic factors prevail when surprise announcements are made, and the price reaction is exaggerated. Even while traders are likely to recognize the excessive price move, most are afraid to act against the majority. This is where the contrarian nature of swing trading adds great advantage. A "contrarian" is not a trader who always acts contrary to prevailing price direction, but one who acts contrary to the prevailing causes underlying price movement. So when a majority is acting out of greed or panic, the swing trader (acting as contrarian) is likely to apply logic in the timing of trades.

Because the greed and panic effect is of very short duration (with prices expected to return to more rational levels within a few trading sessions), swing traders applying rational timing when most others are acting out of greed and panic take advantage of these very short-term uptrends and downtrends.

This is why options soon to expire and ATM or ITM are going to perform quite well in this short-term price trend. Their moneyness and short remaining lives make such options potentially very profitable very quickly.

In the next chapter, the risk issue is expanded upon with a more in-depth view of leverage, especially relating to trading with stock. The traditional swing trading and day trading strategy focuses on stock and avoids options based on some misconceptions. These include the idea that options will not mirror stock price movement well enough to be used for swing trading. This might be true if longer-term or OTM contracts were used. Many stock-based swing traders also view options as being too risky to use in a short-term swing trading program. This belief, too, is unfounded. The leverage risk of stock can be addressed efficiently with options, and a starting point in analyzing this is to study and understand how stock leverage works in a swing trading program.

CHAPTER 4

MARGINAL POTENTIAL: LEVERAGE LIMITATIONS IN SWING TRADING WITH STOCK

> The fatal errors of life are not due to man's being unreasonable. An unreasonable moment may be one's finest. They are due to man's being logical.
>
> Oscar Wilde, *De Profundis*, 1905

MARGIN RULES ARE COMPLEX ENOUGH TO CLOAK THE VERY REAL risks involved in the use of margin but simple enough so that every trader should understand them. To some traders, margin is a great convenience for short-term use; for others, it is a constant vehicle for increasing profit potential—and risk potential.

In both instances, using options to control blocks of stock is a method of leverage that carries lower risk and can overcome the risks of margin-based leverage. The big difference is that when you use margin to leverage, you are borrowing money. With options, you are buying and selling the *rights* to blocks of stock, but no borrowing is involved.

This chapter summarizes margin risks for stock-based portfolios. Although the material covers the basics of leverage, it is a worthwhile exercise to review this material as a prelude to considering using options in place of stock for a swing trading program.

Margin Trading: An Overview

The standard method used by investors and traders is to apply margin to augment capital. For example, with a $20,000 account, you can take up equity positions in $40,000 worth of shares. This means every one-point move up adds two points of profit. However, the risk of a decline is augmented as well since lost value leads to a requirement for you to place more capital into the margin account.

When your equity positions decline, you still owe the 50% borrowed funds to your broker, but your equity value is lower. Using margin to increase the size of positions sounds very promising at first, but it does increase risks significantly. So, ironically, a conservative investor is likely to focus on selecting the best value companies as a first step before buying shares. However, even though a company is considered "safe" based on fundamental analysis, if that same investor doubles the base with 50% borrowed money, that lower-risk stock is now placed in jeopardy in a higher-risk form of leverage. So for many, even the most risk-averse, the leverage risk is assumed daily but remains invisible.

Stock investors who have not analyzed leverage risks inherent in margin should realize one key fact: using your margin account is borrowing money from your broker in order to buy stock. As with all forms of borrowing, the pitfall is to acknowledge the profit potential and ignoring the risk. For example, how often have you heard that your home equity is being left "idle" and could be accessed through refinancing or opening a secured line of credit? The appeal of "putting your equity to work" is the same appeal as in margin investing. It is borrowed money, and the more you borrow, the greater the danger.

The equivalent to the home equity appeal is the margin account. It's so easy to use margin; all you're required to do is to put up half, and then the other half is yours to use. You're putting your equity to work in another way by borrowing $40,000 with only $20,000 worth of equity. In fact, the appeal is so widespread that some investors think it would be foolish to not take advantage of margin. But as is true of all investing decisions, a full understanding of margin risks is just as important as a wise selection of stocks.

The margin account can be opened as one of the two choices when your brokerage account is initiated. The other choice, a cash account, allows you to trade only to the extent of cash you have deposited. But for as little as $2,000 of initial margin, you can create a cash account allowing you to finance (borrow) the same amount again. You can put $2,000 into the account and then invest in $4,000 worth of securities. The perception in an account such as this is that it just makes sense to borrow the maximum, so you would want to double your cash deposit by buying twice as much, with half on margin. However, you do not have to use all of the margin value to trade in this way, a fact that is often overlooked. Another perception about margin is that it would be foolish to *not* use margin to the max and take advantage of the profit potential this offers to you.

Beyond initial margin is a second requirement, called maintenance margin. This is the minimum cash and equity balance you have to maintain to keep that ratio at 50%. For example, if you started out with $20,000 and borrowed another $20,000 on margin to invest in $40,000 worth of stock, what happens if your investment value falls to $37,000? This means you have lost $3,000 (out of an initial cash deposit of $20,000) or 15%. The $3,000 loss is only 7.5% of the full $40,000 value, but you have only $20,000 in cash, so the percentage lost is doubled when margin is maxed out.

The maintenance issue comes up when this happens. Your broker has loaned you $20,000, but your account has dropped by $3,000. So you will be required to deposit more funds (in this case, $3,000) to bring the account back to the 50% level. In other words, when the investment base loses money, this doesn't reduce the entire $40,000; it reduces your share. The broker's debt is still $20,000, but your equity has declined to $17,000.

The broker will then put out a margin call, demanding that you deposit $3,000 to bring the balance back to the minimum maintenance level (which varies by broker) and to remedy the collateral level. Now imagine what happens if the stock declines again. Another margin call has the effect of damaging your equity even more, but throughout you still owe $20,000 to the broker—no matter how far the overall portfolio value falls. And if you are unable to satisfy the margin call, your broker will sell some of your holdings to bring the account back into balance. The margin relationship between your equity and debt to the broker can change every day based on price changes in the stocks held in your portfolio.

In addition to having to maintain the required collateral, you also have to pay interest on the funds borrowed from your broker. Margin balances are loans, so they have to be repaid eventually, but as long as they remain outstanding, interest is going to be deducted from your account every month. If the overall portfolio balance falls, you have a paper loss, a higher margin requirement, and ongoing interest payments. For all of these reasons, a prudent use of margin is as a temporary bridge, with the intention of eliminating the outstanding balance from short-term profits. Unfortunately, many investors and traders use profits to increase their margin levels. Eventually, a loss may wipe out all of the profits accumulated in this manner. The higher the margin dollar value, the greater your vulnerability.

Investors tend to assume that they can use their margin accounts to invest in any stocks they want. However, this is not true. Margin rules are set by the Federal Reserve under Regulation T (see the full text of Reg. T at http://tinyurl.com/9mfoqlx). Reg. T sets standards for initial margin and maintenance; however, your broker may impose stricter standards than the minimums required under this regulation. One limitation the Fed has imposed is that margin cannot be used to invest in penny stocks (generally low-priced stocks not traded on public exchanges), OTC Bulletin Board Securities, or IPOs. Your broker may also restrict margin trading in specific stocks based on recent volatility, news, or earnings reports.

MARGIN CALLS

Anyone using margin for trading activity is vulnerable to margin calls. This occurs any time the required ratio between equity and margin moves out of balance due to changes in the value of securities. This may include both stocks and options.

Beyond the initial margin, maintenance margin is where traders may get into trouble. The problem with a margin call that cannot be met is that it's the broker and not the trader who decides which securities to close. You might discover that the securities you want to leave on deposit to mature into profitable positions are the very ones closed by your broker to meet a margin call. The broker is not required to speak with you either; you may not know which securities were disposed of until after the fact. You have no control over this decision, so the smart move is to ensure that if you use margin, you have adequate capital on account or in reserve.

Returning to the previous example, assume you have $20,000 in cash and you place it on deposit to borrow an additional $20,000. However, if the value of your investments drops to $30,000 (losing one-fourth of market value), your equity declines by 50% to $10,000 ($30,000 less the $20,000 on margin leaves $10,000). If your maintenance margin requirement is 25% you are required to have $7,500 in your account (25% x $30,000).

This example is based on the 25% level, which you meet because you have $10,000 in your account. However, what if your broker's rules demand a maintenance margin of 40%? In this case, you have to keep at least $12,000 on deposit (40% x $30,000 = $12,000). However, your current balance is only $10,000; so you will receive a margin call for an additional $2,000.

This example demonstrates not only the high risk of leverage but also the great disadvantage of using borrowed funds. In case of a price drop, your loss is doubled. The example assumed securities lost 25% of their value, but that meant your equity dropped by 50%. Why? Because with one-half leverage—turning $20,000 into $40,000—all of the loss falls on the equity side. A 25% decline in the $40,000 portfolio translates to a 50% loss on the equity side. This is the risk in using margin, in other words borrowing money, to invest.

The Advantage of Margin

The tendency among traders is to borrow the most they can, with an eye to potential profits only and disregarding potential losses.

The same doubling up occurs when prices rise, of course. If you begin with $20,000 as in this case and add another $20,000 in margin, what happens when your account value rises by $10,000? That $50,000 account consists of $20,000 in margin debt plus $30,000 in equity. In this case, your equity has grown by 50%. The high risk of leverage in this example turns into an accelerated profit rather than a loss. The amount in your portfolio above maintenance margin is given the odd name "excess equity."

In the case of a loss, even losing 50% of your equity as a consequence of a 25% loss in portfolio value is only the beginning. If the price continues to fall, the losses accelerate at the same rate. Another 25% loss wipes out your entire equity value, and you still owe $20,000 to your broker. However, the same argument can be made on the profit side. If you make a 50% gain based on a 25% positive move, what happens if the portfolio value rises 50%? In that case, you make a 100% gain. This is the appeal of margin investing if and when the portfolio positions move in the desired direction.

In contrast, in a cash account—one without any leverage—profits and losses are "1 to 1" and for many that is acceptable. Rebounding from a loss may be desirable compared to the risk of losing everything due to accelerated consequences of losses. For example, a $20,000 account declining by $5,000 is still worth $15,000 (not the $10,000 with margin maxed out). And if the account gains 25%, it is worth $25,000, not the $30,000 possible with maxed out leverage.

Risk Understanding

Too often, traders see only the profit potential involved with leverage. They do not realize that a 25% loss in a fully leveraged portfolio translates to a 50% loss in equity or that a 50% loss translates to a complete loss of equity. This risk is serious, so if you are going to use leverage to invest in stock, it should be with the full knowledge and understanding of the risks involved.

You will find language in your brokerage agreement disclosing the risks of margin trading; however, few traders read the fine print and even those who do often do not believe that the disclosed risks are real or that those risks affect them. But every trader should know exactly what is meant by this language.

The disclosure might read, for example, "Margin trading is engaging in transactions to purchase securities partially through a margin loan, with securities purchased serving as collateral. In the event of a decline in value, an initial margin deposit must be made to secure collateral obligations based on changing values in the securities purchased."

What does this mean? It's exactly what has been described here: If the value of your securities falls, you have to refresh your balances to maintenance margin levels and respond to margin calls promptly. Your losses are accelerated in a fully leveraged account at twice the rate of loss (because you have doubled your base by using borrowed funds).

The broker's disclosure will also remind you that "You may lose more money than the amount deposited in your margin account." This is a profound statement and the core of margin risk (again because leverage itself means doubling the investment base *and* the amount at risk). What many fail to realize is the meaning of this disclosure: In the event of losses, the equity side is where losses are taken, but the debt side remains and has to be repaid whether the portfolio rises or falls.

Another key disclosure item is that the broker has the right to increase the house maintenance margin at any time and also is not required to notify you in advance. Changes take effect immediately, so it is possible to get a margin call when you thought you were within the required levels. If you need time to satisfy this surprise change in margin requirements, you should also remember that under the disclosure agreement, you are not entitled to any extensions. If you don't make up the shortfall based on changed requirements immediately, your broker will liquidate positions without consulting with you.

Confronting the Margin Issues

How can you manage margin risk while still maximizing capital in your portfolio? This is where a few key policies have great effect and enable you to avoid unexpected losses:

1. *Know the rules.* Margin rules are not complex, and disclosure is always provided by brokerage firms to each customer with a margin account. Even so, many of the rules may come as a surprise, including margin calls and unannounced changes in maintenance margin levels. Knowing the rules and understanding what can occur is the first step in mitigating the margin risks every trader faces. Read the disclosures and make sure you are fully aware of all of the risks you face when using margin debt to invest.
2. *Use margin only when your capital base is adequate for unexpected market moves.* If your portfolio is going to be fully invested (meaning you are 100% "at risk"), you may also question whether you can afford to use leverage to increase your market exposure. The tremendous opportunities from margin come with equally tremendous risks. The best use of margin is when it is applied moderately and not to "double down" on risks in the hope of doubling up on profits.
3. *Only use margin when you need to; don't max it out.* That you can borrow up to 50% of the total of your portfolio does not mean you have to. Use margin as a bridge when you are fully invested or as a way to take advantage of exceptional opportunities. The way the system works is that initial margin at 50% is followed by maintenance margin somewhere below that level (for stock positions). This is a potential slippery slope allowing you to continue holding on to positions even as their value declines. The prudent step might be to close a position and take small losses rather than risk larger losses in case the current trend continues.
4. *When you have profits, eliminate margin balances.* You do not need to keep margin open and continue paying interest on borrowed funds. Every investor knows that market moves

often are followed by consolidation, so moving in and out of margin and using excess equity to pay down margin balances is wise. It cuts risk and reduces interest expense. It also means the borrowing potential is there for future use if you decide to tap it later.

5. *Identify ways to reduce margin risk.* Margin risk is going to be a constant if you (a) max out your borrowing at all times and increase positions just because you are allowed to, (b) fail to pay down margin after profits are realized or to minimize losses, or (c) fail to acknowledge the very real risks you face when you max out your margin debt.

To reduce these risks, using options in place of stock makes sense. You can control 100 shares of stock for 5% or less of the cost of stock, which is a smarter form of leverage than borrowing money from your broker. For example, if you buy an option and the price of the underlying moves against you, the loss is digestible at 5% or less of the value of the underlying security. However, had you doubled your position through margin, your realized loss would be twice the rate of loss on the full position (a 25% decline in value equals a 50% loss to your equity). Options solve this problem and also provide much greater control. You are less likely to experience a margin call or unexpected changes in policies on the part of your broker when you use options.

Option trading is subject to margin rules just as stock is and at times even to a greater maintenance margin level. Margin accounts provide borrowing advantages when stock is involved. However, for options trading, margin requirements are not a form of leverage but a collateral requirement. When you open a long option, you are required to pay the full price of the option and cannot leverage it. When you go short and the position is covered, there is no margin requirement. If the short option is uncovered, margin collateral requirement is 100% of the strike value of the option. So a short uncovered call with a 50 strike comes with a margin collateral demand of $5,000 per short option.

Option margin requirements are quite complex when you enter into combinations such as spreads and straddles. To see a complete analysis of margin collateral requirements for options trades, download a free copy of the *CBOE Margin Manual,* at http://cboe.com/LearnCenter/workbench/pdfs/MarginManual2000.pdf

The next chapter explains how leverage with options reduces your exposure to risk while keeping profit potential in place and how margin rules on options trades work.

CHAPTER 5

Elegant Solutions: Options to Address the Risk and Leverage Issues

> Is it progress if a cannibal uses knife and fork?
> Stanislaw Lec, *Unkempt Thoughts*, 1962

THE PROBLEM WITH MOST FORMS OF LEVERAGE IS HOW EASY IT IS to overlook or ignore its high risks. Whenever you borrow money to invest, you create a mathematical increase in the amount of profits, but that same increase applies to losses as well.

For swing traders, using margin to double up shares of stock appears to be a reasonable strategy at first, but that risk can wipe out a series of small profits in one big move in the wrong direction. A solution is to not swing trade with stock, because in that case you live with those risks. Use options instead, where the built-in risk limitation is a feature of the option price. Soon-to-expire contracts at the money are very cheap, and in the typical swing trade you only need a few days for a reversal to make that contract profitable.

What happens, though, if the timing and signals are off and the price moves in the opposite direction? In this case, you will lose. However, because the option is so cheap compared to stock, the loss is not as severe. For example, with a $50 stock, you need $5,000 to buy 100 shares ($2,500 cash plus $2,500 margin). If the price declines 25% to $37.50 per share, you lose half of your cash investment or $1,250. Using an option in the same situation may cost about $250 but allows you to control 100 shares. And you can buy a call to time an uptrend or a put to time a downtrend.

If the price moves in the wrong direction and your option becomes worthless, you lose 100%. But your loss is 100% of $250, which is less undesirable than 50% of $2,500—$250 versus $1,250.

This makes the point that leverage in a swing trading program based on options expiring within one month and at the money carries lower risk and is potentially more profitable than using stock. In addition, on the bearish side of the trade, a long put has much less market risk than 100 shares shorted.

Like stocks, options are subject to margin rules as well. However, with options you are dealing with a much lower dollar level, and so the margin risk is also much lower. Options trading has to be executed in a margin account, but margin has a different meaning in this context than it has for stock-based trading.

The Meaning of Margin in Options Trading

Margin for stock transactions is leverage in the form of borrowed funds. In options trades, margin is the dollar amount that must be placed on deposit when trading options in the brokerage account, specifically if and when you sell options. The deposit is collateral to protect the broker's exposure to loss in the event you lose on your options trade, and in this respect margin for options shares one of the features stock traders know about.

However, the margin is a required level of protection and not leverage in the same way as it is for stocks. You are required to provide initial margin and maintenance margin for options trades based on the rules set by your broker, which have to be at least as stringent as the minimums established by the Federal Reserve, as shown in table 5.1.

The requirements are more complex for nonequity options and for combinations and advanced strategies (butterfly and box spreads, for example). The requirements, as complex as they are,

Table 5.1 Margin requirements for options trades

Trade type	Margin requirements for equity options		
	Cash initial Requirement	Initial Margin	Maintenance Margin
long call or long put (9 months or less to expiration)	pay for the option at 100%	No additional cash deposit is required	None
listed: **long call or long put** (more than 9 months to expiration)	pay for the option at 100%	75% of cost	75% of value
OTC: **long call or long put** (more than 9 months to expiration)	pay for the option at 100%	75% of intrinsic value plus 100% of excess of purchase price over intrinsic value	75% of intrinsic value
short options	cash equal to exercise price	100% of proceeds plus 20% of value of underlying security, less OTM amount if any (to minimum of proceeds plus 10% of exercise price)	100% of market value, plus 20% of underlying value, less OTM amount if any (to minimum of proceeds plus 10% of exercise price)
combined short puts and short calls	cash equal to exercise price	greater of short put or short call requirement plus proceeds from the other side	greater of short put or short call requirement plus proceeds from the other side

Source: *CBOE Margin Manual*, at www.cboe.com.

do not relate to collateral for borrowed funds (as is the case for stock traded on margin), but relate solely to collateral requirements for trading options. "Margin" has a different meaning in each situation.

Leverage risks for option trading are absolutely separate from the margin requirements. The rules apply strictly to how much cash must be left on deposit to protect the broker from market risks, especially for short-side transactions. Leverage risks for options trading are derived from the nature of the transaction itself and not from the margin requirements.

Options are by definition a form of leverage, but they are not based on borrowed money as much as on the degree of exposure. This leverage risk is defined by long versus short, covered versus uncovered, time to expiration, and moneyness of the option. However, options solve the margin risk associated with stocks traded on margin by eliminating the debt aspect. Note that for equity positions, you are required to pay for the option as part of the initial phase. Some types of transactions require initial and maintenance margin at 100% others at 75%. But the market risk of the option-based margin is quite different from that of the stock-based leverage accomplished through margin.

The true definition of leverage for options is found in the contract itself. Every option controls 100 shares of stock, and the short-term ATM option is probably going to be valued at or below 5% of the value of that underlying security. That is, the leverage is built in to the option and is not a matter of borrowed money.

The Leverage Attribute of Options

The great advantage in using options to swing trade is found in the leverage attributes. A relatively low-cost option allows you to control 100 shares of the underlying. In a majority of options trading strategies, the great concern is the offset between time and cost. Where there is more time until expiration, the option cost is higher due to time value. The less time until expiration, the lower the cost but the sooner the position will expire.

This relationship is different for options on the same underlying depending on their moneyness. That is, an option far OTM will experience lower responsiveness between option premium and price movement in the underlying . When time to expiration is greater (for example, over three months), even options that are ATM are not going to respond point-for-point. The move to ITM may be offset by changes in extrinsic value (implied volatility).

These problems are resolved when you use options expiring in one month or sooner and focus on those options that are ATM or slightly ITM. With these, you accomplish maximum leverage. Premium value is going to be closest to point-for-point changes as the option moves ITM. Unlike most option strategies, swing trading is based on the assumption that a swing is going to last between three and five sessions, so that a short remaining life is not a disadvantage. In fact, because time value is all or mostly gone, the impending expiration is a great advantage.

In most types of options trading, timing is focused on a study of volatility. Short positions are best opened when implied volatility is quite high, and long positions are timed when implied volatility is quite low. In a swing trading strategy, this approach can be used; however, volatility often requires more than the three to five sessions swing traders follow. So a different system is recommended for option-based swing trading: using charts to track the underlying.

A majority of traders view charts as useful for stock trades only and implied volatility as the primary means for timing of options trades. However, using price, volume, and momentum signals based on the underlying is also an effective method for timing options trades. This is especially true for short-term (one month or less) contracts that are ATM or slightly ITM. These positions—because of the status of time and proximity between strike and current price of the underlying—maximize the leverage potential of options.

The highly promoted advantages of using margin to leverage stock purchases is appealing because virtually anyone with cash to invest gets approved automatically for margin borrowing. It is made all too easy, and emphasis is placed on the profit potential. Many traders using margin simply have not studied the math enough to understand that losses are doubled in the same way as profits. A 25% decline in a fully margined position means a loss of 50% of equity for traders, and a 50% decline means a 100% loss. With options, these high risks are eliminated by maximum leverage based on the option terms rather than on borrowed money. Borrowing money to buy more stock means not only having to repay the debt, but also having to pay interest on the amount borrowed. The rate ranges between 6.5% and 8.5% depending on the brokerage firm and on the total margin amount outstanding.

The key point to remember in this comparison is that the margin account is leverage based on borrowing money to buy more stock. But with options the leverage is based on the low cost of the option itself and not on any borrowed money. A comparison of risk profiles between margin borrowing of stock and the use of options is shown in figure 5.1.

To an extent, margin requirements for options trading can be avoided with the use of a cash account. In this type of account, the trade has to be fully paid for by settlement date (the day following the options trade). If you enter a swing trading program using only long options, you can trade in a cash account. However, you cannot open short positions; for short-option trading, you must have a margin account.

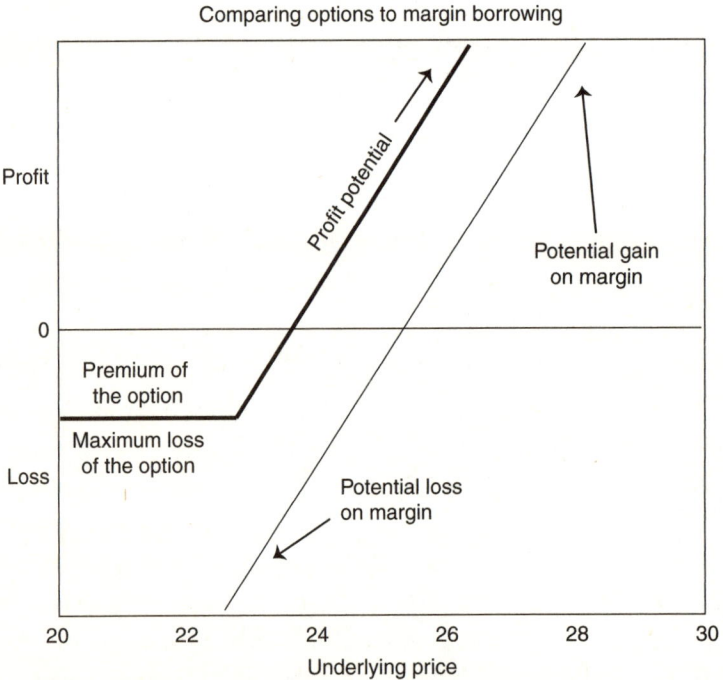

Figure 5.1 Comparing options to margin borrowing
Source: Figure created by author.

Managing the Margin Requirement: Equity Levels Needed

If you trade strictly long positions, you can use a cash account. For some traders, this is preferable simply to avoid the margin collateral requirements. However, your broker may require a minimum account balance to trade options under any conditions, and to maintain flexibility in the use of options it is highly desirable to be able to trade long or short and in combinations. If you have adequate equity in your account, using margin and meeting the collateral demands is not difficult.

For listed long options bought in a margin account, you are required to pay for the entire trade initially. No additional margin is required after this trade as long as expiration is nine months or less. For a swing trading program, this should describe virtually all of your long trades. If you purchase options extending beyond nine months, you can deplete your margin to 75% of the cost (initial) and then up to 75% of current value (maintenance).

For short options, you are not allowed to trade in a cash account. You have to use margin and meet the specific margin requirements. The calculation is complex, but generally speaking you have to maintain cash equal to the exercise price of the short margin (for example, if the strike is 30, you have to keep $3,000 on hand). The initial margin is for an additional 20% of the underlying value (less the extent of OTM points). For combinations including short calls and short puts opened at the same time, the cash has to be at least equal to the exercise price.

The margin requirements for short options provide no leverage whatsoever. In a stock portfolio, you are allowed to margin up to 50% of the long position's value, which increases both profit and loss potential. For options, however, the issue is not leverage but coverage of risk. This is why the collateral requirements are so high.

Leverage Outcomes: Comparing Stocks to Options

Without considering the differences in risk, a comparison between investing in stock and the purchase of a single call option demonstrates the much greater net return that options provide. This leverage cannot be ignored, and it makes using options the most practical method of swing trading. Swing trading using options addresses the complex issues of leverage by the nature of the option contract. This alternative to leverage by way of borrowing money (margin) solves the most serious problem of all, the accelerated losses that every margin trader faces. A second aspect to the options-based swing trade is the means of timing in the trades themselves. In most a trading strategies, distinctions are made between reliance on analytical tools for stocks and options. The options-based swing trade bridges these differences.

Most stock trades are based on analysis of charts and the use of technical tools: price patterns, candlestick indicators, volume, moving averages, and momentum oscillators. Most options trading focuses on the study of implied volatility (IV) and, to a degree, on comparisons between implied volatility (options) and historical volatility (stocks). This distinction ignores the great opportunities in combining both forms of analysis.

The problem in relying on IV as the primary signal for entry and exit is that the duration of IV movement is not certain. Degrees of IV often are too subtle to provide clear entry and exit timing. Changes from low to high (or high to low) might occur very rapidly or might take many days or even weeks. The momentum of IV is uncertain, especially in comparison to the charting and technical signals stock traders use. IV analysis is appropriate for most options strategies, which are likely to be based on several weeks or months of strategic development. In fact, short strategies benefit from a longer "seasoning" of IV as the result of increased and accelerated time decay. The faster time decay occurs, the more likely the short option is to become profitable (even lacking the expected movement in the underlying). Swing trading is a short-term strategy, so relying on IV is not an effective method to manage the trade in a three- to five-day time frame.

For this reason, given the leverage advantages of options over stocks, it makes sense to maximize leverage by using the same timing tools that stock traders use. The options-based swing trading strategy based on chart patterns, volume, candlestick indicators, and momentum oscillators provides a timing advantage that IV cannot. The uncertainty of IV supports this argument and also helps overcome another problem with the IV-based timing strategy: Even the best-timed entry may have offsetting disadvantages as a consequence of time decay.

When the option is close to expiration (one month or less), it will be most responsive to movement of the underlying. This is true for ATM and ITM positions. However, at the same time, IV tends to be less of a factor during this same period. So IV is not as reliable as chart reversal patterns in this last month of the option's life span. Options traders focusing solely on IV will be inclined to use longer-term options, if only to build a reliable base for entry and exit as an aspect of IV analysis. This creates a problem. The swing trade, by definition, is a short-term trade, so swing traders rely on fast development of ITM profits. This is most likely in the last month of the option's life, the very time when IV is least likely to provide the signals required to time entry and exit.

This does not mean that IV should be abandoned entirely. It provides a great form of timing analysis and confirmation. However, even the most effective IV-timed trade is not going to work as well close to expiration as one based on charting indicators.

The relative value of one analytical means over another is a complex part of the timing question. Leverage is the key to all forms of analysis because options are leveraged against the underlying security. However, because this form of leverage does not require the use of borrowed funds, it carries lower risk than margin trading. The timing issues based on IV versus charting only make this comparative analysis more complex.

The IV of an option is likely to be most responsive to changes in the underlying when some time remains until expiration (more than one month). In this period, an ATM option's value consists of an exchange between IV and time value. So as time value declines, IV may be offset with increased premium; the net result is that overall premium value does not change as much as the underlying price changes. While many analysts lump these two attributes together, they are quite separate. Time value is predetermined and will decay at a rate that cannot be altered. Extrinsic value (IV) varies based on changes in proximity as well as time, but it is not so much a time value form of premium as an expression of perceived market risk. With all forms of analysis, the proximity between strike and current market value of the underlying and time until expiration are what determine the IV value (as well as changes in the underlying's historical volatility and, as a consequence, its own market risk).

So for longer-term options strategies, IV analysis is a sensible and necessary methodology for timing option entry and exit. However, for swing trading, IV is not reliable. This is why swing traders and day traders may not fully appreciate the value of charting and reversal analysis as an effective signaling approach. However, because swing trading is most effective when little time value remains (close to expiration) and when options are at or in the money, IV plays little or no role in identifying reversal points.

THE KNOWLEDGE AND EXPERIENCE PROBLEM

The swing trader normally focuses on the leverage issues and timing of trades, assuming shares of stock are the medium for the swing trade. Naturally, the detailed study of stock charts and technical indicators makes sense for this swing trader. The same trader might be dubious about the value of options in swing trading, even with their low cost, low risk, and attractive leverage features. This is where in-depth understanding of options is valuable.

A novice options trader will find IV to be particularly complex but may already be aware of the technical aspects of chart analysis. This is an advantage in entering a swing trading program, assuming that the basic rules and terminology of options can be mastered. However, it remains essential to gain knowledge and experience concerning the nature of options trading and how and why values change. This inevitably means that in order to fully appreciate the use of options for swing trading (even in a strategy completely based on chart analysis), the trader needs to understand how IV works and why values rise or fall apart from what occurs on the underlying chart.

The swings discovered and anticipated in reversal signals form the basis for timing entry or exit. Even so, an unusually high or low option premium relative to premium on other options raises the question of IV as a confirming or contradictory signal. A well-timed entry at the bottom or top of the swing is expected to lead to changes in both the underlying price and in ATM short-term options. Why does this not always work?

The timing of reversal could be perfect. Even so, the underlying moves as expected, but the option value does not change at all or even moves in the opposite direction. This can occur when volatility is exceptionally high or low and subsequently adjusts. Even though you focus on options expiring in one month or less, with little or no time value, and ATM or ITM, the IV value is still a potential factor in changes to the premium value. At this point and proximity in the cycle, the IV offset is likely to be quite short-term, but with focus on a three- to five-day trend, the problem could delay or even offset the specific trade.

Because of this possibility, the reality is that trades are not always going to work as expected. Being aware of the status of IV at the point of entry into a swing trade (top of bottom, long or short, using calls or puts) may help avoid this surprise and eliminates one cause of a failed trade. Beyond this, some portion of trades is going to fail even when IV is not a factor. So IV awareness is one type of analysis for a well-timed options swing trade. However, it is only one of many analytical considerations.

This is where experience and knowledge about the nature of options trading are essential. The most expert chart analyst is going to make some poorly timed decisions, and that is unavoidable. However, in the use of options, the importance of IV cannot be stressed too much, even when primary focus is on chart-based reversal. This is so because the full option premium has only one part that is variable, namely, IV (extrinsic value). Time value as a separate force is predictable even though it works with and offsets IV changes (especially farther away from expiration). Likewise, intrinsic value is simply the degree to which the option is in the money.

You might have noticed that when the underlying moves in the money, the option value does not always move point for point.

This is another version of extrinsic offset. You know that time value offsets and often moves against growth in intrinsic value, but you don't expect to see this offset every day. Time value is more gradual. However, when the underlying moves three points in the money and the option premium moves only two points, the offset is likely to be caused by offsetting changes in IV value. This occurs most often when the strike and underlying price are quite close. The good news for swing traders is that when expiration is very close, this IV (or extrinsic) offset is not much of a factor.

Options with many months to go before expiration tend to be much less responsive to ITM change. This is one of the two reasons that swing trading works best with options expiring in one month or less. The second factor is that time value is at its lowest during this period, further leading to more responsive ITM premium movement.

Pattern Day Trading Risks

Options traders are going to be concerned with the risk of being subjected to the "pattern day trader" rule. This is a special margin requirement developed by the Financial Industry Regulatory Authority (FINRA, www.finra.org) to ensure that high-volume traders provide adequate collateral in their accounts.

In the past, day traders discovered that they were able to enter and exit trades even on very high dollar levels of risk without needing to deposit any funds on margin. Because margin is calculated based on outstanding trade balances at the end of the trading day, moving in and out of positions in a single session provided day traders with virtually unlimited leverage but without any collateral requirements.

As a result FINRA identified a type of trader called a pattern day trader. This is any individual executing four or more trades on the same security within a period of five consecutive trading sessions (and if the value of those trades is greater than 6% of total trading activity in the same time frame). This includes both long and short positions and encompasses stock as well as option trades. Any traders meeting this definition are required to deposit and maintain at least $25,000 on margin (in cash or securities) and to keep this margin on hand for each day on which these transactions are entered. If the equity in an account moves below the required $25,000, the day trading activity is frozen until the requirement is met.

This rule has been in effect since September 28, 2001, and is enforced at various levels by the Securities and Exchange Commission (SEC), National Association of Securities Dealers (NASD), and the New York Stock Exchange (NYSE) and is administered by brokerage firms overseeing customer accounts.

A problem with being identified as a pattern day trader extends beyond the initial $25,000 margin requirement. Once your account has been flagged and you are called a pattern day trader, your broker might continue to restrict you even if you are not day trading after the initial period. The $25,000 also is a *minimum* requirement set by the regulators. A brokerage firm may also impose a higher day trading margin based on the level of activity in your account. The rule concerning margin levels is vague as is the guideline for when the brokerage firm removes the restriction. You might have to negotiate to have the designation and margin requirement removed. It is much wiser to avoid getting flagged in the first place.

You cannot get around the rule by day trading in a cash account (meaning the use of long options but not short options). Day trading in a cash account is prohibited. You are required to pay the purchase price of the option or other security before selling it. This prevents using the day trading margin from going into effect. The practice of closing out positions before the end of the session, called "freeriding," is banned under the Federal Reserve's Regulation T. If you attempt to open and close day trades in your cash account, your broker will freeze your account for 90 days. This freeze does not prevent the purchase of securities, but it does ban all day trading.

The pattern day trading rule can easily interfere with an otherwise elegant swing trading strategy. The potential of moving in and out of a single position four or more times over five days often is attractive, but it is not worth being required to place $25,000 on margin. Some suggestions to avoid this limitation:

1. Don't try to skirt the margin requirements of options trading by limiting yourself to a cash account. This prevents the use of short positions; more seriously, day trading in a cash account is prohibited and could lead to a 90-day freeze. Focus on the collateral requirements of the margin account and don't try to get around the day trading rules. You are not allowed to day trade in this manner.
2. Be aware of the pattern day trading rule and make trades in several securities. There are plenty of swing opportunities available, and you may switch your short-term entry and exit between different securities to avoid falling into the pattern day trader definition. It is worth missing a few opportunities to avoid being restricted under this rule.
3. Remember that options are leveraged without any borrowing requirements. However, the collateral requirements imposed through margin are very specific. So know the rules and employ several different underlying positions.
4. If you overlook the rules and are identified as a pattern day trader, work with your broker to remove the restriction as soon as possible after closing positions on the security that led to this margin requirement. Remember, though, that your broker is not required under any specific rules to change this designation. So it is better to avoid the problem than to try and resolve it later.

Once you understand how margin collateral works for options trades, your swing trading program is going to rely on identification of strong entry and exit criteria. In previous chapters, the basic reversal signals (NRD, reversal day, and volume spike) served as a starting point. The next chapter shows how to use technical analysis to turn an options swing trading strategy into an effective and methodical system.

CHAPTER 6

IN AND OUT: ENTRY AND EXIT CRITERIA FOR SWING TRADING

> It's a delightful thing to think of perfection; but it's vastly more amusing to talk of errors and absurdities.
> — Fanny Burney, *Camilla*, 1796

BEYOND THE BASIC SWING TRADING SIGNALS—NRD, REVERSAL day, and volume spike—there exists a range of very specific and powerful reversal tools. This chapter shows how to put these together to time entry and exit most effectively.

No signal, range of signals, or even strongly confirmed signals can ever be expected to give you a 100% certainty about timing. Traders want to know what degree of improved performance they can expect from the effective use of swing trading signals, and that is a difficult issue to pin down. However, if you begin with the concept of a random walk, then any market decision is a fifty-fifty proposition. If price movement is truly random, then there is an equal chance to prices rising or falling at all times.

Although the random walk is only a theory and is easily disproven by an analysis of market behavior, it serves as a good starting point. Most traders have noticed that prices move in response to market-wide trends, earnings surprises, changes in management's guidance for the future, rumors of mergers or takeovers, and changes in historical volatility. In other words, price trends are reactionary. This is hardly random. However, to address the question of how reliable entry and exit signals are, make a few assumptions based on the random walk theory:

1. Without any charting analysis or knowledge about a stock's price, chances are equally for a rise or a fall in price.
2. Any known effects on price will alter the random starting point. (For example, an earnings disappointment is likely to cause the price to drop, and rumors of a takeover with a 10% bump above the current price will cause the current price to rise).
3. Any improvement you can accomplish above 50% likelihood will improve your overall timing outcomes.

For example, some candlestick indicators (such as the engulfing pattern) lead to reversal up to 80% of the time. When you see a bearish engulfing pattern at the top of an uptrend or a bullish engulfing pattern at the bottom of the downtrend, the pattern serves as a red flag indicating impending change. However, this is only the first phase in leading to action.

Beyond the initial signal, you may find confirmation in another candlestick pattern, a traditional Western indicator (double top or bottom, price gaps, or head and shoulders, for example), volume spikes and indicators, or changes in momentum oscillators. Any and all of these signals confirm the initial signal and improve your timing above a 50% probability.

Because all signals have a chance of failing, it makes no sense to place too much capital into a single trade. In order to ensure that overall timing effectively beats the odds without increasing risks as well, develop a plan to swing trade with a specific amount of capital in each trade. If you can improve your timing to 65% or 70%, you will have more profits than losses. If that change is possible through technical analysis and charting study, then these tools are worth using as your basis for deciding when to enter and exit trades.

A mistake traders are likely to make is to let themselves be convinced by the experience of a few highly successful trades that they have the system figured out. Then they begin making larger trades, putting more capital at risk, and ignoring or forgetting that timing will never be perfect. In this situation, one big loss wipes out a series of small gains and defeats the entire purpose of timing and risk reduction.

The solution is to identify the level of capital you are willing to put at risk in any one trade. Also identify the point where you are willing to take profits or to cut losses. Although swing trading is based on the premise of recognizing trends, there is no flaw in taking profits when they materialize. Equally important, there is no flaw in getting out of a poorly timed trade once you realize the problem. The temptation to hold off in the hope that the trend will turn and move in your direction is common, but that turn usually does not occur. You are better off taking a small loss today and preventing a complete loss next week.

A starting point in timing your trades is to look for reversal setup signals. This is true whether you are looking for the best moment to enter a trade for the first time or to exit a trade you have on at the moment.

The Reversal Setup

Chart analysis is made stronger when repetitive price patterns appear. Analysts will take comfort in recognizing that trading ranges of a particular stock maintain the same breadth even as price swings upward and downward. They also recognize how price behavior changes as prices approach resistance and support. These observations concerning repetitive price patterns enable swing traders to predict and time trades. When losses occur due to poor timing, they tend to be small, and when timing based on price patterns is effective, the outcome tends to be profitable.

For example, note the predictability of price patterns for U.S. Steel over several months, as shown in figure 6.1.

The breadth of trading remained in approximately a two-point range throughout most of the charted period even though a series of sharp uptrends and downtrends occurred consistently. The duration of these trends averaged two weeks. That is, the breadth of trading and duration of offsetting trends were both

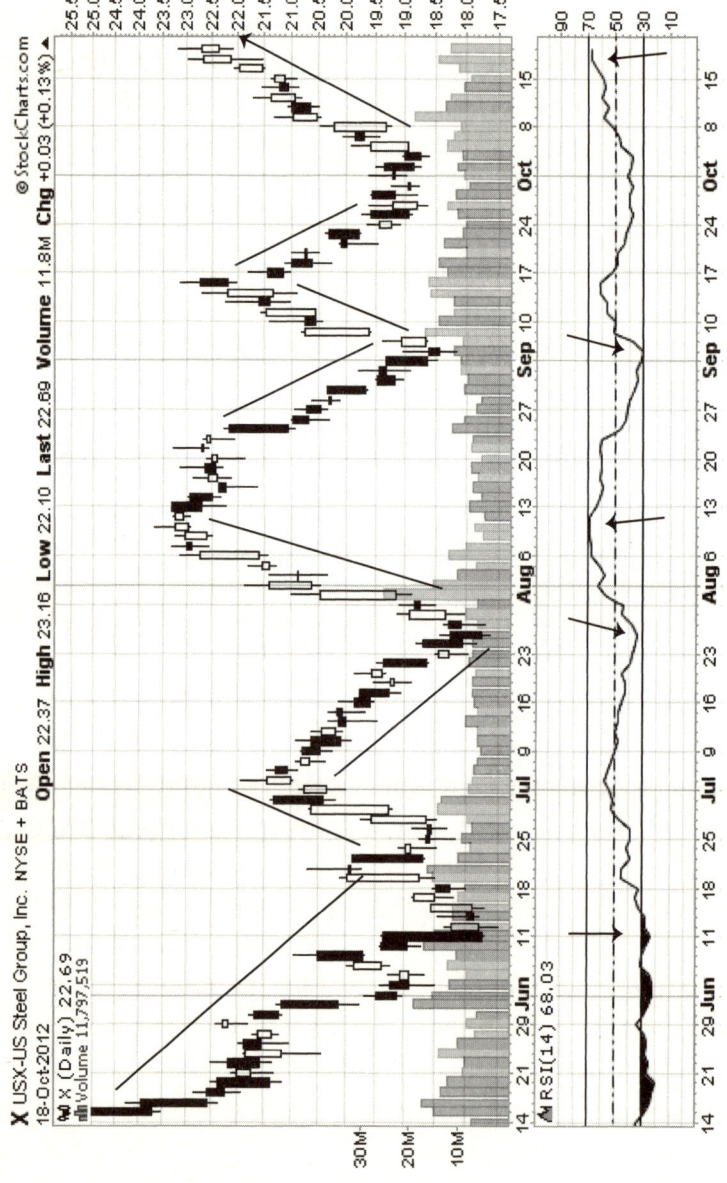

Figure 6.1 Repetitive patterns
Source: StockCharts.com.

repetitive. The established levels of resistance ($23.50) and support ($18.00) held throughout, and as price approached these levels, it reversed. In fact, the appearance of reversal days right at the turning point was remarkably consistent. Adding to this pattern was the movement of the Relative Strength Index (RSI) oscillator, which approached and touched the 70 and 30 lines just as reversal occurred. In each case, the RSI change followed the trend but provided a specific likely turning point in advance of the turn itself.

This consistent pattern by no means ensures that the pattern will continue into the future. However, it does provide a starting point for seeking reversal setup signals. In the case of U.S. Steel the combination of resistance and support holding up and consistent reversal days provides a starting indicator for swing trading. For example, the last session on the chart does not appear to signal reversal. Price was nearly at resistance, but a reversal day (a black candlestick) had not yet appeared.

Reversal setup comes in dozens of different forms, some subtle and others quite obvious. Recognition of repetitive patterns adds strength to the observed setup signals, such as price approaching reversal or support followed by a reversal day. For swing traders studying charts of a range of stocks, this repetitive advantage reduces uncertainty. As a short list of "favorite" swing trading stocks emerges, and the primary reason for including them is their predictability based on a repetition of signals and price patterns.

For anyone dubious about technical analysis, the suggestion that repetitive patterns provide timing help is questionable. However, a study of the effects found in resistance and support, price gaps, candlestick indicators, volume, and momentum oscillators do point to a predictable outcome often enough to draw the attention of even the skeptic. Patterns are reflections of the interaction of buyers and sellers, the orderly exchange of supply and demand, and even of the efficiency of the market. Within the chaos of short-term price movement, repetitive patterns, once recognized, are the basis of setup clues that every trader seeks.

A widely held belief in the market is that cyclical timing contains too many variables to be used reliably in timing entry and exit. Chart analysis is part art and part science, and studying setup signals may encompass both intuitive and visual perceptions of price patterns and logical, mathematical conclusions drawn from indicators as they appear. One example, referring again to the U.S. Steel chart, was seen in the oscillator of RSI, which hinted at the conclusion of both uptrends and downtrends by approaching those "magic" index values of 70 (overbought) and 30 (oversold). Combine this with the visually accessible narrow trading range and trend duration, and you have a clear and discernible pattern.

Setup signals come in many shapes and sizes, and you cannot rely only on a few that you have found often. However, some stock movements do follow precise patterns and rhythms. U.S. Steel's chart is easy to study as a visually clear set of bouncing prices between resistance and support in a highly predictable pattern. Is this simply good hindsight? To a degree it is, but swing traders learn to use combinations to mark reversal and then confirm it. Reversal is most likely to occur at or near resistance and support, a tendency shown strongly in the chart of U.S. Steel. By observing the duration of short-term trends as well as tracking movement in the momentum oscillator, advance timing is improved based on the rhythmic patterns and their repetitive nature.

Channel Analysis

Beyond the tendency of price to follow repetitive patterns, many specific but simple formations make it easier to time entry and exit. For example, channel lines may reassure a trader that the breadth of trading is not changing or warn when it is.

The channel lines track evolving trends, either with a positive or a negative slope. The upper side of the range is resistance and the lower is support, as in all trading ranges. However, the value of the channel lines is that they signal changes in the trading range breadth, usually preceding a breakout from the existing trend.

The channel exists between two parallel lines. In a rising trend, the lower line is the trend line and the upper line is the channel line. These titles are reversed in a declining trend. The channel begins at a point where there are at least two reaction lows (bullish trend beginning) or reaction highs (bearish). These two lines are parallel. Thus, the range between high and low remains the same even as price levels move upward or downward. Changes in that parallel movement define when a trend is on the verge of ending. However, further analysis is needed to determine whether the end of the trend is going to lead to an upside or downside move.

Any price move below support or above resistance serves as an initial signal of a coming change. A second change is the increase or decrease in the breadth of trading. Beyond this, you would also expect to find reversal signals in candlesticks and volume indicators or momentum oscillators as confirmation of the coming change in price direction. The rising channel line is evident in the chart of Amazon (AMZN) in figure 6.2.

The channel extended for nearly two months, with both resistance and support gradually rising. The end of this trend and likely reversal were marked by the highly reliable two-session candlestick indicator, the bearish engulfing pattern. This occurred at the same time that the channel line ended due to the price decline.

The opposite direction reveals the same recognizable channel direction and conclusion. On the chart of Research in Motion (RIMM in fig. 6.3), a highly volatile period consisted of short-term downward channels with clearly marked reversal signals. First was an unusual but very strong double candlestick reversal, the piercing line followed by a harami. The harami by itself is not a very reliable reversal signal, but when it appears in this configuration, it confirms both the end of the channel and the more reliable piercing line.

The uptrend that followed also ended with a clear reversal signal in the form of a bearish engulfing indicator. This is an exceptionally strong signal, especially when it appears after a price run-up *and* immediately after a price gap.

The next downtrend concluded after a one-month downside run with a reversal day and a gap to the upside. This led to a one-week uptrend ending with a gap and then a double top.

The final downtrend consists entirely of sessions with gapping prices and concluded with a reversal day. A comparison

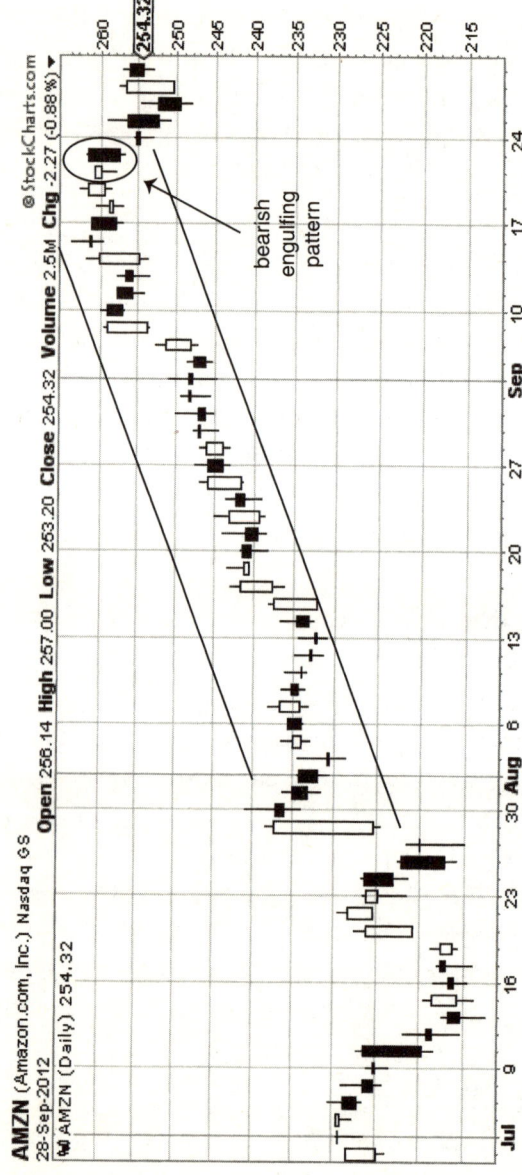

Figure 6.2 Channel lines—rising trend
Source: StockCharts.com.

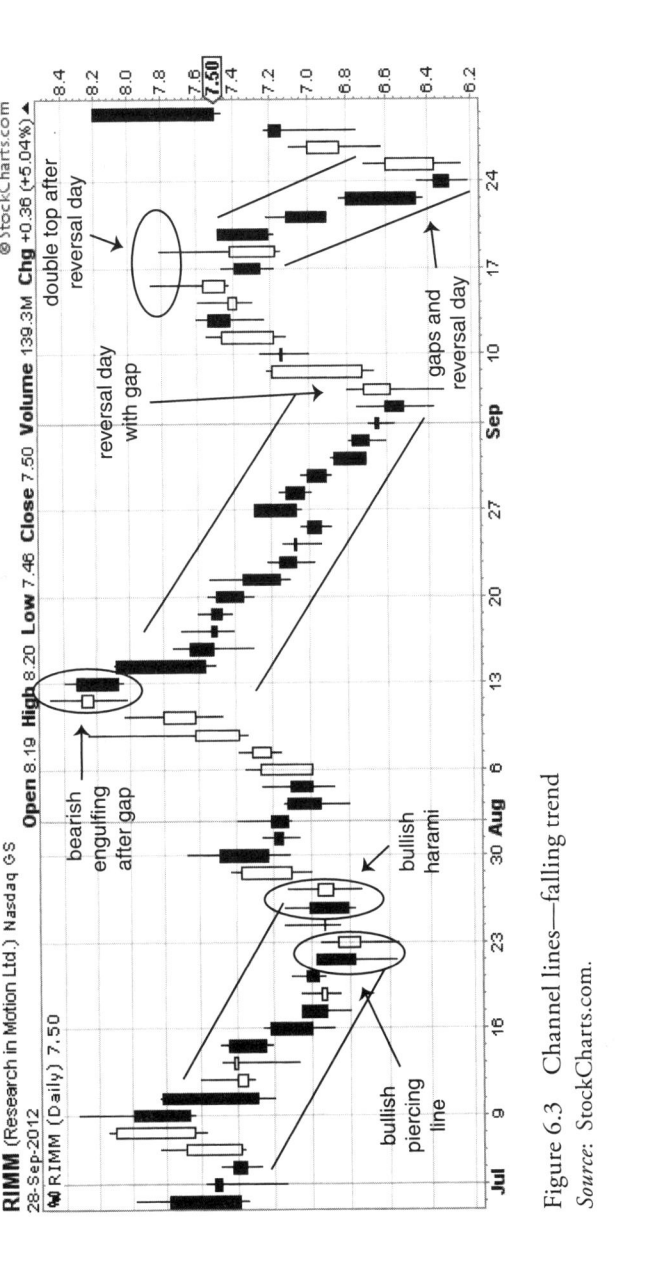

Figure 6.3 Channel lines—falling trend
Source: StockCharts.com.

between the uptrend and downtrend channels shows that these trends lasted varying periods of time. This raises a question: How long does the trend have to continue to be considered a channel? Perhaps the best answer is that duration does not matter as long as it provides clear and strong reversal indication, enabling you to improve timing of entry and exit.

Channels do not always lead to reversal, as in the previous examples. They may precede continuation as well. This is why you need to pay attention to the signals. A breakout above resistance after an upward-trending channel or below support after a downward-trending channel occurs as an acceleration of the established trend. For example, The Travelers (TRV) chart in figure 6.4 consists of upward-trending channel lines, concluding with two weeks of sideways movement and then a strong bullish continuation indicator, the thrusting lines.

This signaled the resumption of the uptrend. Notice the contrast between the narrowing daily range of trading in the preceding sessions to the large and fast-moving upward sessions after this signal. The narrowing ranges were a further signal that a reversal—was likely to occur.

The same observations hold true after a downtrend. The chart of Digital Realty Trust (DLR) in figure 6.5 provides a good example. The downtrend marked by the channel lines extended for six weeks before the gapping jump in price. However, this was followed quickly by a continuation signal, the bearish side-by-side black lines. After this, a stronger downtrend began.

Channel lines are tools for tracking dynamic trends and identifying turning or ending points (or resumption of the trend in some cases). If you are already in a trend, watching the development of channel lines provides early indication of the trend's end and, when confirmed, supports an exit signal (or continuation). If you are not yet in a trade, the same channel lines provide initial entry signals and, once confirmed, help mark the best time to make the trade.

Channel lines often end at a point of reversal. Evolving price patterns of other types, such as wedges, are another form of reversal signals, and triangles most often signal continuation. A

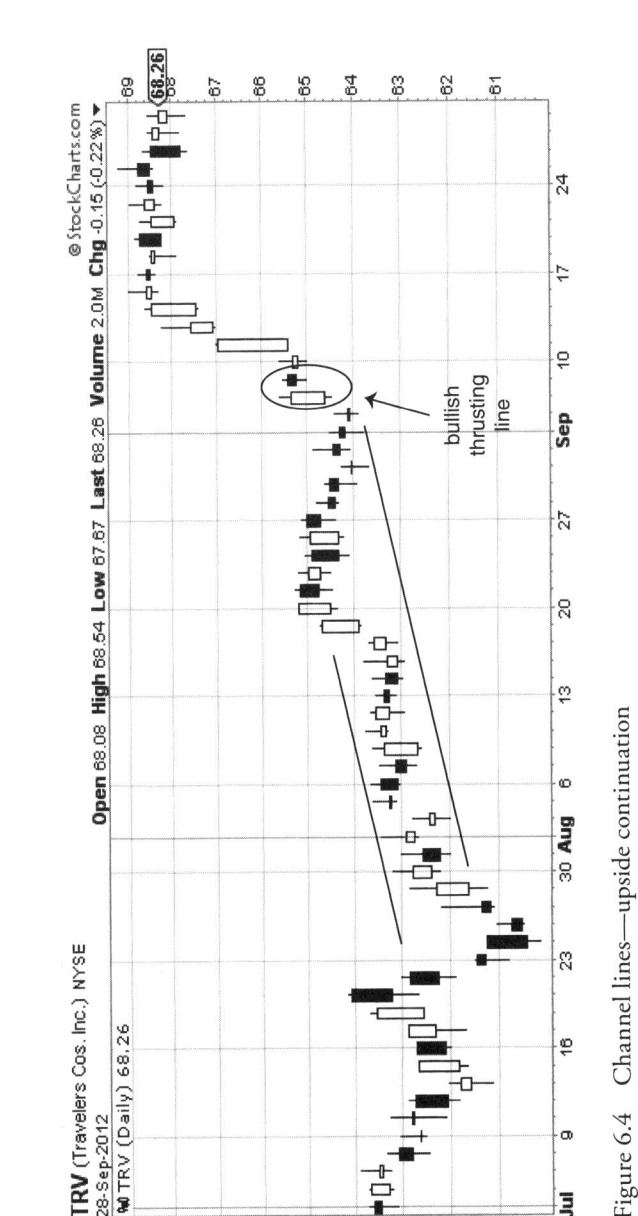

Figure 6.4 Channel lines—upside continuation
Source: StockCharts.com.

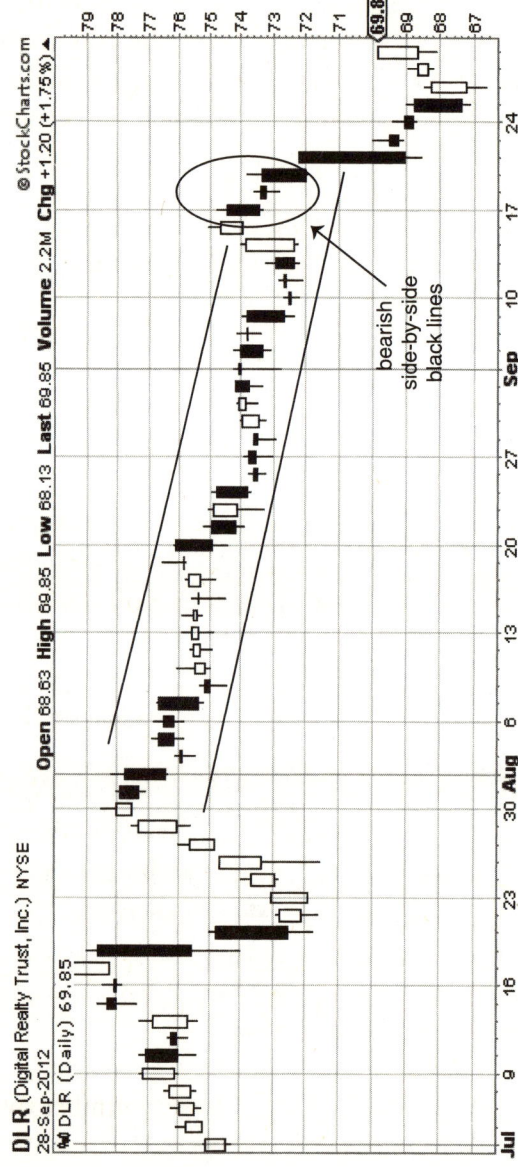

Figure 6.5 Channel lines—downside continuation
Source: StockCharts.com.

wedge consists of narrowing movement in both the upper and lower channel lines, and when these converge, price is likely to turn in the opposite direction. A triangle normally consists of price movement on one side with a narrowing on the other; as the range narrows, the side showing a change is likely to continue its movement in the same direction. Any time you are working with evolving trends of any type, including the parallel trending channel lines, you need to rely on confirmation before taking action.

Retracement and Pullback

In every trend there are likely to be periods of retracement, temporary price reversals moving against the trend's direction. Swing traders can use these price movements to execute entry and exit. One of the ways that the degree of retracement is made predictable is through Fibonacci analysis.

Leonardo Fibonacci was a thirteenth-century mathematician who observed repetitive numerical tendencies in nature. The *Fibonacci sequence* is a set of numbers in which each value is the sum of the two previous numbers:

0, 1, 1, 2, 3, 5, 8, 13, 21, 34, 55, 89, 144, and so forth

Why is this sequence important in chart analysis? When estimating the degree of retracement, you are likely to discover clues in the Fibonacci Sequence. Any number in the sequence divided by the following number yields approximately 62%:

$55 \div 89 = 61.8\%$
$13 \div 21 = 61.9\%$

Any number in the sequence divided by the number two places ahead results in approximately 38%

$55 \div 144 = 38.2\%$
$13 \div 34 = 38.2\%$

A retracement, when price is moving in the opposite direction of its established trend, is distinguished from reversal because there is a lack of reversal signals. Swing traders may assume that retracement is underway and can estimate the degree of retracement based on the Fibonacci sequence. The degree of price change in retracement is likely to exhibit a price pullback of 38%, 50%, or 62%. This is not a certainty, but these price points mark a potential area where the retracement is likely to conclude.

For example, as shown in figure 6.6, Caterpillar (CAT) went through a period of uptrend, from a price of $78 to $91 in about one month or 13 points. The price peaked and then declined. It fell back to $83 or 8 points from the high. This decline represented a 61.5% decline in price from the high:

$$8 \div 13 = 61.5\%$$

This is very close to the 62% level expected for retracement to conclude and for the established trend to continue. The Caterpillar example demonstrates how a retracement can be defined and when resumption of the trend is likely to continue.

The same applies in cases of downtrends. As shown in figure 6.7, Duke Energy (DUK) experienced an extended downtrend over most of a three-month period. This included two distinct retracements. The first retracement occurred after a decline from $70.50 to $64.50, a drop of 6 points, and it was from $64.50 to $66.75 or 2.25 points. This was a 37.5% retracement:

$$2.25 \div 6 = 37.5\%$$

The second retracement came after the resumption of the downtrend beginning at $67.50 and a drop in the price to $63.00, a decline of 4.75 points. The retracement moved from the low of $63 up to $64.75, a rise of 1.75 points. This represented a retracement of 36.8%, close to the 38% target level:

$$1.75 \div 4.75 = 36.8\%$$

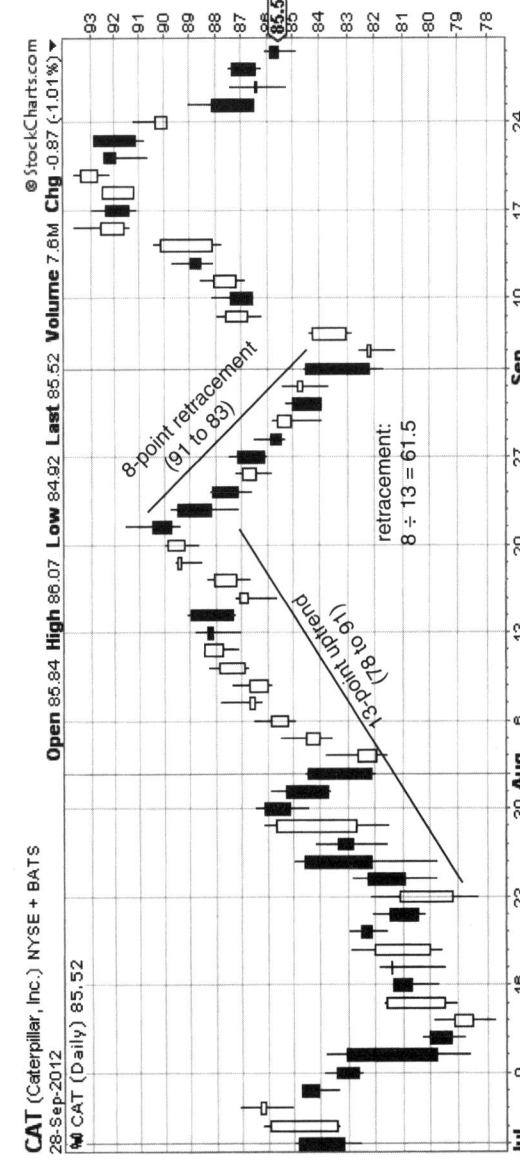

Figure 6.6 Fibonacci retracement in an uptrend
Source: StockCharts.com.

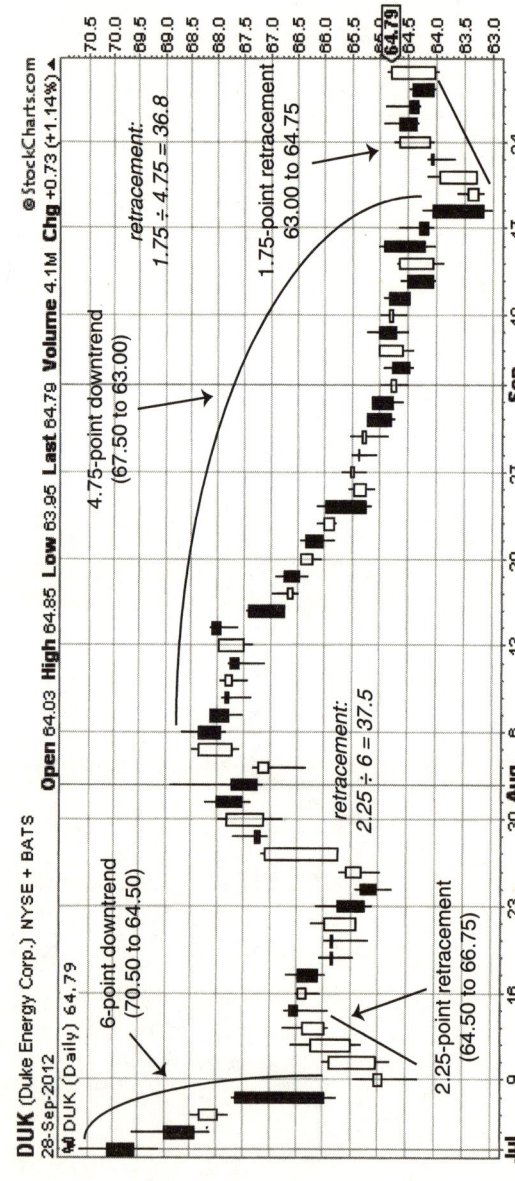

Figure 6.7 Fibonacci retracement in a downtrend
Source: StockCharts.com.

This sequence is useful in identifying where to seek the possible end of the retracement, but it does not provide enough on its own merits. The lack of reversal signals often defines retracement, however, so this natural pattern helps to develop a rationale for the extent of retracement and likely return to the established trend.

COILED MARKETS

A "coiled" market is one poised to make a strong move away from its established trend. Because of the coiled condition, the move may be stronger than it would have otherwise been. For swing traders, this condition represents a typical delayed reaction followed by an overreaction.

The offset of relatively high volatility and fast price movement against inactivity and low volatility is what presents swing trading opportunities. The change in the rhythm of price movement accompanies tests of resistance and support, earnings announcements, and rumors. What might appear as impulsive is in reality the consequence of accumulated and discovered news and the reaction to it by buyers and sellers. Either side is likely to suddenly gain or lose confidence in the trend; this is reflected in momentum. When an extended period of congestion occurs, you cannot know which direction will dominate the next trend, but the longer that period extends, the stronger the eventual movement might be. This coiled spring effect may frustrate a trader who is not paying attention, just as it rewards traders watching for the price, volume, and momentum signals foreshadowing a coming new trend.

Coiled movement is usually thought of as offsetting temporary movement in the direction opposite to the established trend, but it might also be found immediately after the end of congestion. Swing traders are frustrated by the sideways movement of congestion and may fail to recognize the warning signals of a move about to occur. Seeking only immediate and clearly identified reversals means many coiled market opportunities can be missed.

For example, the chart of Alcoa (AA), shown in figure 6.8, consists of a two-month uptrend, interrupted by a period of declining, a form of coiled spring. This began with the bearish inside down pattern as marked on the chart.

The coil offset ended with the reversal to the upside. The continuing uptrend itself concluded at the top of the price range with the bearish inverted hammer. All of the back and forth and signals involved were quite useful to swing traders, who may have entered and exited several times during this period. However, note the longer-term uptrend that persisted throughout even to the end of the period.

Another coiled market example is seen in figure 6.9 in the chart of Hewlett-Packard (HPQ). The difference here is that the coiled market period was moving sideways, representing a brief period of consolidation before the downtrend continued.

The initial downtrend was quite sharp but concluded with a double signal in the form of a narrow range day (NRD) that also served as a reversal day. The congestion coil lasted a month and, during such periods, it may be quite difficult to determine whether the next move will be a reversal or continuation. In this instance, a bearish engulfing pattern (which is reliable for reversal 80% of the time it appears) appeared and was quickly confirmed with an exceptionally long black candle session. The downtrend resumed.

Because coiled markets represent a delay in the current trend, the subsequent movement often is exaggerated, representing a delayed form of momentum within that trend. However, swing traders demand certainty in the form of confirmation, especially with coiled markets. These are not certain and may in fact not be coiled markets at all but the beginning of something new, such as a reversal in the trend. Therefore, confirmation is especially important in identifying the end of the coiled market period.

One signal that the coiled period is ending may be found in the narrowing breadth of the range. This was the case for Alcoa (AA) whose chart is shown in figure 6.8 but less so for Hewlett-Packard

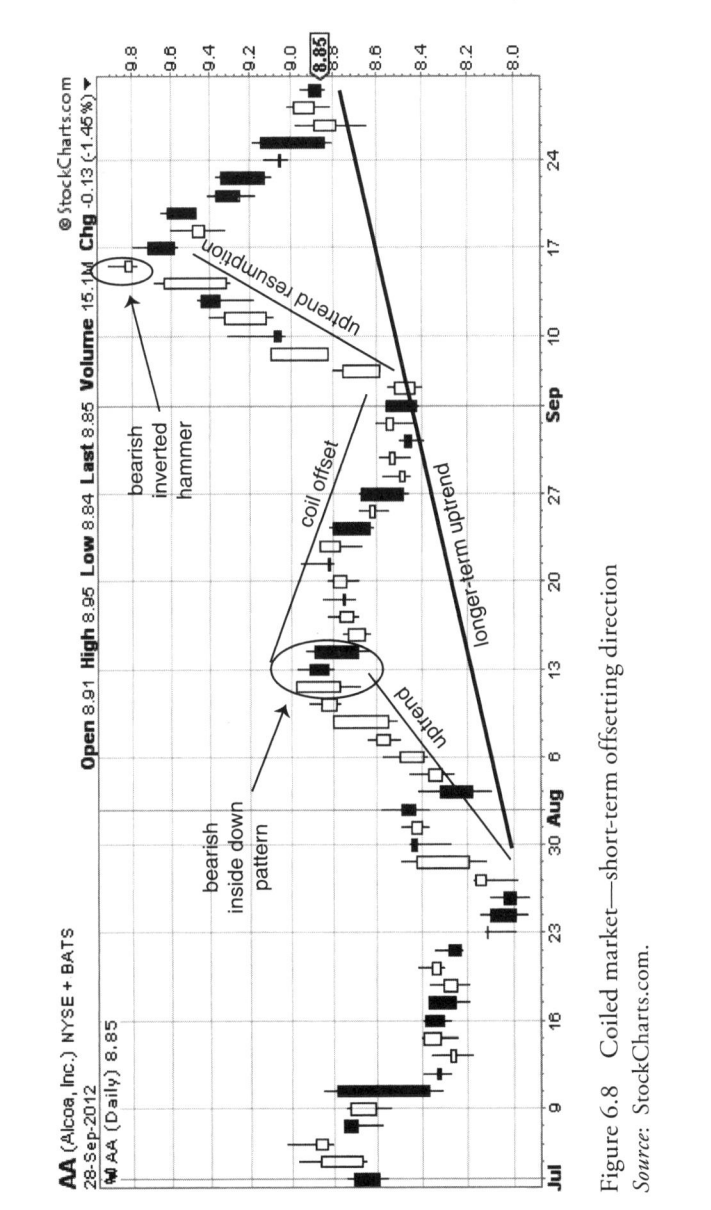

Figure 6.8 Coiled market—short-term offsetting direction
Source: StockCharts.com.

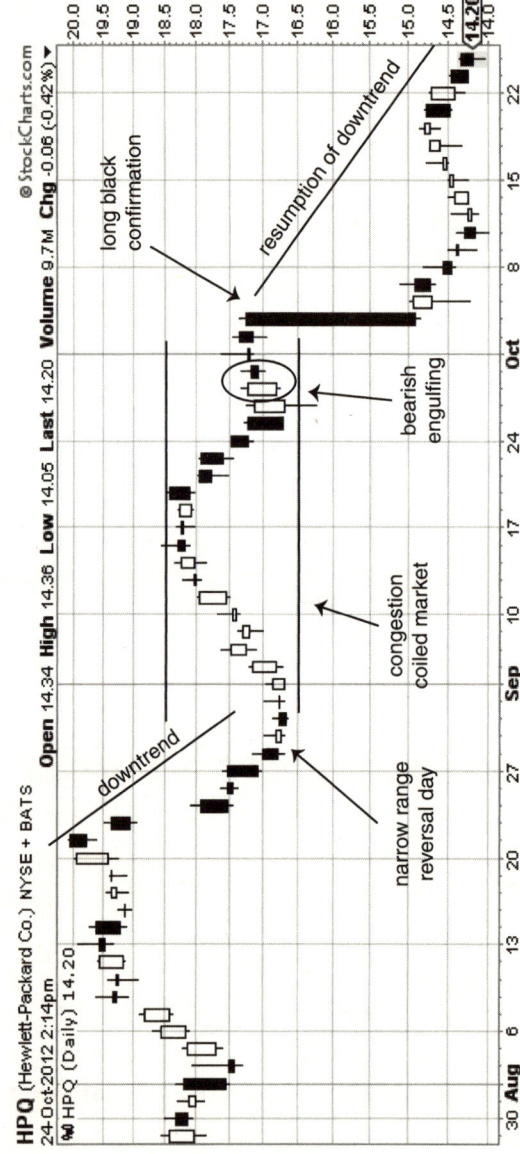

Figure 6.9 Coiled market—congestion midway in the trend
Source: StockCharts.com.

(HPQ). However, whereas on AA's chart the coiled market phase concluded with a narrowing breadth during the decline of the coiled market, HPQ signaled the end of the congestion and immediately provided strong confirmation. Signals such as triangles to signal continuation (or wedges to indicate a likelihood of reversal) are instructive in defining the nature of the offsetting price movement. It may be a coiled market or the beginning of a reversal, and therefore confirmation from additional price, volume, and momentum signals is essential before entering a new trade. Coiled markets are exceptionally difficult for the timing of swing trades although the interim price directions representing short-term uptrends and downtrends offer swing trading opportunities. For the less certain interpretation of offsetting and consolidation periods, the prudent action is to wait until a clearer direction emerges.

Reversal Gaps

One great pitfall in swing trading is to assume that trends reverse quickly. In fact, even after strong reversal signals a period of sideways movement or even continuation often occurs. Some reversals are delayed by a week or even more. So the problem you face is determining not only what constitutes a reversal signal, but also how quickly it is going to go into effect.

One exceptionally strong sign of the possibility for immediate reversal is found in the reversal gap. This occurs as the result of truly surprising news (such as a sharp and unexpected change in earnings news or management's guidance, for example) or a takeover or merger announcement. As a general rule, a strong uptrend is going to continue after a reversal signal due to the crowd mentality among buyers in the moment, and a strong downtrend may continue moving downward after a reversal signal due to strong panic among sellers. However, the surprise is easily spotted by a reversal gap, a price gap moving in the direction opposite to the prevailing trend.

This price gap may signal a very fast turnaround, and the wider the gap, the stronger that signal. This is true when a volume spike occurs also or when tracked momentum oscillators suddenly move into overbought (bearish) or oversold (bullish) conditions. When that reversal gap also occurs at or near resistance (bearish) or support (bullish), this adds strength to the likely fast reversal. Finally, even stronger confirmation is provided when the first reversal gap is quickly followed by another gap.

For example, IBM announced on July 18, 2012, that guidance for the coming full year was being raised from 14.27 to 14.40 EPS. This created an immediate reversal gap, as highlighted on the chart shown in figure 6.10.

A volume spike occurred in the session right after the upward gap confirmed the directional change. The gap was quite large, indicating strong reversal sentiment. The uptrend continued throughout the charted period, moving 25 points from low to high during these three months.

Another example of a reversal gap is more complex because of offsetting news announced soon after the directional change. Procter & Gamble (PG) had a two-week uptrend and then a very sudden downside gap. This took place as management announced guidance based on expected weaker growth and a cut in forecasts of both revenues and earnings. This is shown in the chart shown in figure 6.11.

Once again, a volume spike confirmed the reversal. However, a weak later, Relative Strength Index (RSI) had moved down into oversold territory, indicating that the reaction to the downside may have been exaggerated. As price began trending upward, a strong continuation indicator appeared in the form of three-session side-by-side white lines. As prices continued trending slightly higher, a series of very strong volume spikes also occurred, indicating that price was about to make another move. On July 12, Pershing Square Capital Management, LP, announced it had taken a stake in PG—and prices gapped upward in response.

In this example, the reversal gap was immediate and sharp, but the downtrend did not last long. The news of a new institutional position in the company created just as strong a reversal to the upside.

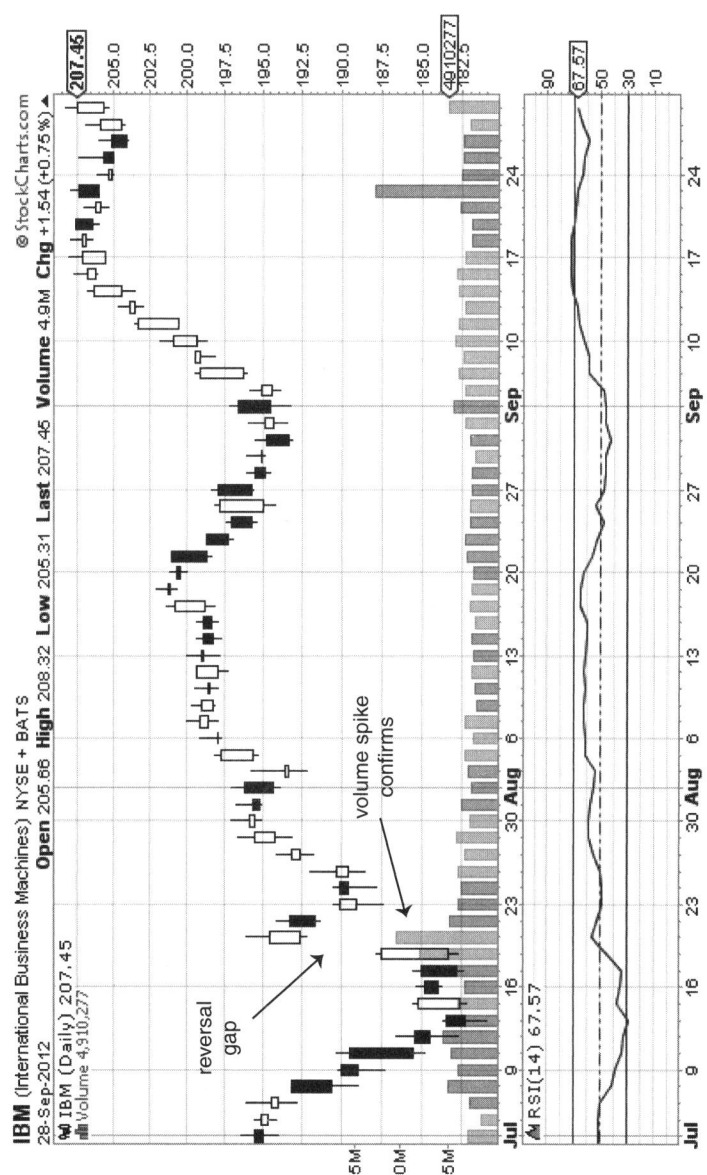

Figure 6.10 Reversal gap on earnings news
Source: StockCharts.com.

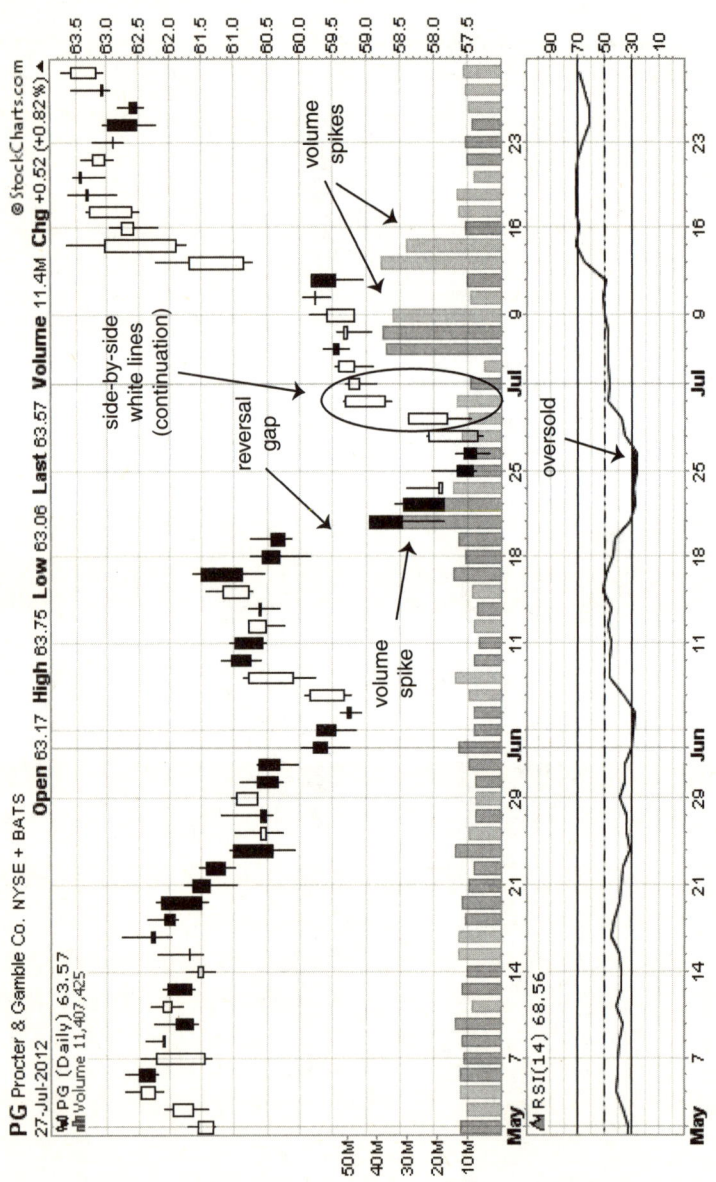

Figure 6.11 Reversal gap on earnings
Source: StockCharts.com.

Cup and Handle Reversals

The cup and handle is so called because it has the appearance of a dipping curve in price (the cup) and then a small adjustment (the handle) concluding with a reversal. As a reversal signal, this works for swing trading as signal or confirmation, often with an exceptionally strong new and opposite trend.

The chart of Exxon Mobil (XOM), shown in figure 6.12, demonstrates this pattern. After a downtrend appeared to stop, it resumed strongly and formed the cup shape. The handle consisted of a gap, a higher open and a lower close, and then a strong uptrend started and continued for two months.

The same pattern works when an uptrend reverses to a downtrend. The inverse cup and handle has the same attributes, as shown in the chart of J.P. Morgan Chase (JPM) in figure 6.13. A brief uptrend concluded with a strong white candlestick that formed the curve of the cup. The handle moved price lower and then higher before it moved sideways for two weeks and then turned downward. Once the downtrend had begun, it proved to be exceptionally strong.

This formation explained an otherwise confusing pattern. Without recognizing the cup and handle, a swing trader might conclude that the consolidation period was volatile and unpredictable. This could also mean missing the signal of reversal. In this case, the cup and handle was quite strong even though the actual downturn was delayed for quite some time. Once you spot the cup and handle, you see that it sets up the reversal and then all you need to do is wait out the eventual move.

The price range began to narrow as the consolidation moved forward, forecasting the downtrend. Once the price moved below support set by consolidation and then continued, the cup and handle pattern was confirmed.

Price Spike Reversals

Great emphasis is placed on Western technical analysis, specifically those signals that test resistance and support. For example,

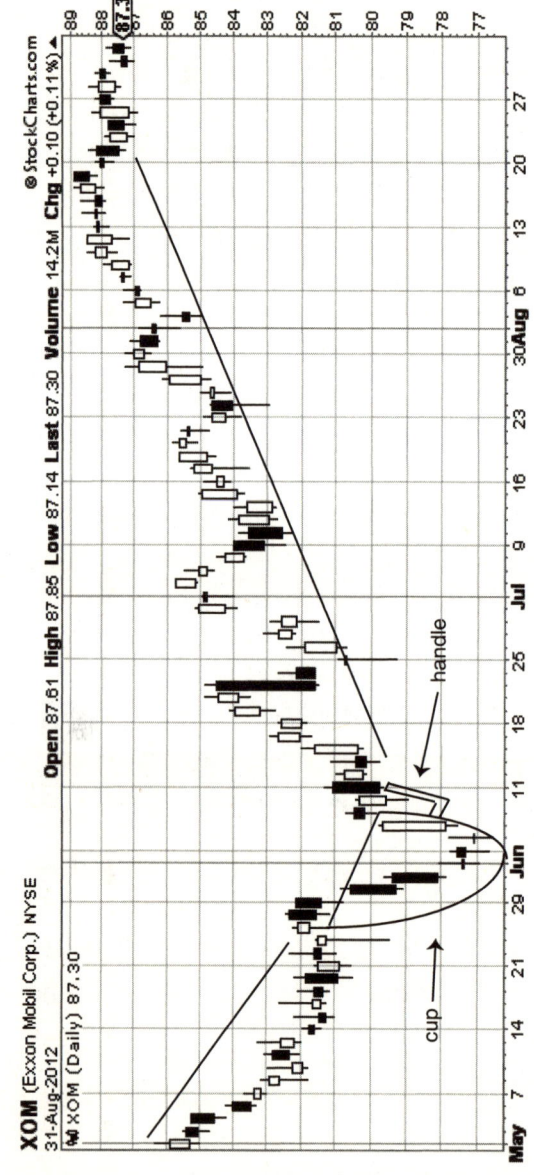

Figure 6.12 Cup and handle
Source: StockCharts.com.

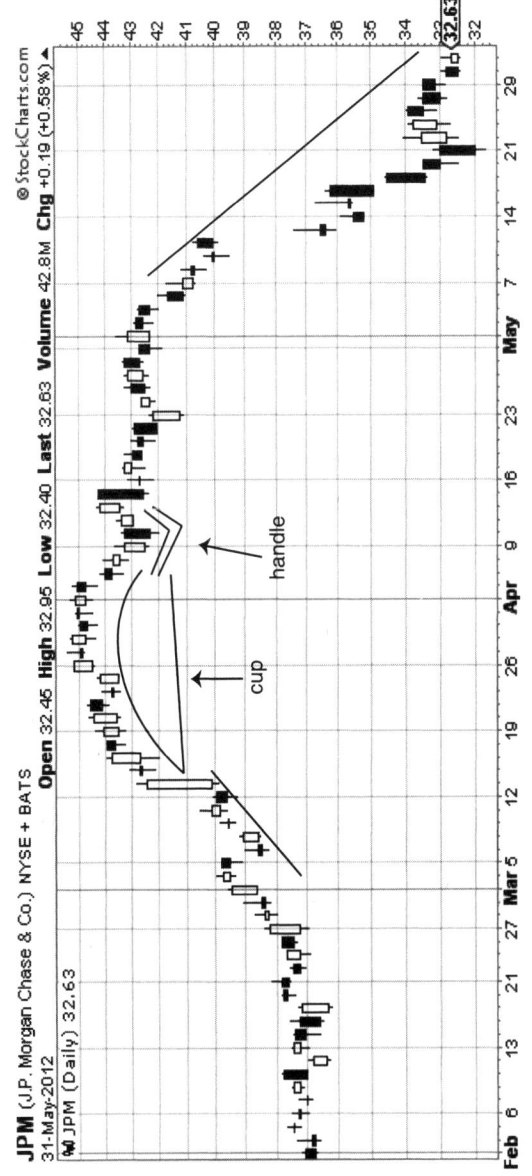

Figure 6.13 Inverse cup and handle
Source: StockCharts.com.

the classic reversal consists of a double top at resistance or a double bottom at support. The test fails, and then price moves in the opposite direction. This type of price movement is well known to provide reliable signals, especially when further confirmed by candlestick reversals, volume spikes, and momentum oscillators.

Even with these reliable tools, one signal often overlooked is the price spike. Seen in the form of candlesticks with unusually long shadows (especially in doji sessions), the price spike represents the last gasp in an existing trend or an early warning signal that a reversal is in the making. So candlesticks, such as long-shadow formations, spinning tops, and hanging man or hammer, are quite strong signals if they appear in the right place:

1. *Doji sessions* are common and not reliable when found alone. However, two additional attributes add strength. The first is when these are found along with other signals, and in that case the doji is a form of confirmation. The second attribute is when the shadow is exceptionally long. At the top of an uptrend, a single session with a long upper shadow reveals lost momentum among buyers, and at the bottom of a downtrend a long lower shadow indicates lost momentum among sellers.

    That shadow is revealing because the price range failed during the session. That is, a very long shadow often is the clear signal that price is about to move in the opposite direction. So look for this to occur at the top of an uptrend or at the bottom of a downtrend, preferably at or near resistance or support.

2. *Spinning top.* This is a session with a fairly small real body of either color, but very long upper *and* lower shadows. The real body is at or close to the center of the session's range. This displays a struggle between buyers and sellers in the session, but its value as a reversal signal relies entirely on where it appears in the trend. It leads to reversal 50% of the time, so by itself the spinning top reveals nothing. However, when it is found at the key point (top of the uptrend at resistance or bottom of the down trend at support) *and* when strong

confirming signals are also found, the spinning top can signal a turn in the trend.

3. *Hammer and hanging man.* This single-session candlestick is simple but powerful. Its real body is usually quite small and can be either color, and it also has a long lower shadow. When the shadow is quite long, the indicated reversal is also strong. When this pattern appears at the bottom of a downtrend, it is a hammer and serves as a signal for a bullish reversal. When it is found at the top of an uptrend, it is called a hanging man and signals a bearish reversal.

All of these signals are exceptionally strong when four conditions are found together:

- long upper (bearish) or lower (bullish) shadows,
- accompanying volume spikes,
- occurrence at resistance (bearish reversal) or support (bullish reversal), and
- reversal is confirmed by momentum oscillator changes.

For example, one way how these price spike reversals occur can be seen in the chart of Verizon (VZ) in figure 6.14; here, a turning point is marked clearly with bearish upper shadows. These upper shadows also represented a double top moving through resistance and failing, resulting in an expected price retreat.

Confirmation consisted of two other indicators: a volume spike and a move in the Relative Strength Index (RSI) into overbought territory. Collectively, these signals strongly anticipated a downtrend. The question, as always, was how far the downtrend would move. The support level was set and tested for 10 sessions, with an attempted decline below that level eventually failing.

Another version of the price spike can be seen in the chart of Pfizer (PFE) shown in figure 6.15. In this case, a hammer (a bullish reversal) combined with volume spikes to signal a bullish reversal.

The hammer had an unusually long lower shadow, and this added strength to the indicated end of the downtrend. The series of volume spikes occurred several sessions later and presented an

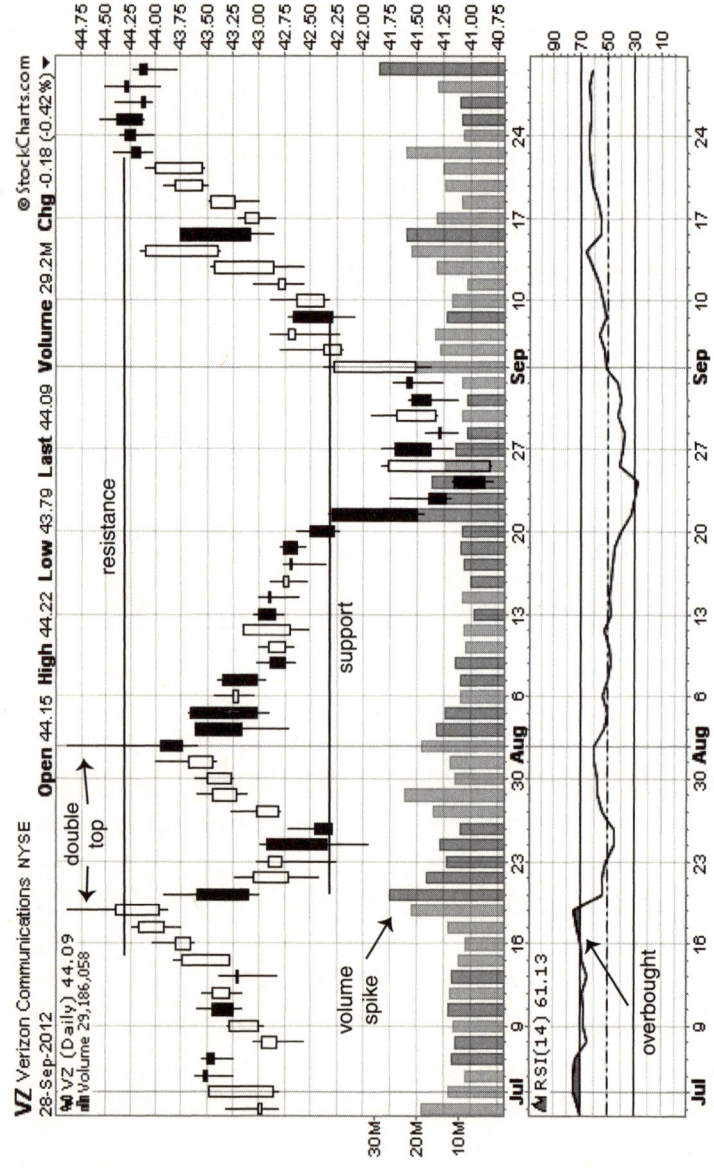

Figure 6.14 Price spike reversal—bearish upper shadows
Source: StockCharts.com.

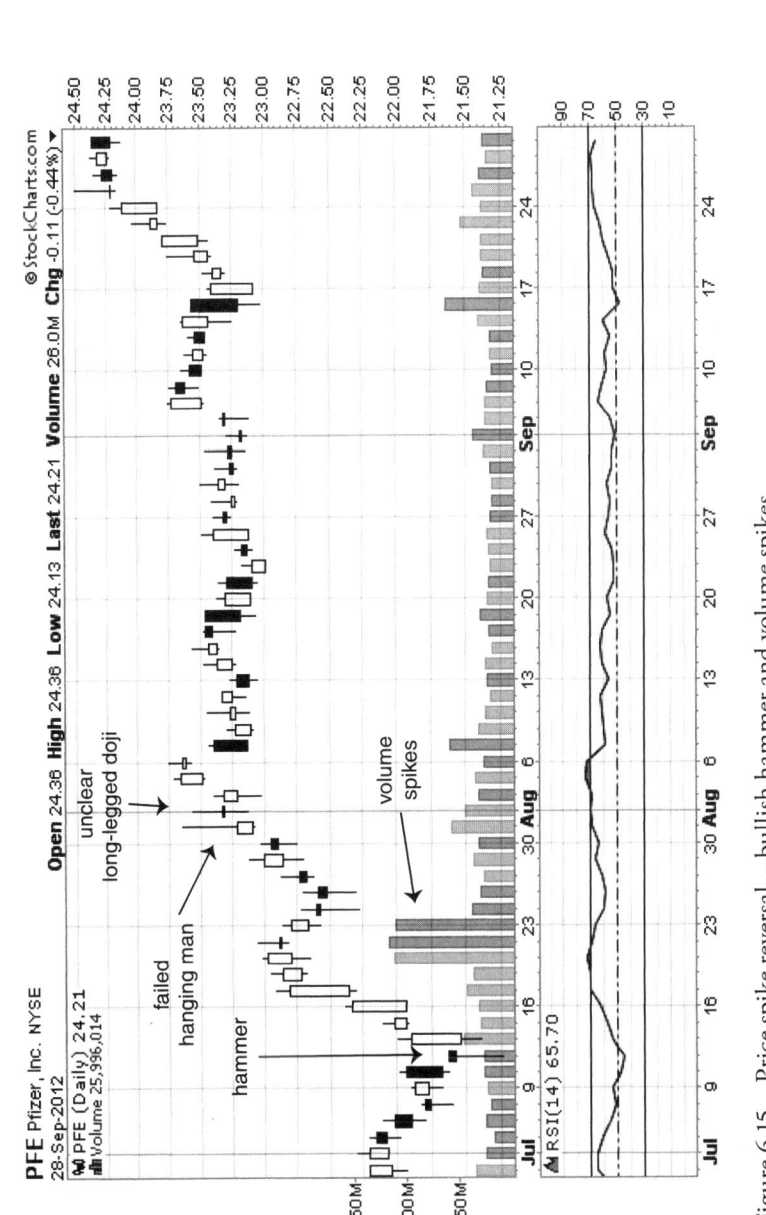

Figure 6.15 Price spike reversal—bullish hammer and volume spikes
Source: StockCharts.com.

interesting struggle between buyers and sellers. The range narrowed as the three high-volume sessions developed, and they were followed by a weak spinning top on the day after the last spike. This was difficult to interpret and could have represented the end of the brief uptrend. However, the signals were confusing after this development.

Three specific signals could have been interpreted as bearish reversals, but even though they confirmed one another, both failed. First, the very strong bearish hanging man (the opposite of a hammer because it is found during an uptrend) appeared. Even with its very long upper shadow, price did not reverse. Second, the long-legged doji appeared. Like many doji sessions, this is not a clear indicator of reversal or continuation; however, when found immediately after another signal, it often serves the confirm that signal. Third, the brief move of RSI into overbought territory occurred. In this case, it looked like a bearish turn indicated in three separate signals, but prices moved sideways for six weeks before finally resuming an upward trend.

Another type of price spike reversal was seen on the chart of Boeing (BA) shown in figure 6.16. Note that the prior support level flipped to a new resistance, an occurrence often seen in charts. That original support level was first subjected to a failed test and then to a second test consisting of long lower shadows that could be called a double bottom. In between these two was an interesting uptrend culminating in a spinning top.

With prior support becoming new resistance, a test would be expected, and one did occur. As price moved through resistance, a second spinning top signaled likely reversal, which quickly followed. This chart provides an example of how price spikes often reverse and are sensitive to the resistance and support levels in effect.

The various entry and exit criteria rely on analysis of signals and confirmation. These come in many forms—Western price and volume patterns, candlesticks, and momentum oscillators. Special attention should be paid to candlesticks in particular, since there are so many strong and highly reliable reversal signals among them helping to time entry and exit. The next chapter explores the role of candlestick analysis in swing trading.

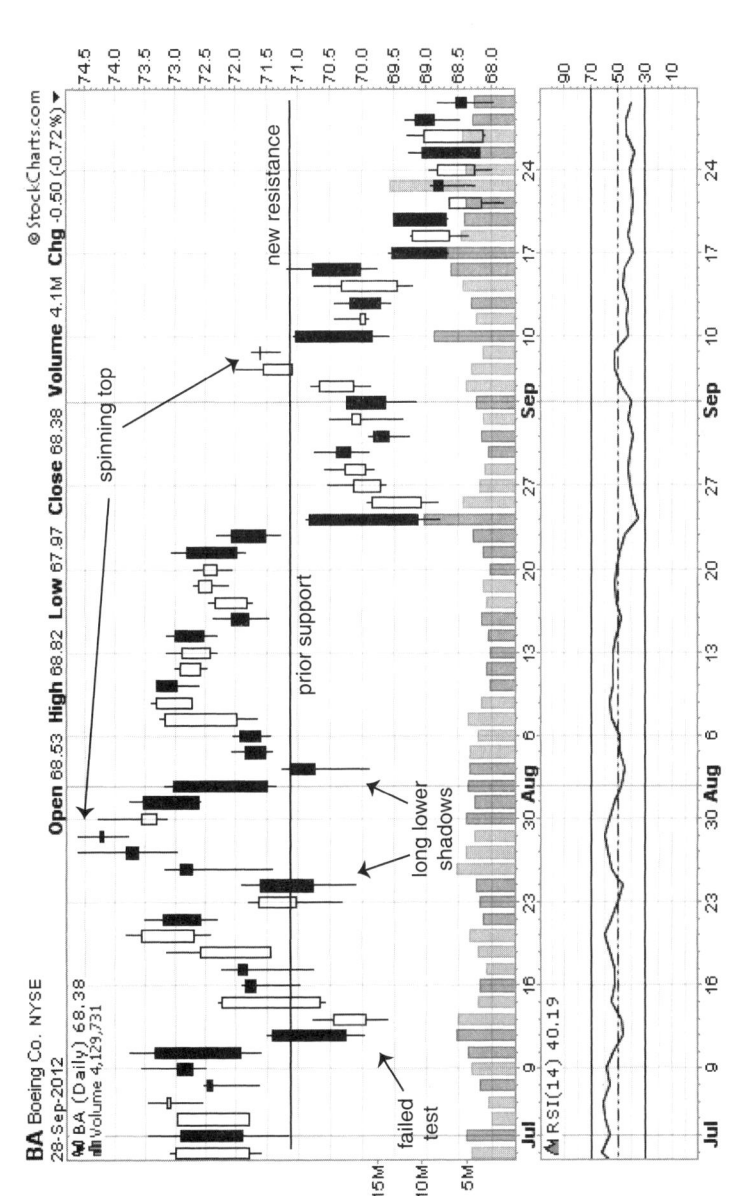

Figure 6.16 Price spike reversal—long lower shadows and spinning top
Source: StockCharts.com.

CHAPTER 7

POWERFUL TIMING TOOLS: EXPANDING SWING SIGNALS WITH CANDLESTICK REVERSALS

> As a rule we disbelieve all facts and theories for which we have no use.
> — William James, *The Will to Believe*, 1897

CHARTING IS A VARIED AND REVEALING TOOL FOR SWING TRADING. Anyone who has used stock for swing trades knows the importance of charting; this chapter explains how those same charts can serve as timing tools for options trades.

Candlestick signals come in dozens of forms. Most are reversal signals, but many others work as continuation signals. The focus of swing trading on reversal signals is understandable because the point of reversal is where you are likely to enter and exit positions. However, continuation is also important, if only to warn you not to enter or exit in the belief that reversal is about to occur. It's all a matter of timing, so both types of indicators serve a purpose.

CHARTING FOR STOCKS AND OPTIONS

Candlestick charts are the most revealing form and the easiest to use of all types of charts. Today, you can find free charts online with ease. This book uses charts provided by *StockCharts.com* because of this ease of use. This site allows you to add and place a large variety of technical signals, including momentum oscillators, moving averages, and volume indicators to enhance your ability to interpret signals.

In traditional analysis, stock charts have been used for stock trading only. The idea is that the Western and candlestick signals tell you when to buy or sell stock. That's true, but it does not mean the value of those indicators is limited to stock trades only. Options trading, in comparison, has focused on a different type of analysis: implied volatility (IV). The use of IV is based on the idea that measurements aid in timing entry and exit into positions. That's true; however, volatility may take many sessions to fully develop, and in the short-term trades associated with swing trading potential problems make IV difficult to rely on if it is used exclusively.

IV is measured along with probability, a test of the likelihood of a trade ending up in the money. So the combined use of IV and probability (especially for short positions) often is effective in timing of entry to maximize premium income and for timing exit to time the lowest possible premium or to avoid losses when the underlying and options move in the wrong direction. IV is further tested and defined through the use of the "Greeks" that measure various aspects of IV:

Delta is a measurement of an option's sensitivity to changes in the underlying price (calls range from 0 to 100 and puts from 0 to −100).
Gamma tests the rate of delta, in other words, the momentum of sensitivity. Using delta and gamma together creates the most reliable IV test.
Vega compares the option's theoretical value to the current volatility or change in volatility. As a test of volatility risk, vega identifies likely IV change in the future.
Theta compares the current option theoretical value to time decay.

These are all worthy tests of IV. However, you cannot know the timing of volatility. Changes, even radical changes, might occur in a matter of hours or days or might take several days to develop. The Greeks are estimates that change with every change in the underlying, so in that respect the Greeks collectively work to compare IV to historical volatility of the underlying security. In comparison, tracking the visual changes found on candlestick charts provides a different type of timing device based on changes in the underlying and anticipation of short-term trend reversal. When you focus your swing trades on soon-to-expire contracts at or close to the money, you know that the option premium is most likely to track underlying price changes as closely as possible (due to low time value and coming expiration).

This means that tracking trends and likely reversal on the underlying chart, while a different approach to timing of options trades than IV analysis, provides many of the same timing benefits. In some respects, chart-based reversal may be more accurate than IV-based trends. The IV may lag behind price change since the option is a derivative of price itself. And so price momentum and actual movement set the standard for volatility of options. Stock price movement leads and option premium follows; in fact, by definition, IV is a reaction to changes in price. The purpose of underlying price tracking is to identify leading indicators in the form of price shapes (candlestick indicators) confirmed by volume and momentum shifts.

Since the candlestick indicators found on charts are specifically used to identify and anticipate price reversal (or continuation), they are strong leading indicators. While IV may serve as a confirming indicator for what these chart patterns reveal, it lags after price, and that confirmation might come too late to time the trade. Since the options-based swing trading strategy is intended to work with contracts expiring in one month or sooner and are at the money or slightly in the money, the changes in IV are not reliable as timing tools. They tend to work more effectively when more time remains until expiration, when time decay is underway, and when the strike levels are trending toward the price of the underlying securities. The timing of IV-based analysis may work more effectively for a longer-term speculative strategy two to three months before expiration.

This does not mean that IV serves no purpose in options trading. It provides great value. But the closer to expiration an ITM contract becomes, the more unpredictable IV is for the purpose of timing trades. One expert described an options strategy aimed at trading close to expiration with this in mind:

> For option traders, the days preceding expiration represent the very best opportunity. During this time frame, traditional approaches to calculating the value of an option contract fail, and prices become distorted. One of the most significant forces, implied volatility collapse, can generate price distortions as large as 30% on expiration Thursday and 100% on Friday for at-the-money options. At the same time, strike price effects resemble the gravitational pull of planets, with stocks as their satellites. Heavily traded optionable stocks tend to hover around strike prices as large institutional investors unwind complex positions ahead of expiration. Option traders who structure day trades that take advantage of these forces can generate more profit in one day than most experienced investors realize in an entire month—sometimes an entire year.
>
> Unlike other trading strategies that are linked—sometimes in subtle ways—to a specific set of market conditions, expiration trading focuses only on the underlying mathematics. It does not rely on any financial predictions, company results, or market direction. In this context, an expiration trader manages ticker symbols and strike prices because the name or business of the underlying stock is irrelevant.[1]

This observation supports the contention that IV analysis cannot be used reliably close to expiration. Although the statement referred specifically to options quite close to expiration, the problem of inaccuracy accelerates throughout the last month of an option's life, further supporting the argument that during this period price charts and trends in price, volume, and momentum are more revealing and more dependable.

The historical separation between charting for stocks and IV analysis for options, has made options-based swing trading an unlikely strategy. By bridging this separation and applying chart analysis of the underlying to price trends of options, you can create a reduced-risk, diversified, and highly leveraged swing trading program. It is based on what you see in chart patterns and on the price changes they predict.

How Reliable Is a Reversal Signal?

There are dozens of candlestick signals, and not all are studied in the following pages. The focus here is on the strongest reversal and continuation indicators, but no signal is 100% accurate. So as a means for reducing risk, it is not wise to place too much capital into any one trade. Keep the dollar value of swing trades consistent to spread risks, acknowledging that in some cases a signal will fail, and your trade will lose.

Among the methods for reducing the likelihood of a poorly timed trade are three trading principles. All of these will help you to maximize your timing and to create more profitable trades:

1. *Be aware of the power of signals at resistance and support.* When a signal of any kind is found at or near resistance or support, it is significantly more meaningful than elsewhere in a trading range. This is true both for reversal and continuation patterns. When a signal includes a price gap, the likelihood of reversal is inevitably part of the equation; at resistance and support, the strength of that reversal indication is increased to a much greater level. In a swing trading strategy, any time the price is at or near these important trading range borders, pay special attention to emerging signals and be ready to act quickly.
2. *Rely on confirmation, even for the strongest signals.* Some signals are reliable for reversal as much as 80% of the time. This is reassuring, so the temptation may be to rely only on those high-probability signals and shun confirmation. This is not advisable. Even highly reliable reversal indicators may fail, so you need to look at the broader picture of what is going on with price, volume, and momentum, and then you

need to time entry or exit based not only on the strong signal that emerges but also on its confirmation. Part of the timing process is the question of what you should do when you discover contradiction rather than confirmation. When signals disagree with one another, what action, if any, should you take? The best approach is to be as conservative as possible. Don't enter a position if you are unsure, and if you can exit at a profit, do so immediately. Confirmation adds strength and certainty to timing, so it is an essential second step when tracking chart indicators.

3. *Become familiar with the rhythm of a stock's price movement.* Every stock develops its own trading pattern, and the duration of trends may be repetitive. Just as a surfer waits out the waves to identify the timing and momentum of each subsequent swell, a swing trader improves the chances of good timing by becoming aware of a stock's tendencies. This occurs because the levels of participation among buyers and sellers, the typical holding periods, and timing of closing positions tend to repeat. Once you are aware of whether short-term trends tend to move in four-day or eight-day terms, for example, you add another form of confirmation to your process.

POWERFUL REVERSAL SIGNALS

In chapter 2, a short list of exceptionally reliable candlestick indicators was introduced and displayed. The context of this was to examine a range of swing trading basics, combining Western technical analysis with Eastern (candlestick) indicators. Expanding on this discussion and moving beyond the engulfing pattern (possibly the strongest of all reversal signals), three white soldiers, and three black crows many additional indicators are worth tracking.

A point worth remembering about all candlestick reversals is also easily overlooked: A reversal must have a trend to reverse. That is, a bullish reversal only applies when it shows up after a period of downward-trending price. It is meant to mark a likely turning point. Likewise, a bearish reversal only applies if you find it at the top of an uptrend.

What does it mean when these reversal signals show up in the wrong place? A bullish reversal showing up during an uptrend or a bearish reversal found during a downtrend cannot just be ignored. In fact, in these instances, the signals serve as indicators of continuation rather than of reversal. It is not enough for price movements to form into well-known patterns; they also have to show up in the right place.

In addition to appearing during specific uptrends or downtrends, signals may also be found after consolidation and in periods of sideways movement. These signals may represent the starting point of new trends. When this occurs, the signals indicate neither reversal nor continuation since no upward or downward trend is in effect. Instead, a candlestick signal may act as a "generating" or "initiating" signal, a sign that a trend in the indicated direction is about to begin. All traders know that after consolidation identifying the starting point of new trends is among the most difficult analytical tasks to perform accurately. However, either reversal or continuation signals do provide either a bullish or a bearish bias. If these can be confirmed by changes in volume or momentum, it will be easier to mark the beginning of a new trend.

More Powerful Reversals in Single Sessions

Beyond the exceptionally strong signals, dozens of other indicators are found in single sessions, two consecutive sessions, or three or more sessions. Among the strongest single-session reversal signals are the hammer and hanging man.

These appear to be the same, but their names rely on where they appear in the price trend. The real body may be white or black and is small. A lower shadow, often quite long, is the second attribute. If it appears at the bottom of a downtrend, it is a hammer. If it is found at the top of an uptrend, it is a hanging man.

Although this signal consists of a single session only, it often serves as the defining reversal step. For example, on the chart of Coca-Cola (KO) in figure 7.1, a hammer marks the turning point from gradually declining prices to strong, gapping upward price movement. In comparison, the chart for Caterpillar (CAT) ended its uptrend with a hanging man and then a last failed attempt to move prices higher, leading into a strong downtrend. Three sessions earlier, another hanging man appeared, but its meaning was unclear. The price fell to create that hanging man, so it did not show up right at the top of the uptrend. Both of these charts are shown in figure 7.1.

Two additional single-session indicators appear frequently, but both provide less certainty than the hanging man and hammer. The long-legged doji is a doji session (little or no difference between opening and closing price) with long upper and lower shadows.

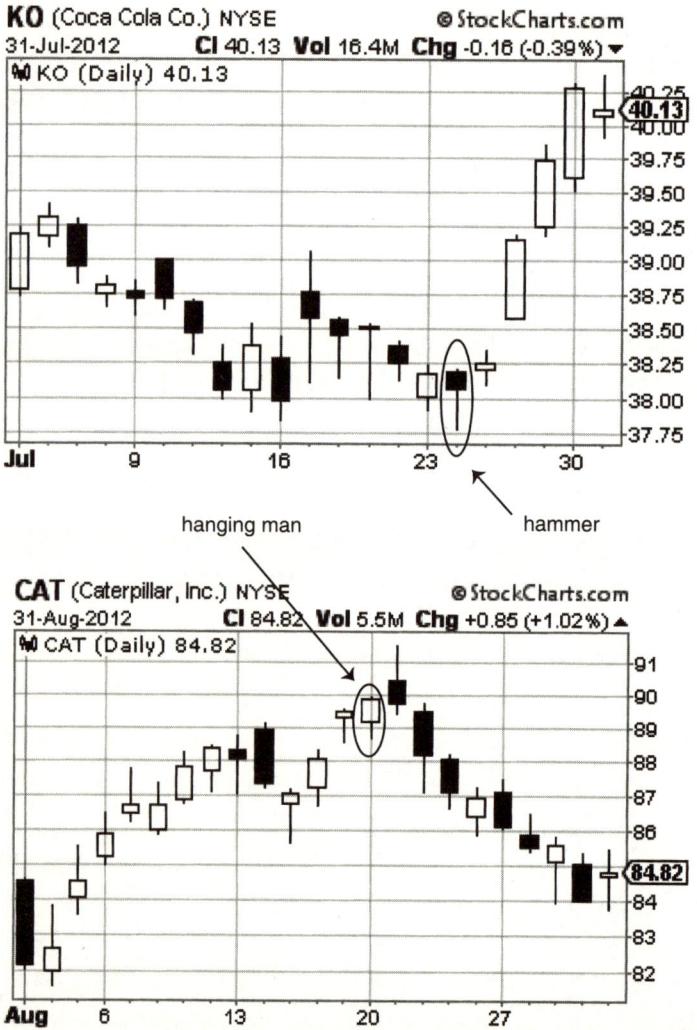

Figure 7.1   Hammer and hanging man
Source: StockCharts.com.

This represents a struggle for control between buyers and sellers and may be either bullish or bearish. By itself it doesn't provide much help, but when it confirms reversal, it can be quite useful.

The second indicator with many of the same attributes is called a spinning top. Like the long-legged, doji, the spinning top has long upper and lower shadows representing a struggle between buyers and sellers, and its value depends on where it appears in a trend. The major difference is that it has a small real body while the doji has no real body. Both of these are shown in figure 7.2.

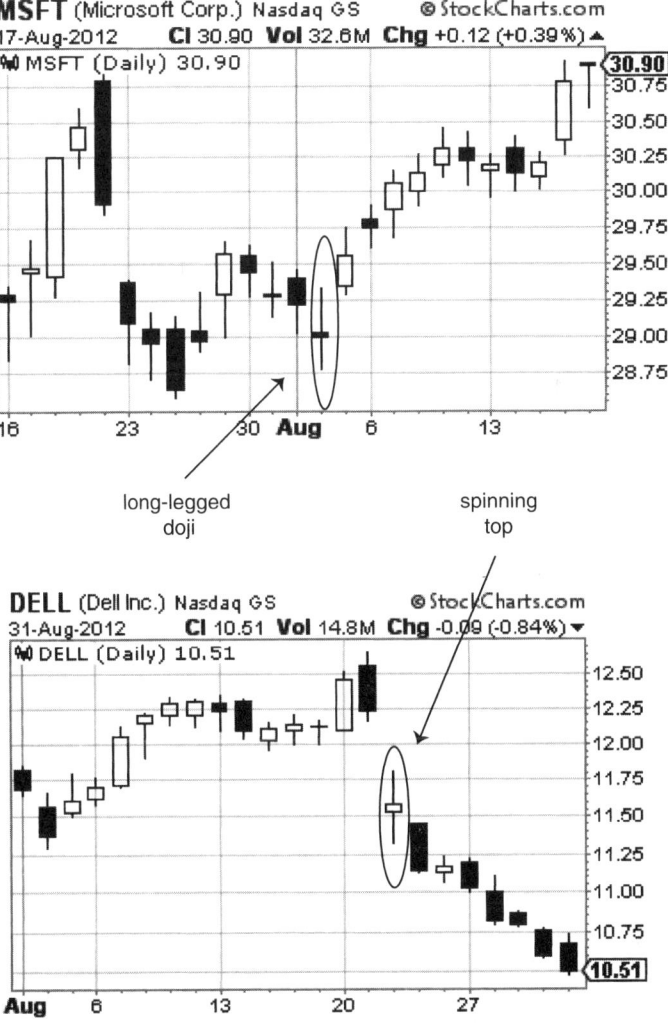

Figure 7.2   Long-legged doji and spinning top
Source: StockCharts.com.

The long-legged doji on the Microsoft (MSFT) chart appeared after a downtrend and sideways movement. It marks the end of consolidation and the start of a new uptrend. However, the gaps on either side of the session make it unclear whether it would lead to an uptrend or a downtrend.

The spinning top found on the Dell chart was unusual in that it showed up followed by a downward gap off the uptrend's high price level. Spinning tops are uncertain signals, but in this case it worked as confirmation of the previous gap. This signaled the beginning of a new downtrend and confirmed the strong gap right before it showed up.

THE DOUBLE-SESSION REVERSAL SIGNAL

Single-session reversals are difficult to analyze because they may lack confirmation and often show up as false indicators. Greater strength is likely to be found in the many double-session reversals, but the mere fact that there are two sessions does not always make the signal more reliable.

For example, the harami is a frequently occurring signal consisting of a session followed by one of the opposite color that opens and closes within the range of the first. However, the harami is one of those fifty-fifty signals, and it takes on meaning only when it confirms another signal. The chart of DuPont (K) shown in figure 7.3 has a bullish harami at an odd placement on the chart. Based on the price movement preceding it, this could be a reversal of a very weak three-session downtrend, or it could work as a continuation signal of the uptrend that began two weeks earlier. Most likely, it marks the conclusion of the preceding three sessions, that is, it indicates not a downtrend but a retracement.

The bearish version is found on the chart of Kellogg (K), also shown in figure 7.3, and it preceded an extended downtrend. However, the bearish harami did not appear at the end of a distinct downtrend but was more likely the turning point at the end of a consolidation period.

Another uncertain two-session pattern is the harami cross. This is like the harami, but the second day is a doji, forming the cross

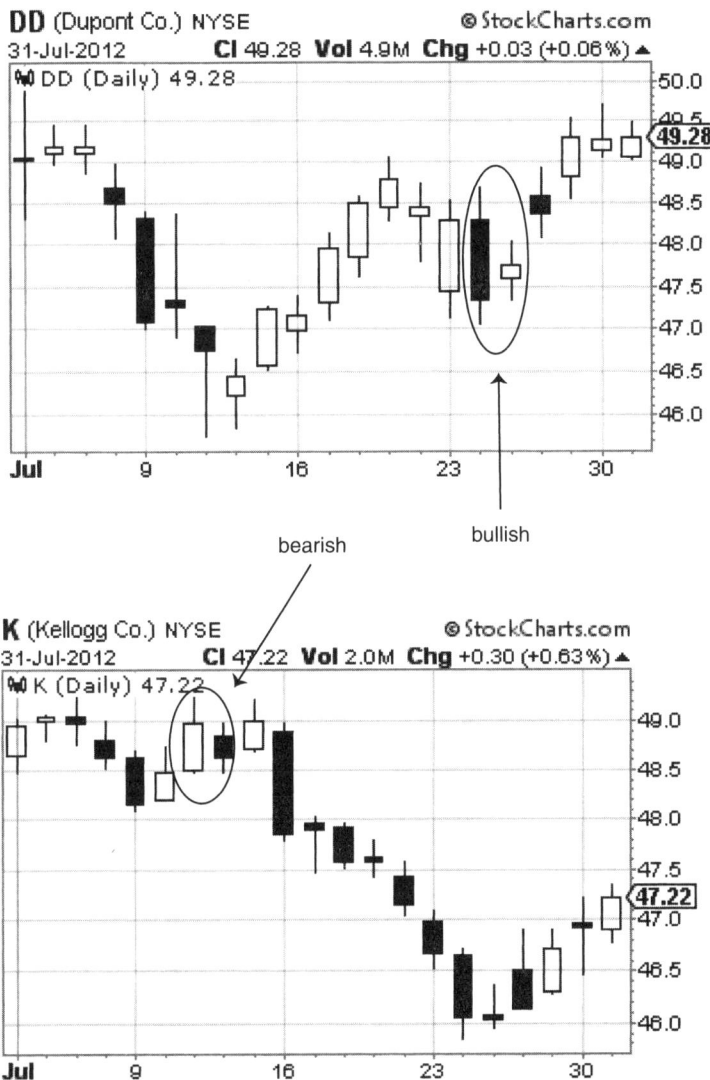

Figure 7.3 Harami
Source: StockCharts.com.

appearance. Like the harami, the cross version works as reversal only about half of the time and as continuation at least as often. Examples of the harami cross are seen in the charts of 3M (MMM) and Hawaiian Electric (HE) in figure 7.4. Neither of these is conclusive in terms of either continuation or reversal, and their appearance would require further confirmation before taking action.

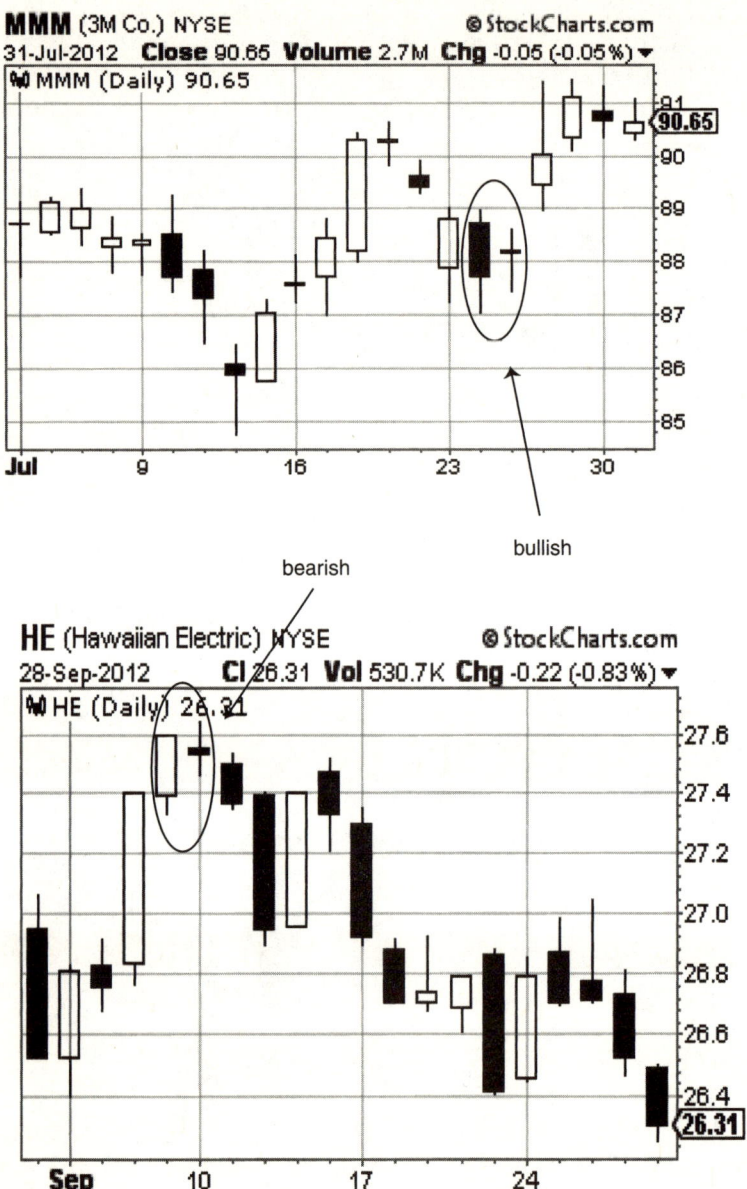

Figure 7.4 Harami cross
Source: StockCharts.com.

The inverted hammer is one of those oddly named indicators, for two reasons. First, as with the "normal" hammer, its real body can be either black or white. However, it is a two-session indicator consisting of a black session and a downside gap (bullish) or a white session and an upside gap (bearish) and then the "hammer" session. In both bullish and bearish versions, the relatively small real body is accompanied by an upper shadow in both bullish and bearish versions. So even the bearish version is called an inverted hammer and is not termed an inverted hanging man.

Examples of these formations are found in figure 7.5. General Mills (GIS) demonstrated the bullish inverted hammer even

Figure 7.5   Inverted hammer
Source: StockCharts.com.

though the downtrend appeared to have reversed by the time it appeared. This means the formation could indicate confirmation rather than reversal even though price then trended sideways. In spite of this uncertainty, the bullish inverted hammer ends up in an uptrend 70% of the time,

The bearish version seen in the chart of Walt Disney (DIS) appeared at the top of an uptrend as you would expect although the downtrend did not begin immediately. The bear version of the inverted hammer is not highly reliable by itself, resulting in reversal only about half of the time.

TRIPLE-SESSION REVERSALS

Beyond the one-session and two-session indicators are the complex reversals. These involve three consecutive sessions and, for that reason, may be more difficult to locate. However, they also tend to be much more reliable than many of the one-session and two-session reversal signals. They tend to reverse more than 60% of the time and as often as 80%.

The first in this group are the bullish and bearish inside patterns. The bullish version (inside up) begins with a session closing down and a second and third upward-moving session. The chart of Home Depot (HD) in figure 7.6 highlights an example of this bullish reversal pattern.

The bearish version is the opposite: a white session followed by two black sessions, such as the case highlighted on the chart of Merck (MRK). While the bullish HD case did result in a strong uptrend, MRK's outcome was less certain. The bearish inside down led to sideways movement for several sessions before the downtrend kicked in toward the end of the period charted. These indicators are 60% to 65% likely to lead to reversal.

The opposite of the inside up and down are the outside up and down patterns. The key to the outside pattern is the second day, which gaps away from the close of the first day. The bullish version begins with a down day, a downside gap, and the two upside days, leading to a bullish reversal; this is reliable as a reversal signal 75% of the time it appears.

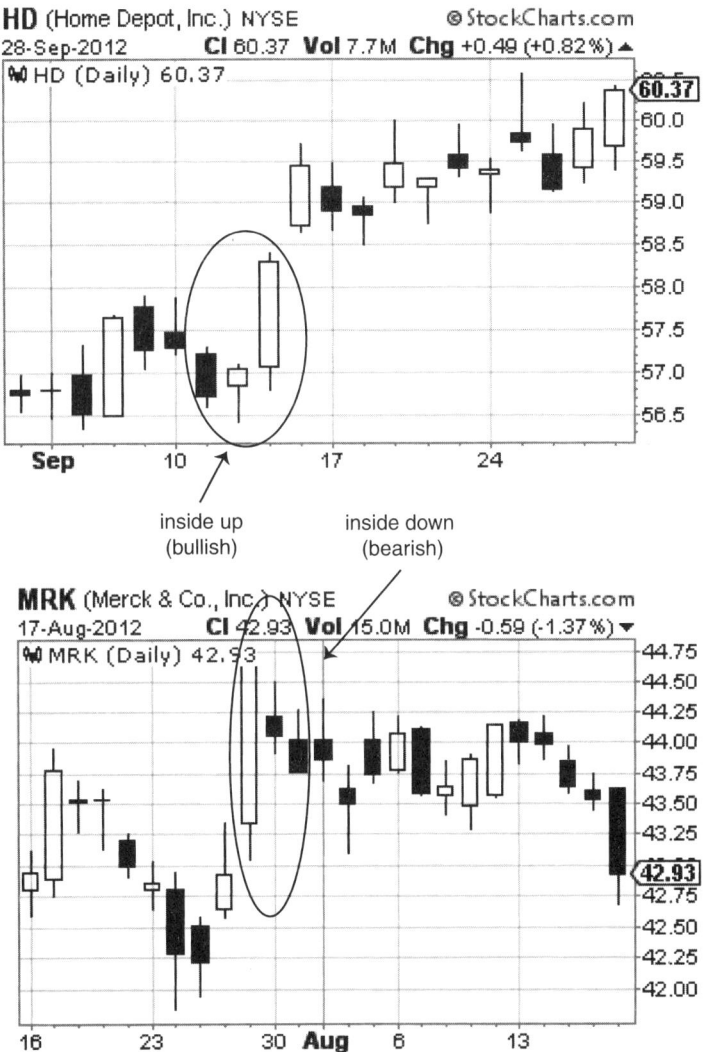

Figure 7.6   Inside patterns
Source: StockCharts.com.

The outside down starts with an upward-moving session, an upside gap, and then concludes with two down days. This is a reliable bearish reversal approximately 70% of the time it is found. Both up and down versions are highlighted on the charts of Wal-Mart (WMT) and Johnson & Johnson (JNJ) in figure 7.7.

The next three-session reversal pattern is the colorfully named abandoned baby. In this pattern, a middle session out of three is separated by gaps from the first and third days. The middle session is a doji or very narrow-range day, and the wider the gap, the stronger the possibility of reversal. The abandoned baby leads to reversal 70% of the time.

The bullish version was found on the chart of General Electric (GE) although the result was not strongly bullish. Prices trended

Figure 7.7   Outside patterns
Source: StockCharts.com.

sideways after the abandoned baby appeared. In contrast, the bearish abandoned baby on the chart of JC Penney (JCP) showed two notable features. First, the middle session had an exceptionally large upper shadow, a strong signal of lost momentum among buyers. Second, the gap after that session was quite large, and prices did trend downward afterward. Both of these charts are shown in figure 7.8.

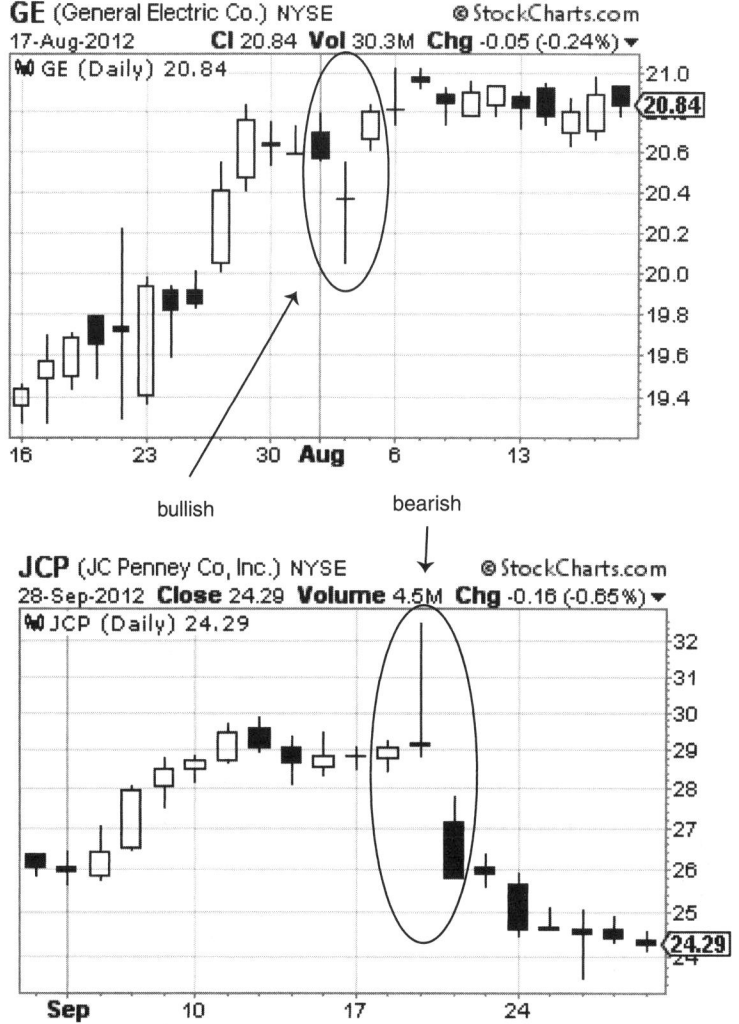

Figure 7.8   Abandoned baby
Source: StockCharts.com.

The squeeze alert is an unusual three-session pattern. The bullish version begins with a black session and is followed by smaller sessions, each opening and closing within the range of the previous session (forming a short-term triangle). The squeeze alert on the bearish side is the same but begins with a white session. In both cases, sessions two and three may move in either direction. The important attribute of the squeeze alert is the declining trading range.

A bullish version was found in the chart of ConocoPhillips (COP) and was a strong example of how the reversal is expected to occur. A weaker bearish version was seen on the chart of Verizon (VZ), and it was weak for two reasons. First, there was no specifically strong uptrend to be reversed. Second, although the ranges narrowed, all were very narrow-range days. The squeeze alert is expected to accurately forecast a reversal about 60% of the time. Both versions can be seen in figure 7.9.

The morning star is a bullish three-stick pattern with a middle narrow-range day. A gap is seen between sessions one and two, but session three rebounds to close within the range of the first session. An example was found on the chart of United Technologies (UTX) in the top half of figure 7.10. The pattern itself marked the price dip before rebounding to the upside. The morning star signals reversal about 80% of the time it is found.

The cousin of the bullish morning star is the bearish evening star. As shown on the chart of Bank of America (BAC) in figure 7.10, it shows up at the top of an uptrend with an upward session and then an upside gap. The third session retreats to close within the range of the first session, marking the reversal and start of a new downtrend. The evening star leads to reversal 70% of the time.

Closely related to the morning star and evening star are the bullish and bearish doji star indicators. As with morning star and evening star, the gapping price is the key to marking the reversal. The bullish version was found on the chart of Cisco Systems (CSCO) shown in figure 7.11, which exhibited a delayed reaction reversal after the preceding downtrend leveled out and moved sideways for a week. The bullish doji star reverses 75% of the time.

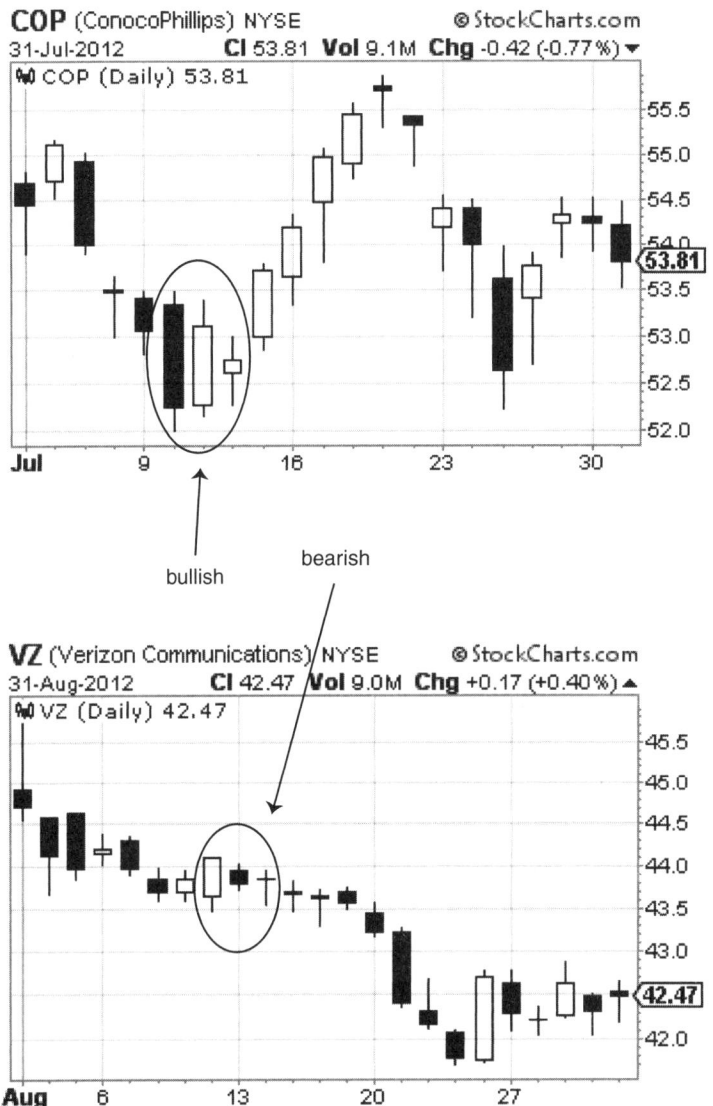

Figure 7.9 Squeeze alert
Source: StockCharts.com.

The bearish doji star is shown on the chart of American Express (AXP). In this case, the first session was a long candlestick, followed by two very narrow-range sessions. However, the price reversed as expected and retreated rapidly. The bearish version signals reversal about 70% of the time it is found.

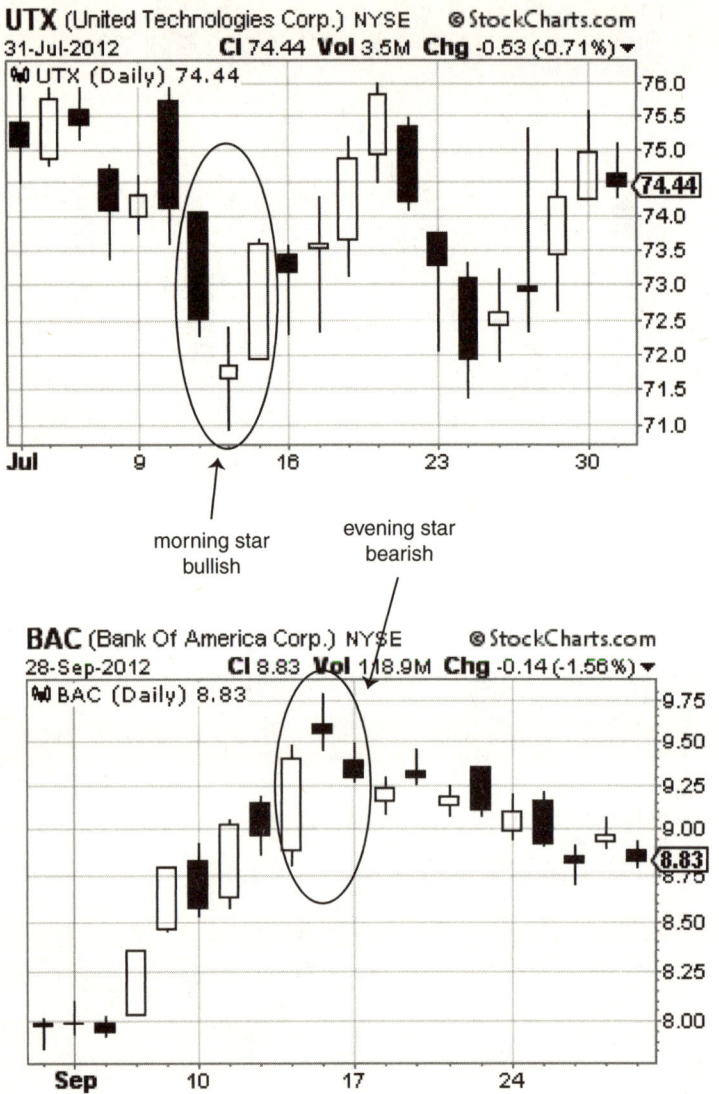

Figure 7.10 Morning star and evening star
Source: StockCharts.com.

Two-Session Continuation Signals

Equally important as reversal signals are continuation indicators. Swing traders want to find strong reversal signals and confirm them. However, continuation signals improve timing as well, preventing exit too early and also preventing reversal entry at the

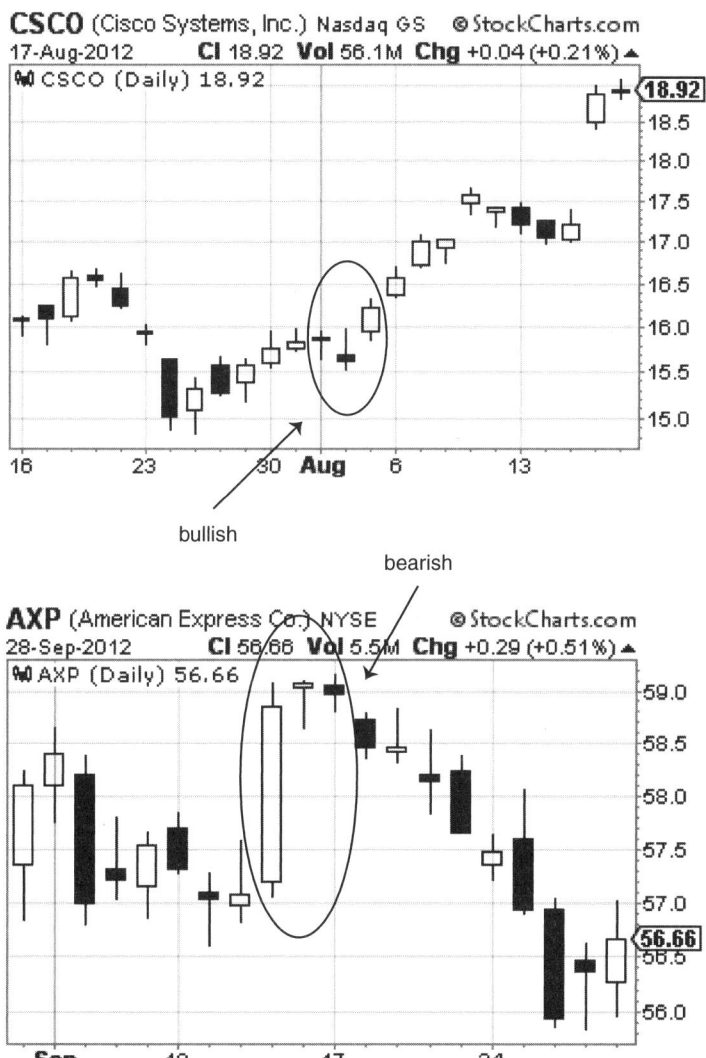

Figure 7.11 Doji star
Source: StockCharts.com.

wrong point in the trend. However, continuation patterns tend to be less reliable than reversals, so confirmation is an absolute requirement before trading decisions are made.

The first continuation signal is called the thrusting lines, but it can be relied upon only about 50% of the time. And so, unless continuation is confirmed by other indicators, this is not a strong signal on its own. The bullish version consists of a white session and then an upward gap to open higher in the second session but closing within the range of the first session. The bearish version is opposite: a black session, gapping to open lower in the second day and then close within the range of the first day.

These indicators are shown in the charts of Unitedhealth Group (UNH) and Digital Realty Trust (DLR) in figure 7.12. The UNH version does, indeed, show up midway in an uptrend, which continues afterward. However, the DLR bearish version fails, and prices reverse to move upward.

The separating lines indicator is somewhat more reliable as a continuation pattern. In the bullish version, a black session gaps upward to be followed by a white session on the second day. This works as continuation indicator about 70% of the time. In the bearish version, a white session gaps downward to be followed by a black session. The bearish separating lines indicator signals continuation about 65% of the time.

Examples of each are found in figure 7.13. Exxon Mobil (XOM) experienced a period of sideways movement and then evolved into a bullish separating lines signal. On the bearish side, Facebook (FB) gapped down strongly after the separating lines appeared and then continued to decline.

The on neck continuation indicator consists of two sessions closing at or very close to the same price. The bullish version begins with a white session, an upward gap, and a second day declining to close to the level of the first day. The bearish on neck starts with a downward session, a gap down, and an upward moving second day that closes at the same price level as the first day. Both bullish and bearish versions are fifty-fifty, and so by themselves they are of little use. In order to read them as continuation (or reversal) signals, you need strong confirmation.

Examples of these patterns were found on the charts of McDonalds (MCD), which clearly consisted of upward continuation, and of Research on Motion (RIMM), which preceded a downtrend although the preceding trend was not a downtrend;

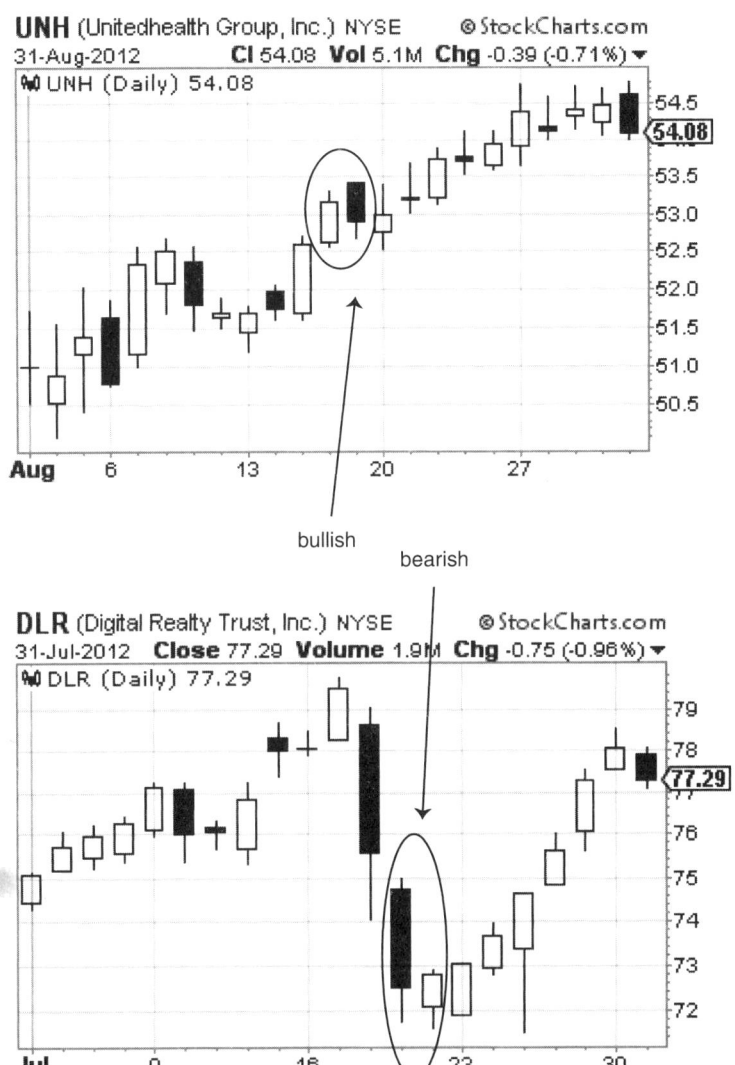

Figure 7.12 Thrusting lines
Source: StockCharts.com.

both are shown in figure 7.14. This is an example of an on neck reversal.

Closely related to on neck is the in neck pattern. These also are fifty-fifty patterns, signaling continuation only 50% of the time. The formations are the same, but the closing prices overlap. In

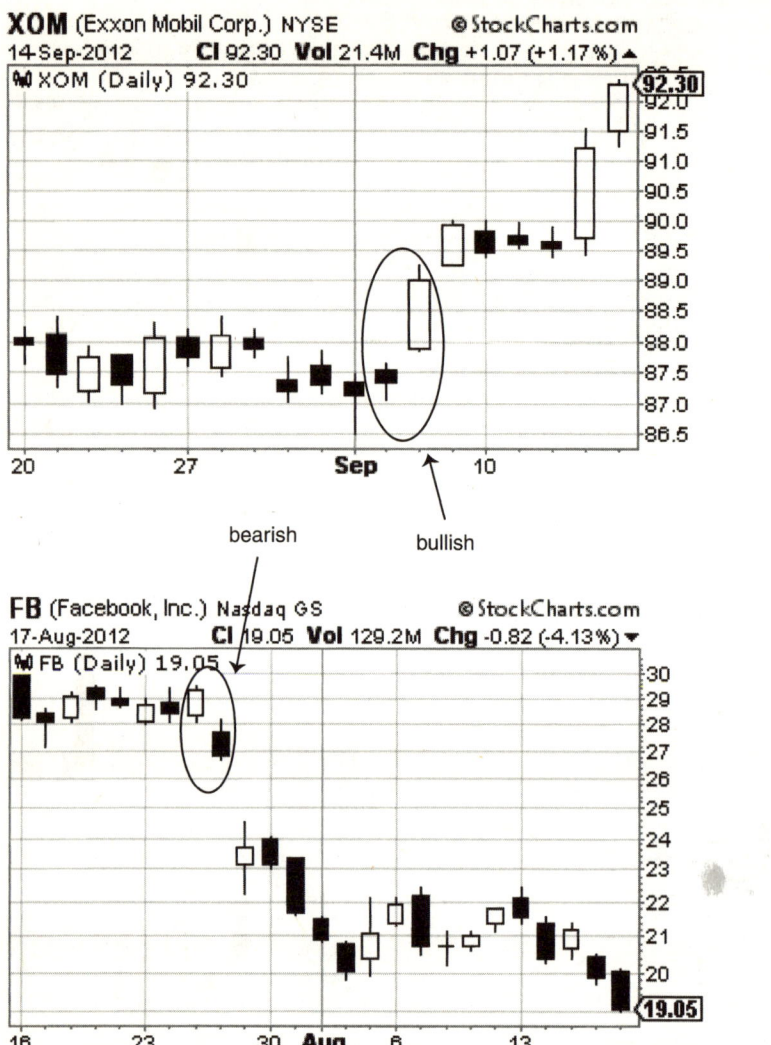

Figure 7.13 Separating lines
Source: StockCharts.com.

the bullish version, the second session closes below the close of the first, and in the bearish version, the second session closes above the close of the first.

For example, the chart of Potash Corp. (POT) included a bullish in neck pattern that reversed the previous trend. And the chart of Duke energy (DUK) included a bearish in neck that worked as a continuation signal; both can be seen in figure 7.15.

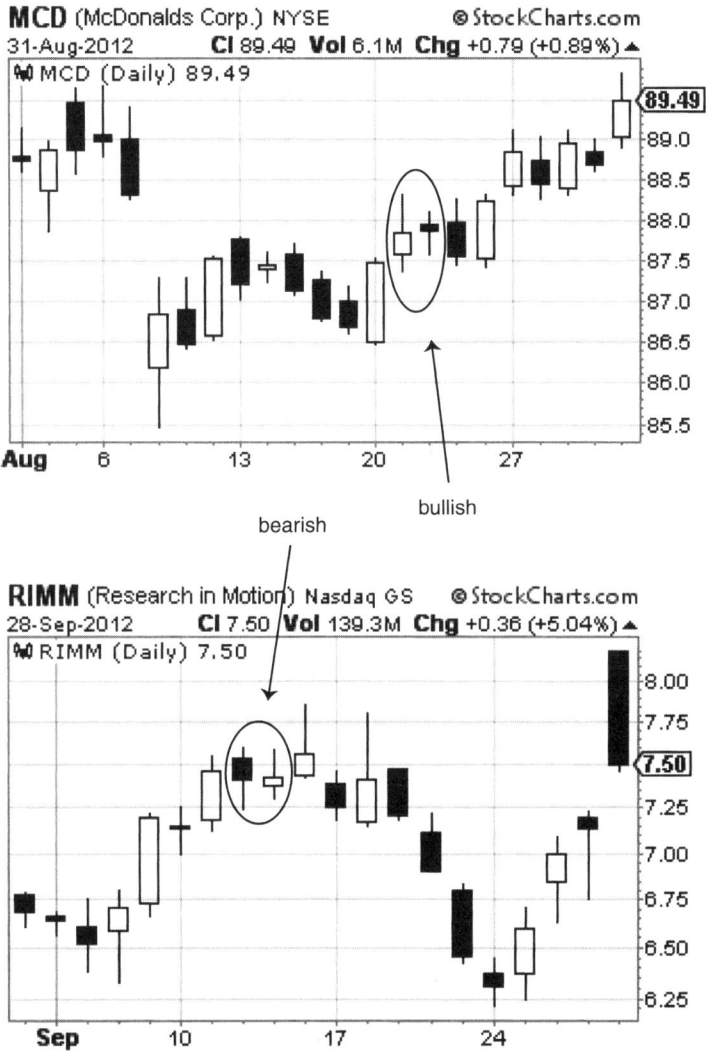

Figure 7.14   On neck lines
Source: StockCharts.com.

Three-Session Continuation Signals

Among the three-session continuation signals are four distinct side-by-side line indicators. First is the white side-by-side, which may be either bullish or bearish. The bullish version is reliable as continuation marker 65% of the time and consists of a white day, an upward gap, and two additional white days. The bearish

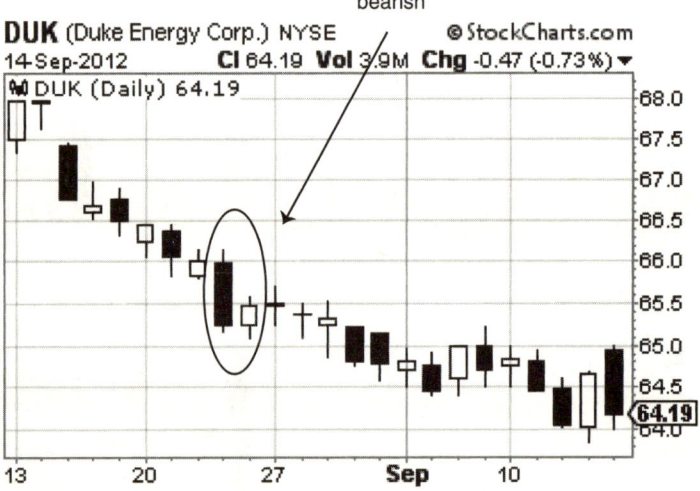

Figure 7.15 In neck lines
Source: StockCharts.com.

side-by-side white lines pattern is reliable for continuation only 55% of the time and consists of a black session, a downward gap, and then two white sessions.

Both white side-by-side lines are shown in figure 7.16. The chart of Travelers (TRV) includes a bullish white side-by-side indicator at the top of an uptrend, and then prices trended sideways. This may have been a pause in the trend or the first

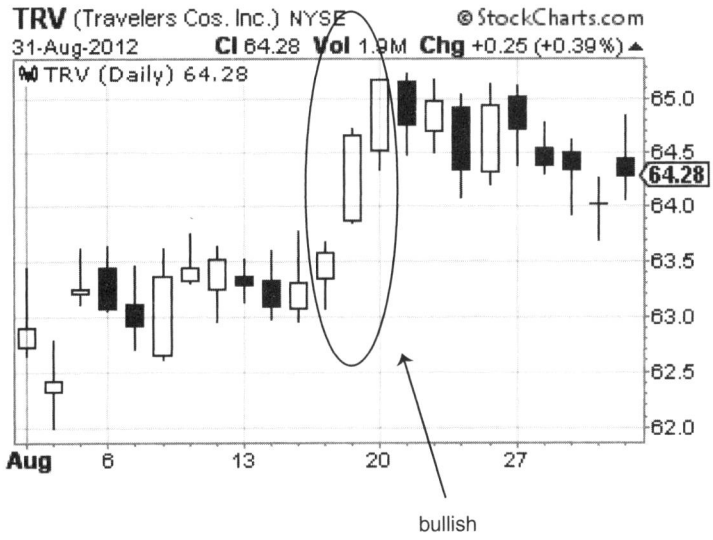

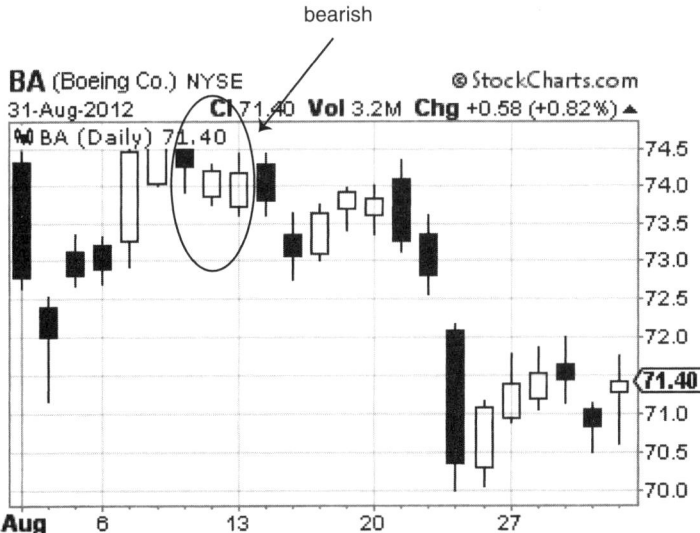

Figure 7.16   White side-by-side lines
Source: StockCharts.com.

signs of a failed indicator. The chart of Boeing (BA) included a small bearish white side-by-side lines signal, a delay, and then a downtrend.

The next two continuation patterns are black side-by-side lines. The bullish version begins with a white session, an upward

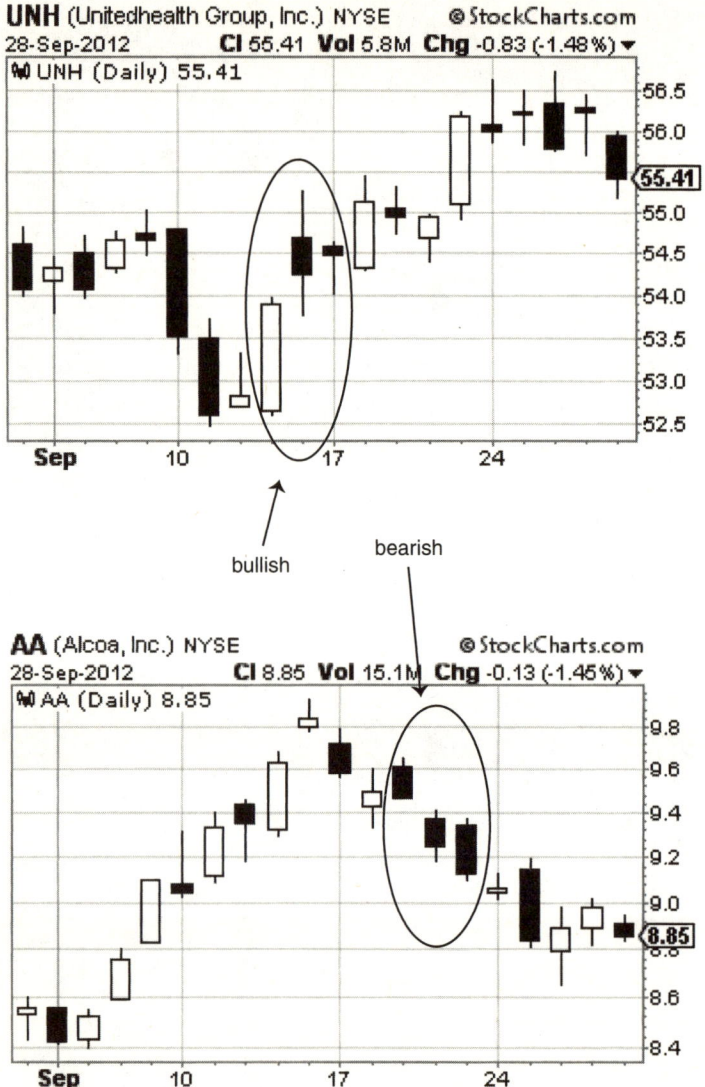

Figure 7.17 Black side-by-side lines
Source: StockCharts.com.

gap, and two black sessions. The bearish side-by-side black lines signal begins with a black session, then a downward gap, and two more black sessions. Both versions are reliable only about 60% of the time.

The bullish black side-by-side lines indicator was found on the chart of Unitedhealth Group (UNH). After a price dip, the continuation pattern appeared, and the uptrend continued. A bearish side-by-side black lines signal appeared on the chart of Alcoa (AA). The downtrend had just begun and worked as a continuation signal through the remainder of the chart; both charts are shown in figure 7.17.

The tasuki gap is reliable only about 55% of the time in both bullish and bearish varieties. The bullish tasuki gap begins with a white session, then an upside gap, a second white session, and a final black session. The bearish version is the opposite: a black session, a downside gap, a second black day, and a final white day.

IBM revealed a strong upside tasuki gap on its chart with a larger than normal price gap. It led to a continuation of the uptrend that had just begun. A bearish version of the tasuki gap was found on the chart of Firstenergy Corp. (FE). Although a downtrend was not clearly set at this point, the signal was followed by a very large black candle session that moved prices lower. Both charts are shown in figure 7.18.

The final type of three-session confirmation is the gap filled. It is similar to the tasuki gap with one important exception: the final session moves down (in the bullish version) or up (in the bearish version) to close within the range of the first day—in other words, to fill the gap. This continuation pattern is reliable only about 60% of the time.

An example of a bullish gap filled was found on the chart of Wells Fargo (WFC). However, this led not to continuation, but to a reversal. A bearish gap filled is highlighted on the chart of Exelon Corp. (EXC), which did not continue the downtrend but evolved into a consolidation pattern. Both charts are shown in figure 7.19.

All candlestick patterns add a rich resource for timing of swing trades. However, none are reliable 100% of the time. Confirmation is essential even for those patterns that come through as expected as often as 75% or 80% of the time.

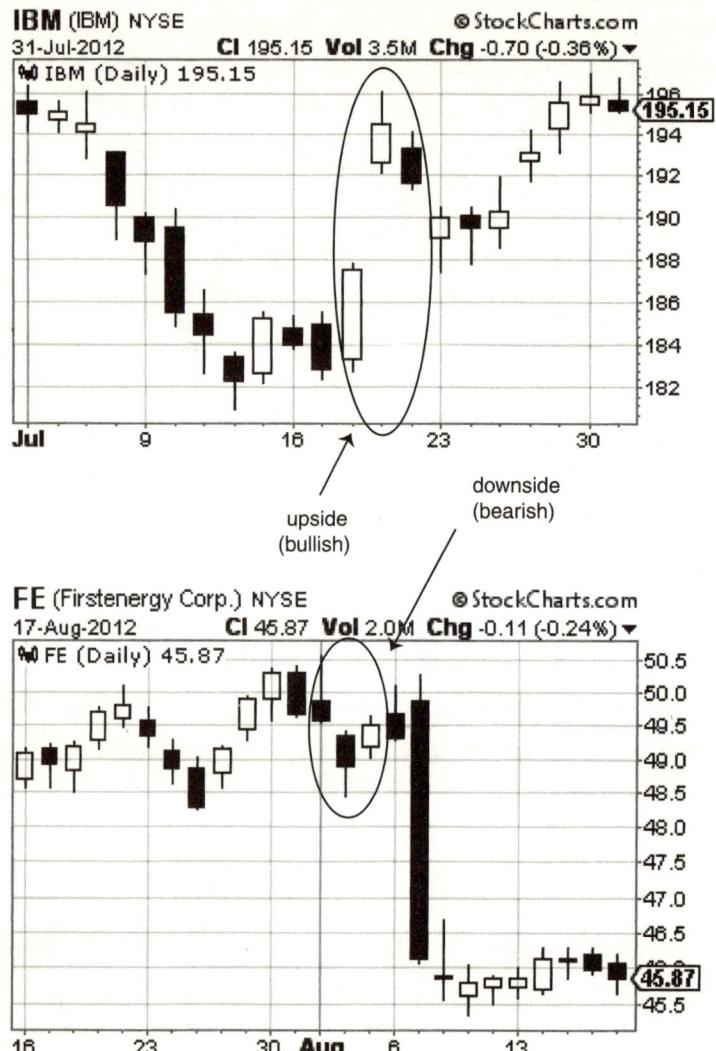

Figure 7.18 Tasuki gap
Source: StockCharts.com.

The next chapter continues the discussion of timing by examining the attributes of options close to expiration. Considering the interaction of time value with implied volatility and the issue of proximity ("moneyness") of the option, reversal signals tend to be most powerful within the last month of the option's life, and the options themselves tend to track the underlying more closely

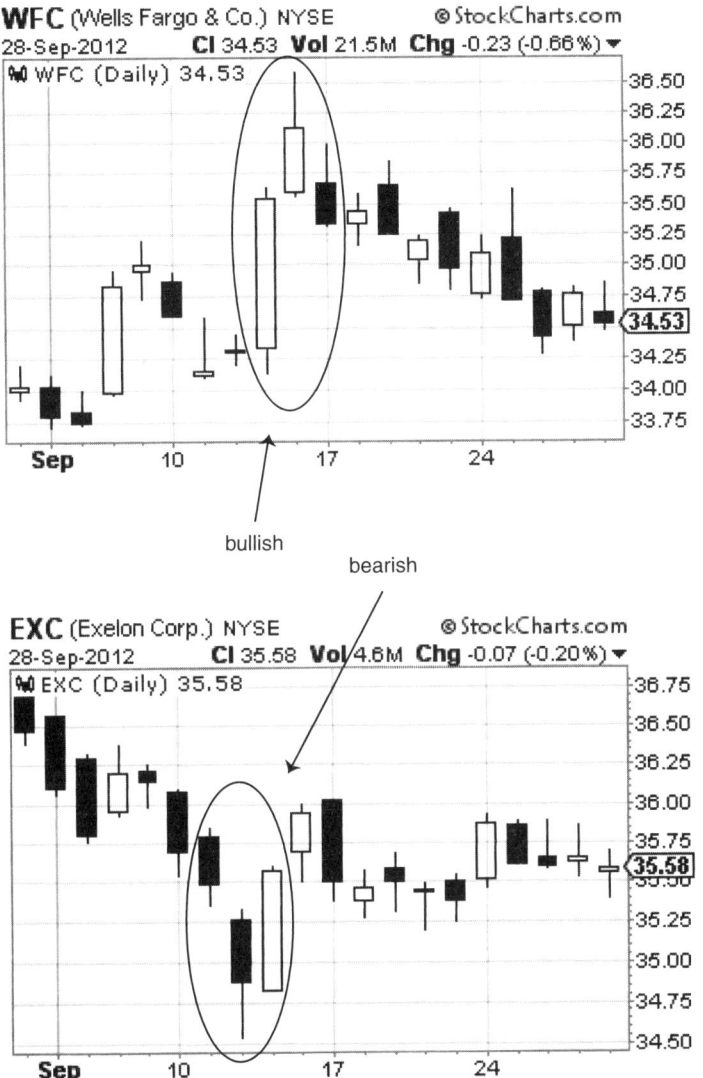

Figure 7.19 Gap filled
Source: StockCharts.com.

than at any other time, reacting to the underlying price movement and making the IV track far less reliable. This change from IV analysis to charting is why short-term, soon-to-expire options are powerful swing trading vehicles.

CHAPTER 8

FLEXING YOUR MUSCLE: THE POWER OF OPTIONS CLOSE TO EXPIRATION

> What I tell you three times is true.
> Lewis Carroll, *The Hunting of the Snark*, 1876

TRADERS TEND TO THINK OF TIME AS THE PROBLEM WITH OPTIONS trading. "Time works against you" and "expiration is a big risk" are common beliefs due to a popular bias in favor of long positions. These problems with time are very real if you restrict your trading activity to the long call or put. However, when you use short options or combinations of long and short, the landscape changes drastically. Trading options close to expiration as part of a swing strategy can turn time decay into a great vehicle for generating profits and reducing risks.

The use of options close to expiration can be a powerful method for taking advantage of rapid time decay. The last week of the option's life will see rapid time decay, and during the same period, implied volatility becomes unpredictable and often useless for the timing you need to make your swings work. This is where charting is effective to boost the elusive timing skills every swing trader needs to master.

A distinction has to be made between time decay and changes in implied volatility. They are not the same attribute, even though the two often work to offset one another. Time decay is related strictly to the passage of time and it accelerates as expiration approaches. Implied volatility (IV) is a separate force, also called extrinsic value, reflecting the assumed risk of each option; it tends to increase as price approaches or moves in the money and to decrease as price moves further out of the money. The confusing aspect of these two forces is that IV may offset changes in time value as well as intrinsic value. So the option value may appear unresponsive to changes in the underlying. This is why swing traders will see the best results when they focus on short-term, at-the-money options. In this condition, time value is close to zero and IV is not a factor (due to the phenomenon of volatility collapse during the final month, in which IV ceases to act as a reliable force on the option's value).

THE PROXIMITY AND TIME ISSUE

Even with options expiring within a few days, a space of two to three points between an OTM option and the underlying strike can create differences in how option pricing responds to or tracks the underlying. The ideal relationship is for the option to be ATM or slightly ITM. These contracts are going to be more responsive than OTM options even if the OTM point difference is small. The closer it is to expiration, the more important this proximity to moneyness becomes.

The relationship between proximity and time helps to identify the option contracts with the greatest swing trading potential. Once you find a reversal signal and have a strong sense of the direction in which the price is going to move over the next three to five days, finding the right option is the next step. Considering that it takes time to overcome OTM status *and* time value, the further away in time and the further away in proximity, the worse your chances. Ideally, you want to swing trade with options expiring very soon and at or slightly in the money.

You can use options deep in the money as well, but these will cost more, and the risk also increases. For example, a long contract five points in the money includes five points of intrinsic value. In comparison, if the option is ATM, there is no intrinsic value so the premium consists solely of time value, which will be minimal. In this case, because premium is so low, your risk in a long contract is also low in comparison to options farther from the money.

On the short side, the opposite argument applies. Picking contracts with little or no time value is a disadvantage because you want value to decline—when it does so, you can enter a "buy to close" order and take the profit. This is accomplished in two ways. First, if the underlying price moves as you expect, your short position loses value, creating a net profit. Second, the passage of time itself also reduces time value even if the price of the underlying remains unchanged. If time value is quite low, your maximum profit is capped at the level of time value itself, since that is the full extent the price may drop. But if the time value is high, your short position opportunity is maximized, since that time value premium will drop out as expiration approaches.

Is the potential profit of short ITM options worth the risk? Perhaps a better question is: Do options provide a better opportunity for profit than stock *and* is the risk any worse? If you open a short contract that is five points ITM, the market risk of those five points is the same as the market risk associated with owning 100 shares of stock, but your cash and margin risk is drastically reduced because you use the option in place of 100 shares of stock.

For example, as of October 31, 2012, IBM was valued at $194.53 per share, as shown in table 8.1. The options available for the next five expirations were:

The expiration dates were 1, 16, 51, and 79 days away. An analysis of nonintrinsic premium (time value and extrinsic or volatility value) shows how the curve occurs. A similar analysis on the same day for Apple (AAPL), which closed at $595.32, is shown in table 8.2.

To view the curve of the nonintrinsic value for calls, check figure 8.1. Note how the curve of the increase is very close for both companies even though the underlying values are much different.

The same phenomenon occurs with puts. Figure 8.2 shows a comparison of the nonintrinsic changes in value for all four expiration dates.

Table 8.1   IBM: Strikes and premium values

call strike	Expiration			
	Nov 2	Nov 17	Dec 22	Jan 19
190	5.15	5.25	6.90	8.90
195	0.80	2.25	4.35	5.95
200	0.05	0.66	2.39	3.65

put strike	Expiration			
	Nov 2	Nov 17	Dec 22	Jan 19
190	0.13	1.57	3.57	4.90
195	1.26	3.55	5.75	6.92
200	5.60	7.10	8.65	10.02

Source: Listings from Charles Schwab & Company at www.schwab.com.

Table 8.2   Apple: Expiration, strike, and option premium

call strike	Expiration			
	Nov 2	Nov 17	Dec 22	Jan 19
590	8.40	16.75	28.07	36.00
595	5.52	13.95	25.40	33.05
600	3.25	11.30	23.25	31.00

put strike	Expiration			
	Nov 2	Nov 17	Dec 22	Jan 19
590	3.20	13.45	24.45	31.80
595	5.05	15.88	26.75	34.30
600	7.85	18.65	29.68	37.05

Source: Listings from Charles Schwab & Company at www.schwab.com.

Again, the curve of the line is very similar even though the price points and underlying values are quite different for these two companies. You are likely to see a similar and predictable curve for most underlying stocks because the changes tend to reflect a current take on valuation. In the example, that "take" (closing price as of October 31, 2012) applied equally to the expiration calls and puts of the same number of days and in a very similar manner.

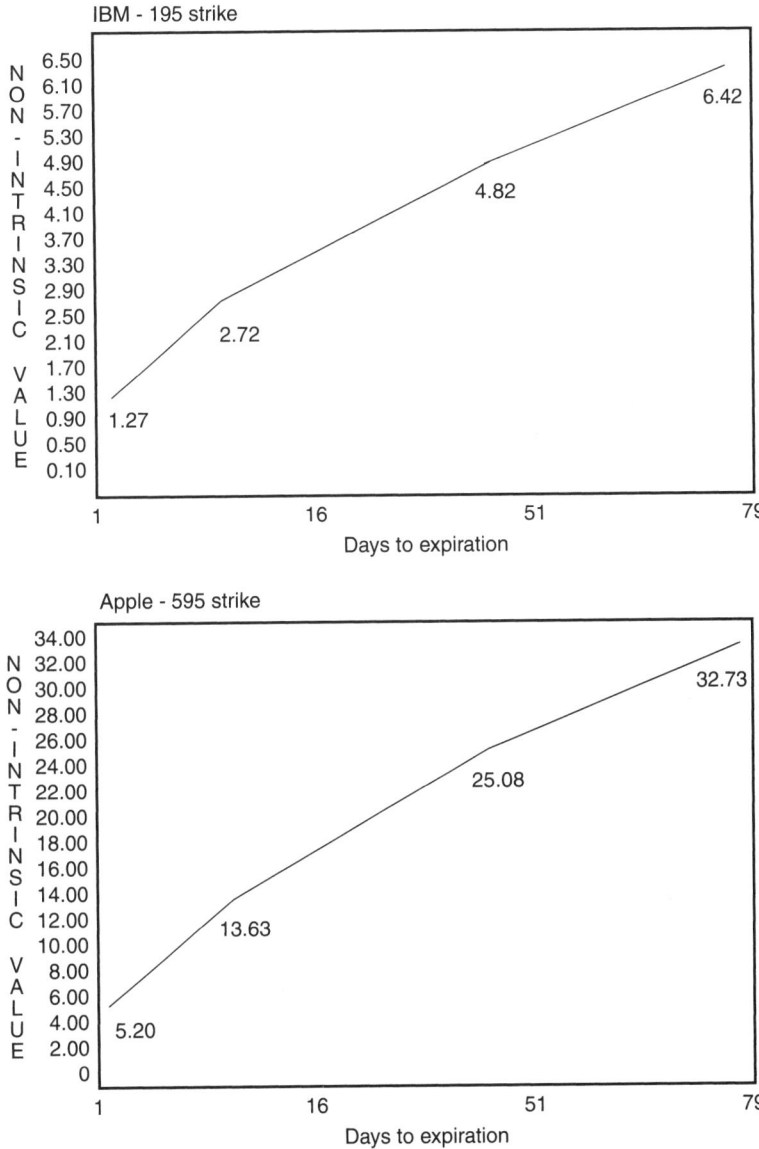

Figure 8.1 Non-intrinsic value of calls
Source: Figure created by author.

For swing trading, the lower the nonintrinsic value, the better the prospects for long positions. For short positions, you want nonintrinsic value premium, but you also have to contend with the time issue. The farther out the expiration of an option, the

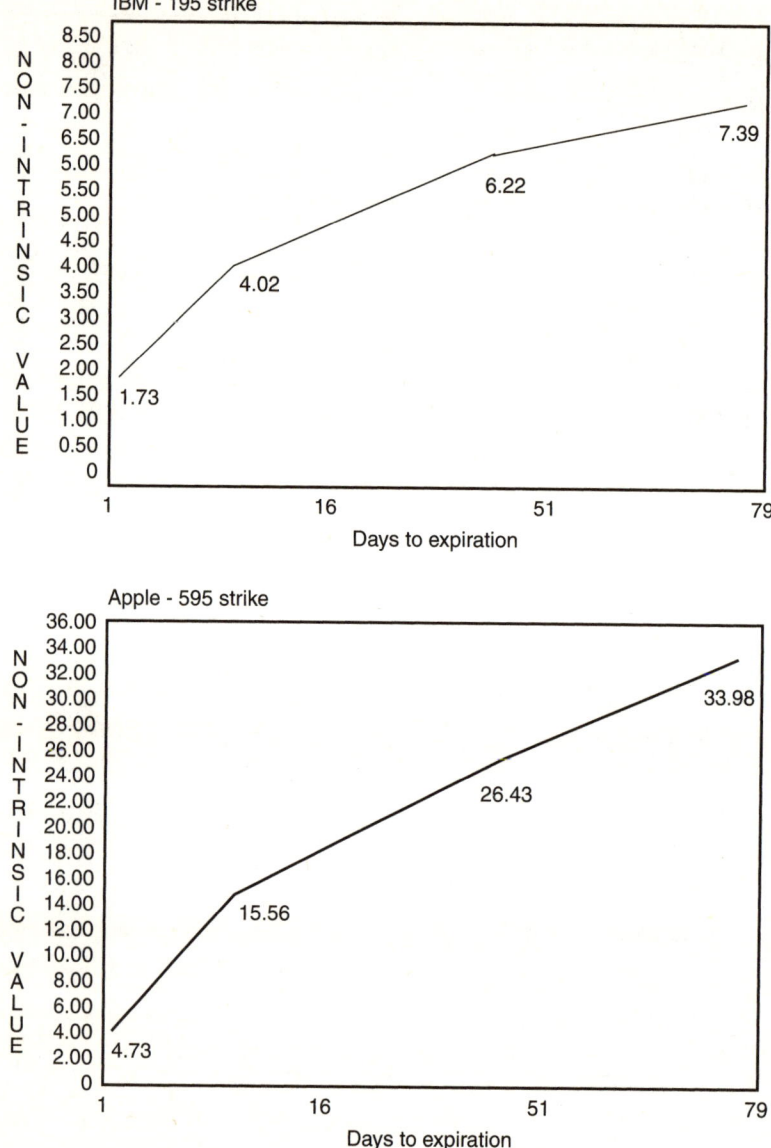

Figure 8.2 Non-intrinsic value of puts
Source: Figure created by author.

less responsive the overall premium is going to be to intrinsic movement.

Because of the different motivations of long and short positions, a sensible swing trading strategy has to be based in relative nonintrinsic value for each expiration. As a general rule, use long-position options that expire as soon as possible. In the example provided, it is likely that you would select long options expiring in 16 days. The closest choice expires in only one day, and this is not enough time to develop a trend, which should last two to five days or longer.

Use short positions expiring with adequate time and extrinsic premium but not so far out that the overall price will be unresponsive to underlying price movement when those positions are ITM (in the example, the IBM 195 or the Apple 595). Based on pricing at the point of this analysis, the 16-day calls and puts provide enough nonintrinsic value to make them attractive; using the 51-day positions nearly doubles the premium income, so choosing between the 16-day or 51-day expirations depends on your perception of how rapidly nonintrinsic value is likely to fall. For example, if you think time decay will be faster in the 16-day calls, then these would be the best choice for opening a short position. Even though time value is higher in the 51-day short calls, time decay will not take place as quickly. A major determining factor in this decision is how much price movement you expect in the underlying within the immediate future. IBM has tended to be a moderate issue with nice, short-term swings in evidence over most of the three-month period shown in its chart in figure 8.3.

Toward the end of the chart, this rhythm was disrupted by a negative guidance announcement from management. The effects of this pessimistic report accompanied by only slightly disappointing earnings cannot be known based only on what is shown here. However, this demonstrates that even a predictable rhythm—in this case a trading range of 10 points for a $200 stock (a 5% swing)—is not going to last forever.

Apple presents a somewhat different case but with the same swing degree of 5%. In this case, the swings average 30 points, but the starting and ending price during this chart period was $600 per share. The swings also tended to be longer-term when defined within channel lines, as shown in figure 8.4.

In both cases, the selection of an option at various points in the swing makes a lot of difference in how well those contracts are

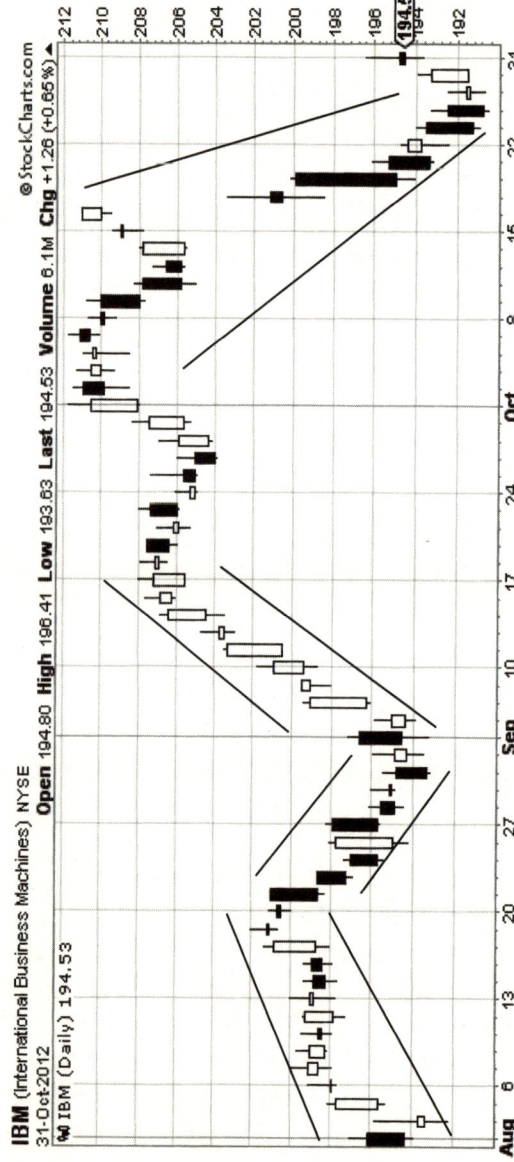

Figure 8.3 10-point trading range
Source: StockCharts.com.

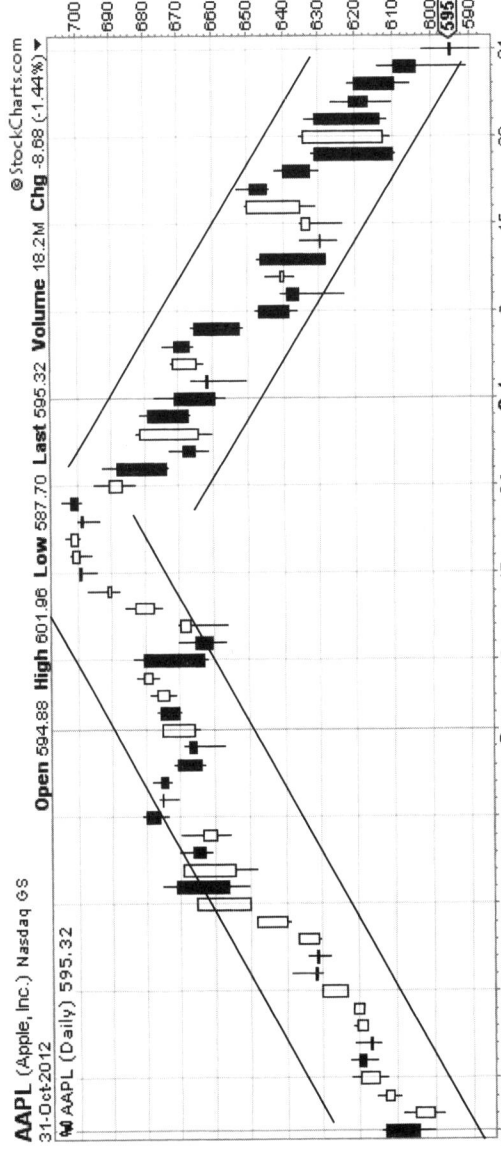

Figure 8.4 30-point trading range
Source: StockCharts.com.

going to track the underlying price. Both of these stocks experienced relatively low volatility, but an oddity of options trading is that the usual definition of volatility—degree of movement and breadth of the trading range—does not matter. What does matter is the number of points by which the underlying moves and how much ITM movement is seen in the corresponding option. As a result of significant and rapid movement of soon-to-expire options at or in the money, a swing trading profit can be realized quickly regardless of whether the historical volatility of the stock is high or low. What matters are the points of movement, and that is going to have the greatest impact ITM or ATM for options with little or no nonintrinsic value.

Short-term options have become more desirable for swing trading because of their flexibility thanks to the introduction of weekly options for many stocks. These weekly options are extremely short-term positions that are offered in addition to expirations on the third Saturday of each month. That is, if you enter a position in the first week, you can often find a weekly contract expiring in one or two weeks rather than monthly contracts expiring in three weeks. These add great flexibility to a swing trading program based on technical reversals of the underlying stock (as opposed to longer-term analysis of implied volatility) and may even enable movement in and out of swings more than once per month—while maintaining the ideal of using options expiring within one to two weeks.

Traders who have used weekly options along with monthly contracts within one to two weeks of expiration have observed that ATM positions tend to move quickly and dramatically in response to price movement in the underlying. This movement often results in close to a point-for-point change within one to two days when implied volatility and the related Greeks do not operate as reliably as they do for longer-term contracts. The risk element of these positions is quite low as well. For example, given the proximity issue (ATM) and small time window (one to two weeks), you may want to focus on contracts priced between 0.05 and 1.00 ($5 to $100). Entering these positions as long-side swings carries very low risk. If they expire worthless, the loss is minimal, but if they move ITM, profits can accumulate rapidly. A 1.00 ATM option grows to 3.00 when it moves two points ITM in a single day, for example.

You will have losses focusing on these low-cost, close-proximity, soon-to-expire positions. However, the profit potential is high enough and will occur often enough to make this an approach worth considering. The chances for profit are greatly increased when you also time your trades based on reversal signals found in Western technical price patterns, candlesticks, volume, and momentum oscillators.

THE SWING TRADING QUESTION: LONG OR SHORT?

For any swing trading program based on options, the question of risk has to be addressed. Do you use low-cost long options or short positions expiring later and having more time value?

The many variations on swing trading involve long and short positions and combinations of both and are explored in detail in coming chapters. For now, the question is focused on how specific contracts are selected for swing trading based on proximity (thus, price reaction) and time to expiration.

In long options, the selection of the very close proximity of strike to underlying stock price, combined with equally extreme short time to expiration, makes perfect sense. You are going to experience maximum price reaction when these two attributes are matched up. That is, options ATM and expiring within two weeks or sooner are optimum for a long-option swing trading strategy. For short options, the selection is quite different in terms of price movement and risk. Picking ATM or ITM contracts presents greater risks than you face with OTM positions. In the event the underlying price moves against you (up for short calls or down for short puts), you face the prospect of loss. The hope in these cases is that time decay will offset increased option premium, and this occurs frequently, especially during the last month before expiration. However, if price moves dramatically, you could face a big loss with uncovered short positions. For example, referring back to the chart for IBM (fig. 8.3), the price on October 8 was $210 per share. By October 16, the price had declined 30 points to $190. If you had sold 210 puts at the beginning of this decline, you would face a severe risk of loss if those positions were exercised. This threat can be offset, delayed, and even overcome by rolling the short puts forward and waiting out the price movement in the hope that prices will eventually return to the $200–210 level.

This points out, however, why using OTM options is a smart approach for reducing the risk of swing trading with short-side options. For example, in the case of Apple, shown in the previously cited figure 8.4, the analysis of options expiring in 16 days demonstrates how a 5-point price cushion reduces risk and still generates attractive income. The 16-day expiration for calls and puts is shown in table 8.3

In both of these cases, the cushion of five points generates less premium income but vastly reduces market risk. If you were bearish and wanted to sell uncovered calls with 16 days to expiration, by picking the OTM 600 contracts over the ATM 595 you would get 2.65 ($265) less premium, but you create a 5-point cushion. If you were bullish and wanted to sell uncovered puts, by picking the OTM 590 contracts over the ATM 595, you would get 2.43 ($243) less in premium.

In both of these examples, if the underlying price moves against you, remember that the entire premium was nonintrinsic. As expiration nears, most of the premium would evaporate. This means that a premium reduction would offset underlying price

Table 8.3   Apple: Strikes and premium values

calls
strike 595   13.95 premium
strike 600   11.30 premium

puts
strike 595   15.88 premium
strike 590   13.45 premium

Source: Listings from Charles Schwab & Company at www.schwab.com.

movement. It would take considerable movement for the intrinsic price to exceed the time decay that is going to occur over 16 days. This is likely to give you ample opportunity to close the positions, in many instances at a small profit.

For short option strategies, it makes sense to focus on OTM contracts, preferably ones expiring within half a month or sooner. The farther out expiration is, the higher the risk that unfavorable movement in the underlying stock price will result in a loss. However, even with the focus on short-term OTM contracts with high time value, you can have losses by writing short options in swing trading.

With this in mind, smart rules for managing risk for swing trading with short options include the following:

1. Avoid short option swing trading when earnings announcements are scheduled prior to expiration.
2. Avoid short option writing if ex-dividend date will occur before expiration. The chance of exercise is high right before ex-dividend date for ITM positions.
3. Keep trading levels consistent among different trades to spread market risks; don't put too much into a single short trade.
4. Be prepared to close positions when underlying prices move against you. If this means taking a small loss, this is still wiser than holding off and potentially suffering a larger loss later.
5. If expiration is close and your short options are in a loss position, roll forward to avoid unwelcome exercise.
6. If your swing trade can be closed at a profit close to expiration, close it. Don't wait a few more days for expiration, recognizing the possibility of a last-minute move in the underlying stock price.

THE STRIKE PEG

Most traders observe that options pricing follows stock pricing and thus lags as a responsive market. However, in one respect the opposite is true. Options may lead the market when the expiration date approaches. The tendency for stock prices to gravitate to the closest strike price is called the strike peg.

This occurs because traders may transact stock positions with open option contracts in mind. Both long-stock holders and short sellers affect prices in this manner, and the strike itself can become a target price for the stock in the short term, such as the last three to five trading sessions before option expiration. The strike peg may occur for any number of reasons or combinations of reasons, but it is one of many tendencies to be aware of in developing an options-based swing trading program.

The next chapter examines another oddity in the swing trading landscape: the effect of the ex-dividend date. Short traders know that the most likely date for exercise is the last trading day, whether for calls or puts. However, for traders with short options, a second date is equally as crucial: the ex-dividend date. Anyone who places a purchase order before this date earns the current dividend, so anyone whose short calls are ITM before the ex-dividend date is at risk of early exercise. This does not occur in every case. The long-option holder on the other side of the trader has to be able to generate a net profit from exercise, and this is based on two criteria: the net difference between current value and strike (plus dividend to be earned) versus the original cost that trader paid for the call. If the cost is higher than the potential benefit of exercise gain and dividend, then the long call will not be exercised.

Swing traders planning to use short calls as part of their strategy are smart to focus on underlying stocks whose ex-dividend date does not occur before expiration of the option. The next chapter explains how this is accomplished.

CHAPTER 9

SWINGS MAXIMIZED: TIMING THE SWING WITH EX-DIVIDEND DATE

> Every thought derives from a thwarted sensation.
> Emile M. Cioran, *The Trouble with Being Born*, 1973

SWING TRADING WITH SHORT POSITIONS IS QUITE DIFFERENT FROM swing trading with long positions. Sellers have specific advantages but also face a different set of risks. This chapter provides examples and compares long and short options in swing trading strategies and examines how risks differ between the two.

Some of these differences are obvious. Using long options means you pay for the option, and as a result your maximum loss is the option premium. This is an advantage because it caps the loss; it's a disadvantage because you have to balance the double problem of time and time value and must overcome both to create a profit.

Using short options means you *receive* the premium. This also presents both a positive and a negative side. On the positive side it is always preferable to open a position with a credit, and time decay reduces the value of the short option. As value declines, it becomes possible to enter a "buy to close" and realize a net profit. With the short position, the sequence of events is "sell, hold, buy" so short option positions benefit from a declining option value. Profits in short positions are created in two vastly different ways: from the increase in intrinsic value growing from well-timed swing trades and from time decay, enabling you to close at a profit or wait out expiration. On the negative side, short options may move in the money and result in exercise, an outcome most swing traders want to avoid.

So swing traders need to decide whether to focus on long or short positions or on combinations of both. As this and coming chapters demonstrate, remaining flexible and using both long and short positions (on both calls and puts) enriches the potential of your swing trading strategy. For combination strategies, extra care is required because a even a well-structured hedge can be undone if the ex-dividend date interrupts the control of losses or if the temporary changes in the underlying affect the swing trade. Even beyond the usual reversal signals, acknowledging the effects of the dividend requires that a swing trade be carefully coordinated.

THE TIMING OF EX-DIVIDEND DATES

If you own stock, you want to be in that position before the ex-dividend date. The rule is that if you buy shares *before* the ex-dividend date, you are entitled to the current dividend (which will be paid out usually three to four weeks later). You will be a stockholder of record on the record date, which is the day two trading days after the ex-dividend date. If you buy shares the day before, for example, it takes three days for the purchase to get settled, so that is two days after the ex-dividend date. If you buy stock on or after the ex-dividend date, you are not a stockholder of record for that quarter.

For example, if a stock's ex-dividend date is Tuesday next week and you purchase shares on Monday, the record date will be Thursday (three days later), which also is two days after the ex-dividend date. You will earn the dividend for this quarter. However, if you place your order on or after Tuesday, you will not be a stockholder of record in time to earn the current dividend.

With the potential problems of the ex-dividend date in mind, investors in long-stock positions must be keenly aware of timing for their purchases. Missing the ex-dividend by one or two days is unfortunate, to say the least, and is easily avoided by timing the purchase with the dividend in mind. To earn the current dividend, stock must be purchased at least one day prior to the ex-dividend date.

The dividend timing issue affects swing trading in several other ways. Beyond timing the ownership of stock in order to earn the dividend, options positions are also affected by the sale timing problems or advantages. This depends on what type of options you use and how each position is going to be affected by the dividend.

Long calls: If you plan to buy calls as part of your swing trading strategy, it is wise to avoid having positions open during the period when dividends are earned. A general assumption is that the stock price will decline on or near the ex-dividend date (or on record date) to reflect the payment of a dividend. So if the dividend is $1, you would expect the price to decline by $1 on or near this date. This does not always occur for several reasons (for example, offsetting bullish sentiment, no reaction among long-term stock owners, especially institutions, and earnings announcements when these coincide with dividend season). However, if you accept the premise that the price might decline due to dividends, then swing trading during that week with long calls exposes you to the risk of that decline. For example, if you buy a call and pay 2.00 ($200) and the dividend is one dollar per share, your position could lose 50% of its value due solely to the impact of the dividend.

Short uncovered calls: With any short calls, a decline in market value is a benefit because it enables you to buy to close at a profit. So a swing trade benefits from good timing of bearish reversals as well as from time decay. However, you face exercise risk if you have a short call open during the ex-dividend week. Most exercise risk is associated with the expiration week, especially the last trading day. Early exercise is a remote possibility only. However, any ITM short call is at exercise risk just before the ex-dividend date as well. As a swing trader, you probably don't want exercise, not only because it creates a net loss (between current market value and strike), but also because it destroys the swing trade.

How great is this risk? Not every short call will be exercised early before the ex-dividend date, but some ITM calls will be. The further your short call is ITM, the greater your risk. In order for the long-call owner on the other side of the trade to engage in early exercise, the net cost of buying the call has to be lower than the combined value of the price difference (current value minus strike) as adjusted by current dividend. The profit required is not always possible. Since the call value has risen as it has moved ITM, exercise has to be compared to the appreciated value. For example, if the buyer paid 2 ($200) and the call is now worth 5 ($500), should the position be closed at a $300 profit? Or is it better to buy shares and earn the dividend?

The risk is limited but real. As a safe move to avoid unexpected loss, if you use uncovered short calls for swing trading, avoid opening positions during the ex-dividend month. Focus on underlying issues whose ex-dividend date occurs in the month before or the month after.

Short covered calls: The discussion above applies equally to covered calls. However, upon exercise, there is a difference. With uncovered short calls, early exercise means you have to pay the difference between current market value and strike. For example, if the underlying stock is at $48 per share the day before the ex-dividend date and the strike is $45, early exercise not only wipes out your swing trade but creates a $300 loss. Exercise occurs at the strike, which is below current market value, *and* because shares are called away, you also do not earn the current dividend. This points out the importance of monitoring covered calls around ex-dividend date to avoid this double problem—by closing the option or rolling it forward.

It is wise to avoid covered call positions in the ex-dividend month, whether as part of a swing trading strategy or as part of a more basic covered call. Most covered call writers do not want exercise but prefer to move in and out of the position and take profits, hopefully in a repetitive manner from month to month. Exercise not only disrupts this income stream, but it also creates a capital gain in the underlying, which as a covered call writer you might not want. Unless you have large carryover losses to absorb, the tax liability may easily offset the modest capital gain. As a swing trader relying on the conservative nature of the covered call, you take unintended and unnecessary risks by writing calls during the ex-dividend month.

Long puts: Long puts are advantageous as swing trading choices. If in fact the underlying price does decline at or near the ex-dividend date, the long put will increase in value. So even a soon-to-expire long put may benefit from intrinsic downward movement *and* the dividend effect. Of all options to pick for months including ex-dividend dates occurring before option expiration, long puts are the best selection. They are designed to maximize bearish price movement and also hedge the dividend effect by increasing in value to offset the potential price decline.

Short puts: The short put presents a problem for swing trading strategies. If the ex-dividend date occurs prior to expiration of the option, a decline in the underlying price due to the dividend effect will increase the premium of the short put; you are seeking an increase in premium to be able to close the position at a profit. The decline due to the dividend may also move the short put ITM, making your risk of exercise greater than it is when ATM or OTM. You rely on the combination of favorable time decay and bullish reversal signals to either offset increased intrinsic value or simply to track the put's deterioration in value to make the swing profitable even in a modest uptrend. The short put is a worthy option choice for swing trading, but you have to avoid opening this particular one in the ex-dividend month.

LIKELIHOOD OF EXERCISE

How likely is exercise of your short call immediately before the ex-dividend date? Any swing trader relying on short calls is vulnerable to this possibility. Assuming you do not want to have long shares called away (or, if using uncovered calls, be hit with having to pay up the difference between current value and strike), swing trading, by definition, does not recognize exercise as desirable even when using short calls *is* desirable.

The best way to avoid this problem is to not write calls during the ex-dividend month, and if you have open short contracts and they move ITM, roll forward or close to avoid exercise right before the ex-dividend date. You also avoid the problem by avoiding dividend-paying stocks and swing trading only on issues for which ex-dividend exercise is not a possibility.

Early exercise is a fairly rare event, but it does happen when three conditions are present:

1. The short call is ITM.
2. The buyer can create a net profit from exercise given the initial cost of the call compared to the amount of the dividend plus the paper gain (difference between current value and strike).
3. Dividend is attractive enough to justify purchasing shares through exercise of the call.

Because not all three of these elements exist in each case, early exercise might or might not happen.

The call owner faces a dilemma, however. If the stock behaves as you expect and falls on the ex-dividend date, then the dividend is offset by decline in the value of stock. It is possible to sell stock right at the open of the ex-dividend date (and the dividend will still be earned since the purchase of shares occurred the day before), but it is not always possible to beat the system. It's likely that the stock will open at the reduced price. So in a practical sense, the exercise of the call is going to make sense only if the dividend is higher than the original cost of the option. For many call owners, this will not be the case, so exercise won't happen unless the call owner is simply not aware that it is not a profitable move. This is always a possibility; don't just assume that long-call traders are always aware of their profit and breakeven price points.

The big disadvantage to exercise—from the long trader's point of view—is that the action takes their time premium away. Given that at this point the call has moved ITM, it is likely to be more profitable to just sell and close the call than to exercise it to get the dividend.

In considering the potential consequences of having your short call exercised before your swing trades have matured, it makes all the difference if your position is covered or uncovered. If you are swing trading with a covered call, you have taken on a highly conservative strategy. Assuming you timed the short call based on strong reversal and confirmation, you expect the price to decline so that you can close the call at a profit. However, in some instances, the underlying price will rise, and then the risk of early exercise becomes a reality in some instances.

As long as your strike is higher than your original basis, you will earn a profit from the capital gain as well as from the call premium; early exercise in this case is not entirely negative. In fact, giving up the dividend might turn out a wash in terms of profitability. If the stock price falls on the ex-dividend date (but your short call was exercised the day before), then exercise is a positive outcome for you.

Strategies for Swings with Stock and Options

Although a premise of the options-based swing trading strategy is focused on short-term price movement, it is also possible to incorporate options with stocks in various configurations. Many of these will reduce risks; many others open up possibilities for conservative uses of existing long positions as cover for short-call swing trades with no added market risk.

The most apparent of these options and stock strategies is the covered call. Chapters 12 and 13 examine this strategy in depth. There are three primary methods for covered call swing trading:

1. *The covered call as a one-to-one strategy.* The one-to-one reference is a match between 100 shares of stock and one short call. In this strategy, a trader either buys 100 shares or already holds them in a portfolio. If these shares have appreciated since original purchase, this adds flexibility to the swing trade and also opens up many possibilities for variations of the swing trade.

Under the basic and best-understood swing trade, a strike is selected above the original basis in stock; this ensures that if the short call is exercised, it will produce a net capital gain. Thus, swing trading resulting in exercise produces profits from three possible sources: capital gain on the stock, premium on the short call, and dividends (if stock is owned before the ex-dividend date). Even if the call is exercised, these three sources apply. If the covered call is not exercised, traders are free to close short calls at a profit, roll them forward, or allow them to expire and then write a subsequent covered call.

If the basis in stock is well below current market value, traders may enhance the strategy by writing calls with strikes at or above current market value, which is a prudent strategy. However, greater downside protection is gained by writing ITM calls. In the event the stock price declines sharply, the ITM call offsets that loss with intrinsic value to the extent of the difference between initial value of shares and the strike of the short call. Relying on the swing advantage of time decay, the short call that also happens to be deep ITM can accumulate profits from a decline in stock price, rapid acceleration of time decay, or forward-rolled additional premium.

An alternative is letting the call continue open as exercise approaches and even to accept exercise. In this case, the trader realizes a full profit on the sale of the call and also on the shares (this assumes that the strike, even though lower than current market value, is higher than the original price per share of the underlying). However, this also poses a potential unintended tax consequence. The "qualified covered call" rule states that a call opened that is deep ITM may be unqualified for treatment as long-term capital gains on the underlying upon exercise. A "qualified" covered call is determined by a complex combination of stock closing levels, time until expiration, strike price limits, and the range of price per share. A summary is shown in table 9.1.

Table 9.1 Qualification of Covered Calls

Previous Day's Stock Closing Price	Time until Expiration	Strike Price Limits
$25 or less	More than 30 days	One strike price below prior day's closing stock price (Exception: you cannot have a "qualified" covered call if strike price is lower than 85% of the stock price.)
$25.01 to $60	More than 30 days	One strike price below prior day's closing stock price
$60.01 to $$150	31–90 days	One strike price below prior day's closing stock price
$60.01 to $150	More than 90 days	Two strike prices below prior day's closing stock price (but not more than 10 points in the money)
Over $150	31–90 days	One strike price below prior day's closing stock price
Over $150	More than 90 days	Two strike prices below prior day's closing stock price

Source: Ernst & Young, "Taxes and Investing," 2007; updated edition from CBOE at www.cboe.com/LearnCenter/pdf/TaxesandInvesting.pdf.

2. *Expansion of the covered call to a ratio write.* The ratio write is a strategy involving stock and short calls; however, more calls are written than are covered by stock. For example, if you own 300 shares and write four calls, this creates a 4:3 ratio write. This can also be looked at as a 75% covered and 25% uncovered call or as a combination of three covered calls and one uncovered call.

As long as the strike is higher than current value of the stock—that is, all the calls are OTM—the ratio write makes sense initially. By focusing on soon-to-expire options and relying on rapidly declining time value, the risk level of the ratio write is not as great as it would be otherwise. For example, a ratio write can be created using four-month calls ATM or even OTM. The initial premium income will be quite attractive, but the risk level is considerably greater than that for the typical swing trading option—ATM or slightly ITM and close to expiration (meaning rapid time decay).

The ratio write is a strategy whose market risk depends on the time and proximity issues, just as in all short options. However, this strategy can be used to increase income from swing trading without the level of risk that is found with an uncovered call by itself.

Any swing trader interested in ratio writes should be keenly aware of when the ex-dividend date occurs. If it falls between the day the position is opened and expiration of the short calls, the risk level is vastly increased. Swing trading with a ratio write is best executed in months with no ex-dividend date, on stocks that pay no dividend, or on securities that are exercised European style.

3. *Expansion of the covered call to a variable ratio write.* The ratio write can be modified to reduce risks through the *variable* ratio write. In this version, two different strikes are used instead of one. For example, if you own 300 shares currently valued at $38.50, a variable ratio write of 4:3 could consist of two 40 calls and two 42.50 calls. This is another method of opening short calls beyond the cover of shares owned, but the use of two strikes reduces your exercise risk.

If the underlying price begins to rise toward the first strike, several actions can be taken. One or more of the short calls can be closed or rolled forward, for example. Calls at either strike can also be exchanged for a higher strike to reduce the chances of exercise. Even though the ratio write is not as risky as uncovered call writing, it does carry risks. These risks are reduced substantially by using the variable ratio write.

As with any position including short calls, it is best to avoid the ex-dividend month or to focus on stocks that do not pay dividends. The risk of exercise, especially when you have written more calls than you can cover with stock, is too great to expose yourself to.

CONVERTING THE EXERCISED SHORT OPTION INTO A DIFFERENT SWING TRADING STRATEGY

A swing trading strategy using short puts involves opening positions upon discovering reversal signals at the bottom of a swing. Once confirmed, the short put acts in the same manner as a long call. With short puts you face a different market risk than you do with short calls. With short puts, everything is opposite of short calls: Puts increase in value for each point lost in the underlying. When you short puts, you want the underlying to increase so the put will lose value. If the underlying value declines, the short put increases in value, which is a negative for you. The deeper the decline in the underlying, the larger your potential loss in the short put. You can take several actions to avoid this loss. These include closing and taking a small loss, rolling forward to a later expiration (or forward and down to a later expiration and lower strike), or acceptance of exercise.

If you accept exercise, 100 shares are put to you for each ITM put you sold. When that occurs, you have a new dilemma: You own stock you bought above current market value. So you may wait out the price hoping it will rise once again and cover your paper loss. Or you can pursue a "recovery strategy" in some form. If you believe that the stock price is going to rise and you locate reversal signals and confirmation supporting this possibility, the alternatives include:

1. *Selling an uncovered put.* You can create additional income by writing another uncovered put. This reduces the gap between the strike and the lower current value of shares. However, the danger here is that if the price continues to decline, you increase your losses. In a recovery strategy such as this, the risk is that you may increase your paper losses and move far away from the original plan to swing trade on short-term trends.

   An alternative is to sell shares and take the loss, freeing up capital and collateral to pursue different swing trading opportunities. The only time to use a new short put is when you want to acquire more shares and consider the strike a

fair price or when the declined value of shares is so slight that the short put wipes out the paper loss.
2. *Buying one or more calls.* A more prudent approach is to buy long calls because the risk is limited to what should be a very small premium cost. In comparison, the short-put risk could be substantially higher if the underlying price declines. In addition, you could end up with even more shares when the short put is exercised. Based on these points, the long call is a more sensible recovery strategy.
3. *Entering a low-cost or no-cost combination such as a synthetic long-stock position.* A synthetic position involves a long call and a short put (synthetic long stock) or a long put and a short call (synthetic short stock). The net cost of the synthetic position should be close to zero or even a small credit. If your timing is good and the underlying price rises, the synthetic position duplicates intrinsic movement point for point. This is similar to buying a long call, but due to the short put, the net premium cost is very small. In exchange, that short put represents risk in the sense that if it is exercised, you will have 100 shares put to you at the strike. Exercise risk is avoided by closing the short put or rolling it forward.
4. *Writing a covered call.* Now that you have acquired shares of stock, a covered call may be the most practical and lowest-risk alternative for recovery. However, make sure that the strike is high enough to create an overall profit if the short call is exercised. This is equal to the difference between the strike and your basis in stock minus the premium you receive for selling the call and less any dividends you expect to earn in the near future.

If the current price is far below the strike, which means that you own stock acquired well above market value, a covered call could be impossible. Exercise could result in a net loss, in which case you are better off using one of the other strategies or waiting out the market in the hopes that prices will rise once again.

Is the covered call a better strategy than a naked put? In cases when you cannot create breakeven or better with a covered call, think again about writing a naked put as an alternative. The risk profiles of covered call and uncovered put are identical. You might consider the uncovered put to be a higher risk, but it actually is not. In fact, in many respects, it has better profit potential.

For example, if the underlying price declines, the short put can be closed or rolled to avoid exercise. This avoidance strategy can go on indefinitely. In comparison, with a covered call your downside protection is limited to the amount of premium you receive for selling the call.

If the underlying price rises as you hope, the short put will become worthless, and you keep the premium, perhaps even writing a second uncovered put. However, with the covered call, a rise in price could result in unwanted consequences. Even if you set up the position to create a profit, exercise of the covered call represents a lost opportunity since the underlying will have risen above the strike of the call. Exercise can be avoided by rolling forward or closing at a profit, and one closed covered call can be replaced with another; that is, the covered call should not be dismissed without weighing both it and the uncovered put as possible recovery strategies.

The risks associated with dividends and the ex-dividend date can be managed by simply avoiding the ex-dividend month, focusing on swings using stocks that do not pay dividends, or restricting swing trades to securities with European exercise. The risk is easily avoided, but some swing traders have made the mistake of not being aware of early exercise risk. As a result, they may have their shares called away before the ex-dividend date, and they lose the dividend and their swing trade is destroyed.

This and preceding chapters laid the groundwork for an effective swing trading strategy built on the many different uses of options. Beginning with the next chapter, specific strategies are described based on options in long or short, call or put configurations. The first topic is the most basic: the use of long options as the basis for your swing trading strategy.

CHAPTER 10

STRATEGY # 1: LONG-OPTION APPROACH, A BASIC SOLUTION

> He can't think without his hat.
> Samuel Beckett, *Waiting for Godot*, 1955

LONG OPTIONS OFFER ADVANTAGES FOR SWING TRADING. THEY are inexpensive, highly leveraged, and limited in risk. They also come with disadvantages because they lose value rapidly due to time decay, and long positions held to expiration expire 75% of the time—or is the number 80% or even 90%?

The problem with this statistic is that it is not a certainty. The key qualifier—"held to expiration"— affects actual outcomes. The observation has led many to claim that 75% or *all* long options will expire worthless, but that is not the case.

THE 75% "RULE" AND HOW IT REALLY WORKS

The number of long options that expire worthless is based on holding the positions open until expiration. In a swing trading strategy, you would rarely, if ever, do this. However, the statistic has led to the myth that "most options lose money."

The selection of options and timing of entry have everything to do with profitable outcomes or losses. The assignment of a 75% loss ratio is inaccurate. It is true that sellers have specific advantages. They receive money instead of paying, so time decay works in their favor. Selecting a short position allows you to benefit from reversals in the same way as with long options but with less worry about time decay or volatility. In fact, a short option may become profitable even when the underlying price works against you. This occurs when time decay outpaces intrinsic value. So it's true that short-option traders have considerable advantages over long-option traders, but they also have risks.

Among the risks of short trading the most obvious is exercise risk. Exercise can be avoided by closing to take small losses and avoid bigger ones later, rolling forward, or covering exposed positions. It can also be avoided by restricting activity to covered calls. While this ensures that exercise will not result in a loss (if the right strike and expiration are selected), it does not protect against potentially severe downside risks. Covered call writing also requires that you own 100 shares for each option you sell.

A long option, in comparison, controls 100 shares of stock and replaces outright ownership at a small percentage of the cost. A 50 strike option may cost $250 or less, depending on strike, expiration, and moneyness. Owning 100 shares costs $5,000. This is the essential benefit to long-option swing trading: leverage and profit potential.

Even so, what about that 75% statistic? A widespread perception is that options are simply too risky for buying because three out four become worthless. In swing trading, though, you do not intend to hold options until expiration. The ideal trade will last between three and five days—sometimes more and sometimes less.

The 75% is a misleading conclusion as well. In fact, on average only 10% of all options get exercised in a current cycle. But this does not mean the other 90% expire worthless. Another 60% of options are closed before expiration. The remaining 30% are likely to expire worthless, and so 30%—not 75%—is a number closer to fact. This affects long-options traders negatively, but remember that is also affects short traders positively.[1]

There are three qualifiers for picking the best long option, and these are why long positions contain less risk than short options but have just as much profit potential. These three are:

1. *Select options expiring in one month or less.* During the last month of an option's life cycle, nonintrinsic value (time value and extrinsic or implied volatility value) are closer to zero. The closer expiration becomes, the lower these nonintrinsic portions of the premium. This means that without time decay or implied volatility offset, the option premium is most likely to mirror intrinsic price movement point for point. An option is not going to ever achieve the perfect one-to-one price change with the underlying, but as expiration nears, the relationship between underlying price and intrinsic movement of the option becomes closer.
2. *Focus on strikes at the money or even slightly in the money.* Given the short term of the typical swing trade, you want to avoid time value. Even a two-point OTM option has to absorb two points of favorable movement in the underlying before intrinsic value begins to operate. So a two-point movement in the underlying might result in no net gain for the option. ATM strikes or strikes one point or less ITM provide the most favorable conditions for swing trading.
3. *Time your purchase based on reversal indicators and confirmation.* In working with long options, when should you enter a position? It is not enough to merely pick the option whose strike is closest to current underlying value and that is due to expire within the next few weeks. The timing has to be based on a study of chart patterns, including price, volume, and momentum. The ideal long-position swing trade targets the top or bottom of the current short-term trend, with the goal of buying a call (at the bottom of a downtrend) or a put (at the top of an uptrend). If this timing is effective, profits are possible in a very quick turnaround.

The Need for Defensive Long-Option Strategies

The danger of the intended short-term trade is that reversal does not always occur right away (or at all) even when expiration occurs very soon, strikes are ATM or ITM, and you find strong reversals and confirmation. Some signals fail, and that is reality. Some reversals occur but not right away. If the signals are correct, but reversal is delayed beyond option expiration, you will lose on the trade.

You will not lose 75% of the time that you find strong reversal and confirmation. In fact, requiring these signals as a prerequisite to entering the trade is more likely to increase the percentage of profitable swing trades. Relying on reversal indicators and confirmation will enable you to have more profitable trades than losses.

Because trades do not always work out, a defensive strategy should be employed in trading with long options. When you use short options for swing trading, you can wait out the declining value of the option, and the more it declines, the more profitable the trade becomes. In fact, when using short options, you have an advantage when picking options with a longer time to expiration—two months, for example—because higher time value represents more potential profit. With long options, you do not have the luxury of waiting out time value. Your trade will lose if the option value declines between entry and expiration even if the signals are proven to be right in the longer term.

Defensive strategies for long options include:

1. *Diversify your swing trades.* A great advantage to trading with options is that with the smaller incremental cost, you have more flexibility. You need to maintain adequate security and cash in your account to provide required collateral for option trades, but the difference between the cost of one option and that of 100 shares is the key. You can trade in many different underlying securities at the same time, some bullish and others bearish, all depending on the signals you discover in each case. Diversify to avoid losses you cannot afford.
2. *Keep dollar amounts approximately the same for each trade.* Closely related to diversification is the strategy of keeping all trades at about the same dollar value. For example, if your target trade price is $400, you may be limited to one option in some cases whereas in others you can buy four options priced at 1.00 each. The temptation is to gradually increase trading amounts. If you have a string of profitable trades,

the rationale is that by increasing the amount placed in each trade, you will also increase your profits. The danger of this outlook is that the higher your trade amount, the more disastrous a loss will be. By keeping a series of trades at about the same dollar value, a loss is not going to destroy the entire program. And losses will occur, so this rule is sensible.

3. *If the trade moves against you, sell to cut your losses.* A small loss today is better than a larger loss next week. Not every swing trade will move in the direction you expect, so when you realize that your confirmed signals have failed, cut your losses, close the position, and move to a different trade. Don't look back either. A very destructive habit for options traders is to play the "if only" game with themselves. "If only I had stayed in that trade" or "if only I'd invested much more in that trade." These self-punishing hindsight judgments are destructive to your self-confidence. Not only do some trades fail, some traders look back too much of the time and prevent themselves from moving forward to the next trade. In other words, accept a percentage of loss as part of the strategy and strive to increase the percentage of profits based on smart analysis or reversal signals and confirmation.

4. *Never make a trade in a hurry.* Options values move quickly, so as a consequence, traders may make a decision without enough research. A reversal signal as yet unconfirmed is not adequate justify jumping into a trade. You might miss some opportunities by taking your time, but hurrying into a trade too quickly is going to lead to more losses, and your goal is to create situations for more profits.

THE LONG-OPTION DILEMMA: TIME AND COST PROBLEMS AND SOLUTIONS

Every option trader has had to face the dilemma of time and cost. The longer the time to expiration, the more opportunity for the underlying price to move. If it rises far enough and fast enough, the long call becomes profitable. If price falls far enough and fast enough, the long put becomes profitable.

However, the longer the time to expiration, the higher the cost. When time value is high, it takes considerable price movement (and in the right direction) just to offset time value and even before intrinsic value may begin to accumulate profits.

This is the dilemma of every long-option trader. It is not enough to be correct about the direction of price movement. You also have to be correct with enough time to overcome the time and cost constraints.

The solution when using long options for swing trading is to focus narrowly on those contracts with favorable proximity. This concept—proximity—normally refers to "moneyness" or the relationship between the current underlying price and the option's strike. That is one attribute of great concern, and the other is proximity of time, namely, between the opening trade date and the expiration date.

Thus, proximity has to involve both price and time in order for the best possible options to be identified. Once a reversal or continuation signal is located and confirmed, you next need to decide which option to trade to take advantage of the trend you expect to find. The "right" options are those meeting a few important criteria:

1. *Proximity in terms of moneyness.* The most obvious of criteria for picking the right option is the distance between current price and the strike. The ideal positioning of moneyness is going to be at the money (ATM). Assuming your selection is correct in terms of price movement, a call is picked when your signals point to an uptrend, and a put is picked when your signals point to a downtrend. If you are correct in regard to direction, the ATM option will immediately begin moving in the money (ITM), meaning intrinsic value accumulates as the underlying trends favorably *away from* the strike and further ITM.
2. *Proximity of time.* The ideal movement relies on the contract having as little extrinsic (volatility) value as possible *and* as little time value as possible. Both of these conditions are found only when an ATM option is due to expire within one

month. Even better, if expiration is due to occur within two weeks or less, then you have the most favorable proximity of time. In those last two weeks, time value is very close to zero and volatility collapses. This concept is applied to options throughout their life span, but specifically this collapse is important to swing traders during those two weeks before expiration. At this time, volatility collapse can be relied upon more than at any other time. With the relatively recent introduction of weekly options, focusing on contracts expiring in two weeks or less is possible throughout the monthly cycle. The relationship between nonintrinsic value (time and extrinsic) to the optimum proximity for swing trading is summarized in figure 10.1. Assuming that you focus on ATM options during this period, both time proximity and price proximity are optimal.

3. *Strength of the signal compared to recent price movement.* Swing trading relies on price, volume, and momentum trends, of course, but the timing can also be enhanced by studying the pattern of recent price movement. This refers to price volatility and also to the timing of typical short-term trends.

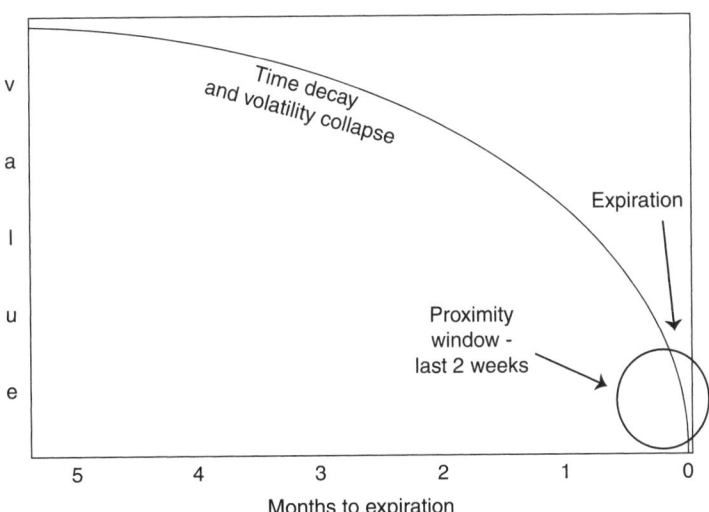

Figure 10.1   Optimum proximity for swing trading
Source: Figure created by the author.

Some stocks experience a two-week swing over long periods of time, and others go for a full month, and some have no discernible rhythm in short-term trends. In quantifying a current signal and confirmation, you must be aware of the current price and its position in the rhythm of recent price trends. This is by no means a reliable timing indicator, but it does add to the strength of a signal when the reversal fits with established cyclical price changes.

4. *Location of price within the current trading range.* A reversal is most likely to occur when price is close to resistance or support. These trading range borders may be tested several times without a breakout, and most of the time, this failed breakout leads to a trend in the opposite direction. This is one of the basic concepts in Western technical analysis, in which strong signals such as exhaustion gaps, rising or falling wedges, double and triple tops and bottoms, and head and shoulders patterns often occur right at resistance or support and provide strong signals of coming reversal. This is especially strong when price does move above resistance or below support in a gapping pattern, and then the likelihood of reversal is even stronger.

LEVERAGE AND DIVERSIFICATION WITH LONG OPTIONS

One aspect of options for swing trading most often overlooked is the ability to diversify. As long as you have adequate capital in your account to provide collateral for your options trades, controlling 100 shares of stock with a relatively cheap option is a powerful form of leverage, and because of the cost advantages of low-cost options close to expiration, you are also better able to diversify among many different underlying securities.

The combination of these two attributes has great potential. Even so, this presents a danger to every trader as well. The temptation to overuse both leverage and diversification may increase risks rather than reducing them.

Leverage risk exists within the option as part of its design. Because a single option costs as little as 5% (or less) of the cost of 100 shares, having adequate collateral in a portfolio may invite excessive play. When options are used to swing trade, having a large amount of collateral may expose you to great danger in the sense of leverage. The leveraging power of options may lead to excessive swing trading in markets that are more volatile and less certain than average. Simply having the advantage of a leveraged instrument is not always a benefit; it may also end up being a liability.

Diversification risk also exists because with the relatively low cost of options it is possible to spread collateral and capital among many more issues than would be possible by trading shares of stock. Because each option controls 100 shares, the power of diversification will seem advantageous at first glance. However, expanded diversification can also translate into broader risk exposure. If the market acts or reacts in the same direction due to a widespread panic, for example, having many long-call or short-put positions on at that time can create unexpected losses. And any time you are surprised by sudden and fast market moves, losses are likely to accumulate rapidly.

These risks—leverage and diversification—point out the need for a few swing trading rules designed to limit risks. These include the following:

1. *Maintain a predetermined trading increment for each swing trade.* Select the dollar amount of your typical swing trade. Even though specific strategies may have better than a fifty-fifty chance of success, do not vary this exposure. The amount should be what you can afford to lose on one trade, never more. The temptation to violate this self-imposed rule exposes you to profoundly higher risks and can quickly destroy an otherwise well planned swing trading program.
2. *Decide in advance the total capital committed to swing trading.* Not every trader will want to use up to 100% of available cash and collateral for swing trading. Most traders will

want to split assets between permanent long positions and a swing trading program. Decide how much you are willing to devote to swing trading based on assets, risk tolerance, and knowledge about the market and options trading. This should not be the maximum available; remember that if any positions move against you, collateral requirements will rise, and you will have to deposit additional funds. So keep the maximum capital commitment at an affordable level.

3. *If markets move against you broadly, take defensive actions— cover or close.* No matter how carefully you analyze and confirm signals and study the market, a big unexpected move in the broad market is always possible. Once you see that a broad market move is taking place, take action to defend against losses in all positions affected negatively by the move. Cut losses in the moment without concerning yourself with possible turnaround. If you cannot afford the kinds of losses that such a move may incur, close those positions immediately. If covering is possible, that presents an alternative, but in most negatively affected markets, closing exposed positions before losses grow makes the most sense.

Long Puts to Offset Short Risk

Aside from the threat of a broad market move, swing traders are continually faced with the dilemma of how to trade bearishly without shorting stock. This is one of the primary reasons why it makes sense to swing trade with options rather than with stock.

Swing traders using stock may observe the problem with options: time value and the looming expiration combine to make options difficult even for short-term trades. An ATM or OTM option is likely to be unresponsive to even positive price movement in the underlying, so that the desired short-term trend is not going to be effective in creating profits. This problem is overcome by focusing on buying options expiring in the next month (and preferably in the next two weeks) and on short options expiring in the next two months (recognizing that time value may play an equal or even greater role in creating desired profits).

Another consideration is the risk-reducing effect long puts have on bearish swings. In the traditional stock-based swing trade, one of two systems is used. First, the swing trader focuses only on long stock at the bottom of a swing, exits at the top and then waits for the conclusion of another downward swing, or he finds a different underlying for the next bullish move. Second, the trader uses long stock at the bottom of the swing and short stock at the top. The advantage to this approach is that it allows the swing trader to swing in both directions, whereas the restriction of long stock eliminates all bearish swings.

The risk of shorting stock keeps many swing traders out of the bearish side of swing trading, and that means that half of all opportunities are passed. The market risk exists because the underlying price might rise, creating two problems. First, it creates a loss on the short position that has to be resolved by closing and taking that loss or by waiting out the market and hoping the price declines once again. Second, each time the price increases, the margin maintenance required also changes, and the trader is required to deposit more equity. Throughout the entire time the short stock is open, the trader also has to pay interest on the shorted stock.

These complexities and risks make shorting stock impractical for those interested in swing trading in very short holding periods and with very low risks. The solution is to replace short stock with long puts. Even swing traders who decide to continue swing trading on the bullish side with stock may discover the advantages of long puts for the opposite, bearish swing.

Long puts not only overcome the risk and cost aspects of shorting stock, but they also represent very low risk levels. Even though collateral requirements on margin apply, buying long puts for a small percentage of the equivalent 100-share value of borrowed stock is a far smaller risk, margin, and market risk exposure.

Long puts are also flexible in terms of loss reduction. If short stock increases in value as the stock price rises, the risk exposure worsens as margin requirements grow. The further it grows, the greater your losses and the more expensive it becomes, not only to get out but also to remain in the position (due to margin requirements and interest expense). In comparison, if you swing trade with a put and the price of the underlying trends bullishly, the put simply becomes worthless. The small investment in the put is the maximum loss you can suffer.

EXAMPLE # 1: CHART-BASED REVERSAL SIGNALS

In examining a stock chart, any number of signals and confirmations are likely to be found. The swing trading goal is always to identify the starting and ending points of short-term trends. It is not enough to locate reversal days, as these occur often and some end up as false signals, or to find narrow-range days (NRD) also known as dojis or near-dojis, since these also appear often and are notoriously unreliable by themselves to signal reversal, or to see a volume spike.

These three basic swing trade reversals are good starting points for determining whether a current trend is coming to an end. However, there has to be more in the form of candlestick or Western technical indicators and patterns, volume indicators, moving average crossover, and momentum oscillators. These are all used collectively to (a) identify likely reversal and (b) add confirmation to the likelihood of the initial signal's validity.

Some examples of chart analysis for long options include the chart of ConocoPhillips (COP), shown in figure 10.2.

This is a very busy chart and signals are numerous:

1. *MA crossing below price indicates bearish reversal.* Both moving average (MA) lines decline below price, indicating that price is likely to decline. This may signal the close of any open positions based on previous bullishness and the opening of a long put in anticipation of a coming downtrend.
2. *Bearish harami.* The harami at the top of the uptrend confirms what the MA crossover predicted. The trend then turned and moved downward.
3. *Hammer.* The bottom of the downtrend was clearly identified with the appearance of the hammer, a bullish reversal signal. This was the point to close long puts and open long calls.

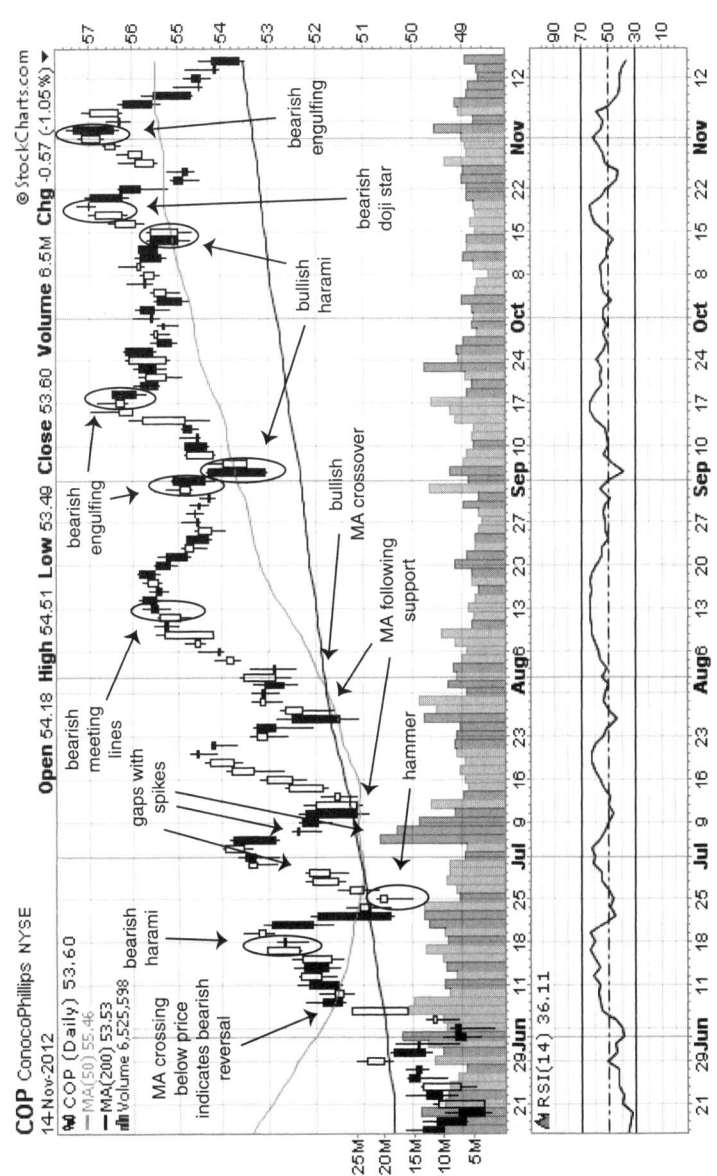

Figure 10.2 Swing trading with long options—example #1
Source: StockCharts.com.

4. *Gaps with spikes.* Although the trend moved upward strongly, the series of price gaps complicated the question of whether the trend was over or likely to continue. The upward gap could have been a bearish sign, but it was quickly followed by a similar downward gap. This indicates a likely continuation of the uptrend.
5. *MA following support.* Both MA lines tracked support very closely, confirming the likelihood that the overall trend was bullish.
6. *Bullish MA crossover.* When the shorter-term MA crosses above the longer-term MA, it is a bullish signal. This confirms the uptrend and is interpreted as a place to buy calls or, if already open, to keep them open.
7. *Bearish meeting lines.* Price outpaced the moving averages until the bearish meeting lines pattern occurred. This was a likely signal that the trend was topping out. At this point, any open long calls should be closed and replaced with long puts.
8. *Bearish engulfing and bullish harami (twice).* The first two-signal occurrence happened very quickly; in fact, the bullish signal happened right after the bearish signal. When the first one appeared, it would make sense to close the calls and replace them with long puts. However, two sessions later, the reverse is indicated: sell the long puts and buy long calls. However, due to the rapid occurrence, if you were to wait for confirmation, the bullish signal provides contradiction instead, so no action would be taken.

    The second double signal lasted over a longer period of time. The initial bearish engulfing pattern signaled the tine to close long calls and buy long puts. The downtrend was gradual and lasted a full month. However, the second bullish harami signaled the likely end, so it was time to sell puts and buy calls.
9. *Bearish doji star.* The bullish trend was very brief, and it ended with the appearance of a very strong signal, the bearish doji star. It is made strong by the gap on either side of the

doji session. This was time to once again acknowledge the reversal: sell open calls and replace with long puts.
10. *Bearish engulfing pattern.* The downtrend was quite fast and was followed by an equally fast uptrend. This ended with the bearish engulfing pattern at the top, one of the strongest reversal signals with approximately 70% reliability. At this point, any open calls should be closed and replaced with long puts, or if long puts are open, they should be held onto in anticipation of the new downtrend.

Example # 2: Chart-Based Reversal Signals

Another example of how to use charting signals to manage long-option swing trading is seen in the chart of Firstenergy Corp. (FE) shown in figure 10.3.

In this case there are about the same number of reversal signals. These are:

1. *Morning star.* This candlestick is easy to miss, but in this case it confirms that the previous downtrend has ended and a new bullish uptrend is likely to follow. This would signal the time to buy calls.
2. *Bullish piercing lines.* This signal appeared after the previous uptrend retraced. It confirms that. in fact, the uptrend is still in effect and that calls should not be sold yet.
3. *Three outside down.* This three-session bearish signal appeared after the extended uptrend and should have sparked disposal of long calls and their replacement with long puts.
4. *Long black with volume spike.* The long black candle session confirmed the strength of the three outside down signal, especially as it was further confirmed with the volume spike. In this situation, the long puts should be held until an opposite signal appears because the downtrend was unusually strong.
5. *Oversold signal in momentum oscillator.* An early warning that the downtrend would soon be ending was the leading indicator in RSI as the line moved down to the oversold level. At this

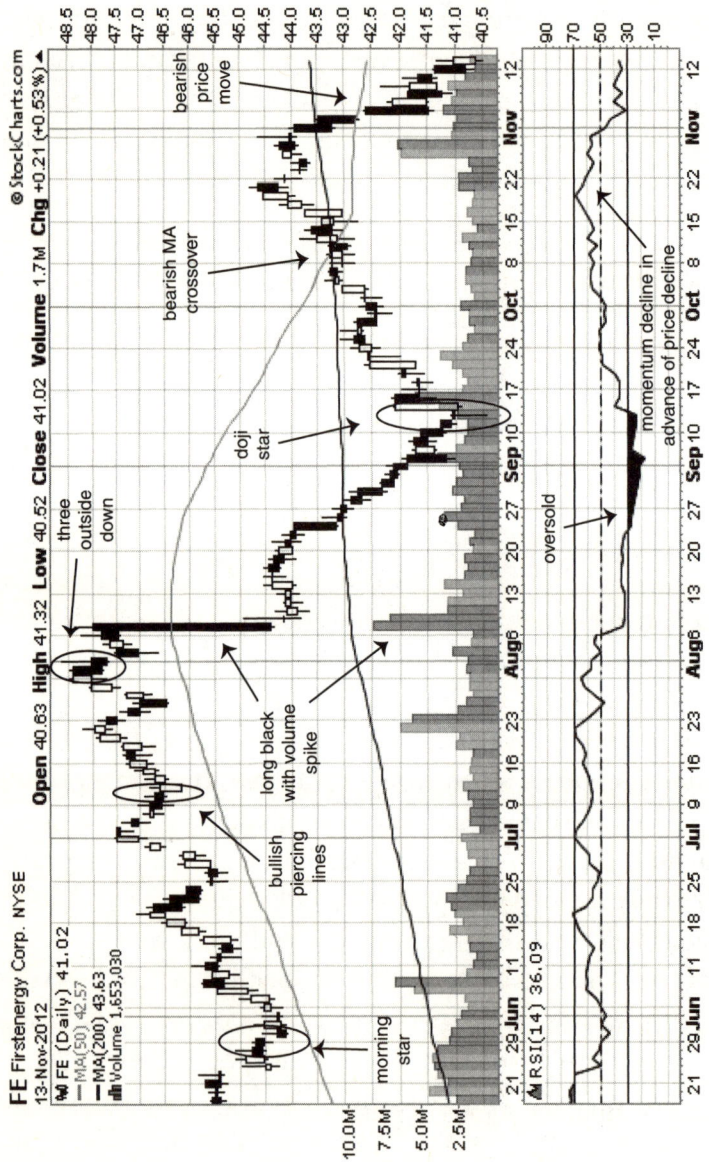

Figure 10.3 Swing trading with long options—example # 2
Source: StockCharts.com.

point, puts should be sold or confirmation should be waited for because it became likely that an uptrend would soon follow. This is unconfirmed at this point, however. A prudent swing trade would be to sell the puts but wait for a further bullish signal.

6. *Doji star.* The bullish doji star strongly confirmed the RSI signal. And this was exceptionally strong as well, with the very long lower shadow. This confirmed the loss of seller momentum, as price could not be driven down any further. An uptrend was very likely, so this was the point when to buy calls.

7. *Bearish MA crossover.* Notice how the shorter-term MA crosses below the longer-term MA right as both crossed below the price level. This is a strongly bearish signal, even though a delayed reaction in price followed. At this point, calls could be disposed of or held while awaiting further bearish confirmation.

8. *Volume spike.* As the price trend weakened, the volume spike confirmed the end of the uptrend. If calls were still open, this could be the place to sell. However, further confirmation of a new downtrend was needed before opening new long puts.

9. *Momentum decline in advance of price move.* The RSI index level began falling even before price declined. It began touching 70 and quickly fell all the way to 30. Although the index did not cross into oversold, this trend was a bearish signal and a leading reversal indicator. This would be a good time for buying long puts.

10. *Bearish price move.* The price trended downward, confirming what the volume spike and RSI change foreshadowed. If puts were not yet bought, this decline would be a good time to finally go long in puts.

EXAMPLE # 3: CHART-BASED REVERSAL SIGNALS

A final example of reversal signals and confirmation for a long-option strategy is found in the chart of Bank of America (BAC) shown in figure 10.4.

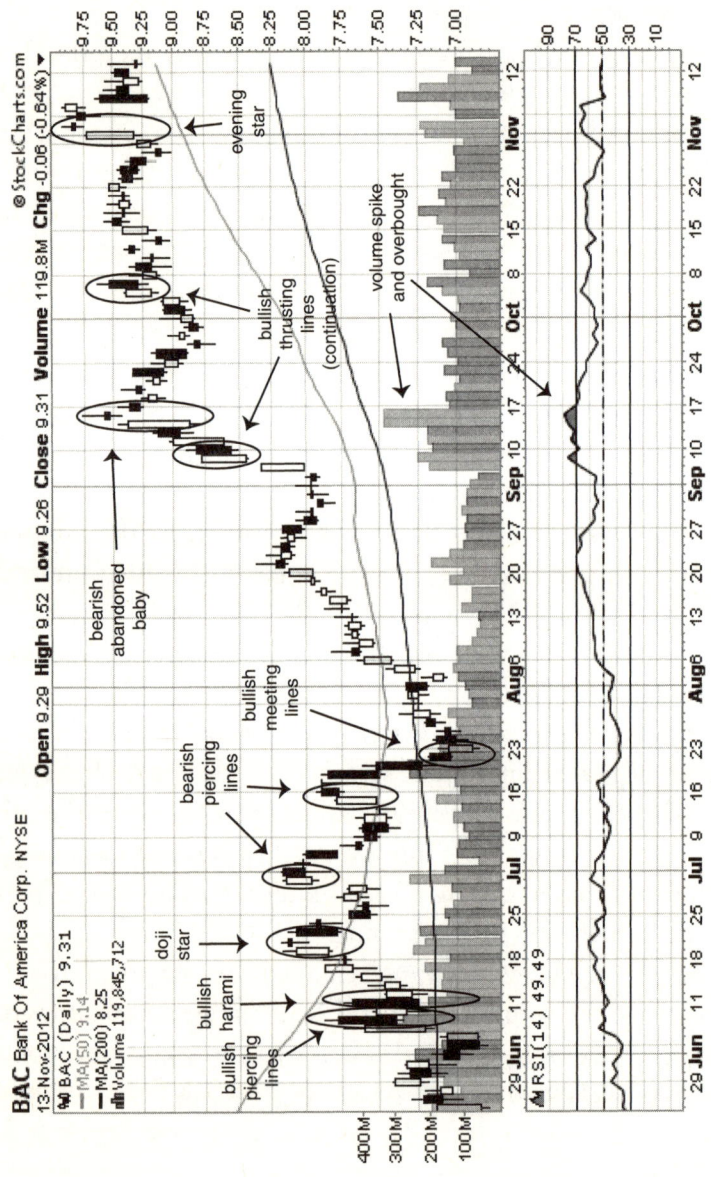

Figure 10.4 Swing trading with long options—example #3
Source: StockCharts.com.

Reversal indicators in this case are just as clear and with just as much confirmation:

1. *Bullish piercing lines.* The first signal is a strong one, the piercing lines. This forecasts an uptrend.
2. *Bullish harami.* This is unusual because it appears right after the piercing lines. By itself, the harami is a fifty-fifty signal, but when coupled with another bullish indicator, it works to confirm.
3. *Doji star.* This bearish signal is the first warning that the uptrend might be over. This is a good point to dispose of long calls. However, until the signal is confirmed, it might be too early to buy puts.
4. *Bearish piercing lines (two).* These are both confirmation that a downtrend is about to begin. It was true, even though the downtrend was short-lived.
5. *Bullish meeting lines.* This easily missed turnaround signal showed up at the bottom of the rapid but brief downtrend and turned out to be the start of a very long uptrend reversal.
6. *Bullish thrusting lines (confirming).* Even though the uptrend had gone on for some time, there was no reversal signal to be found. In fact, the bullish thrusting lines pattern is a continuation signal. No action was needed; just keep those long calls in play.
7. *Bearish abandoned baby.* The uptrend's reversal did finally arrive and in a big way. The bearish abandoned baby should signal disposal of long calls *and* opening of long puts.
8. *Volume spikes and overbought.* Confirming the abandoned baby were two additional strong signals. The volume spike occurred at the same time as the candlestick indicator, and the RSI oscillator also moved into the overbought range. It was time to transition into long puts.
9. *Bullish thrusting* lines *(confirming).* A second continuation signal appeared soon after, telling you that action during September was an offsetting retraction, and the previous

uptrend has resumed. This indicated it was time to sell puts and move back into long calls.
10. *Evening star.* A bearish reversal was signaled by the evening star, the final signal and yet another turn, this time to bearish. It was a signal to sell long calls and buy long puts.

* * *

Long options are the most basic of swing trading strategies and, because no short exposure is involved, probably also the safest. However, there are many other ways to swing trade with options. The next chapter expands the discussion to show how you can combine long and short in a call-based strategy. It involves risk on the short side when the call is uncovered, but if the circumstances warrant it and you are comfortable with the risk, the call long/short swing trading strategy is worth further study.

CHAPTER 11

STRATEGY # 2: LONG/SHORT-CALL STRATEGY, UNCOVERED SHORT SIDE

> Trust everybody, but cut the cards.
>   Finley Peter Dunne, *Casual Observations*, 1900

THE LONG-OPTION STRATEGY IS BASED ON EMPLOYING LONG CALLS at the bottom of the swing and long puts at the top. Although this solves many problems (both options-specific risks and stock-specific risks of short-side trading), it also has limitations. The endless struggle between time and cost adds risk of another type to swing trading with long options only.

That risk—losses due to price not moving rapidly enough before expiration or moving in the wrong direction—can be partially mitigated by combining long and short positions. With calls, this version of swing trading consists of entering long calls at the bottom of a downtrend in anticipation of a reversal and then closing them at the top and entering short calls at an identified top in anticipation of a reversal and a downtrend to follow.

For many traders, an uncovered call is too risky to even consider. However, the question to be addressed as a risk-averse traders is whether you can reduce the exposure by relying on exceptionally strong reversal signals? If the reversal indication is truly exceptional, the likelihood of a downtrend translates to less risk, not more. This risk is further reduced when you consider the two ways that a short call can become profitable: from downward movement of premium, as you expect in your swing trade, and from time decay itself. Because a short position benefits from time decay (since the position can be bought to close for a lower amount), time decay is beneficial on the short side. So there are two short-aside advantages: downward movement of the underlying and time decay.

Overcoming the 75% "Rule" on the Short Side

With long options only, you will naturally be concerned with expiration, and the closer that is, the greater the risk. Various percentages have been cited about options expiring worthless, the most common being 75%. The statistic is misleading, however. It is more accurate to state that 75% of options held until expiration expire worthless. However, overall, this does not translate to 75% of all options. Many are closed early at a profit, exercised, or rolled forward. Many more are closed on the last trading day; overall, only a relatively small number of options simply expire worthless.

When it comes to short options, expiration is desirable. Since you have sold the option and received premium, worthless expiration translates to profit. If an option expires worthless, you do not have to take any action. Once it has expired, you can write new short positions and then wait out time decay again. So whether you use the 75% rule or some other standard, the higher the rate of expiration of short calls, the better your shorting strategy works. Only about 10% of all options are exercised in each cycle; 60% are closed before expiration, and the remaining 30% expire worthless. So when you write short calls, even though uncovered, worthless expiration is a positive outcome, not a negative one. A bigger potential problem is the outcome if and when the underlying market value rises. If growth in intrinsic value outpaces time decay, you will face the risk of loss upon exercise or when you close to avoid exercise.

You can usually see this coming. If you write OTM short calls, which means that you are going to rely on level or declining price in the underlying. Because you benefit from time decay when you have gone short, you should become concerned if instead the underlying price rises. When this occurs, a prudent course is to close the short position immediately and write off any loss and then try again elsewhere. If you write ITM options expecting a rapid decline in intrinsic value, you face the same problem but with a different—and perhaps higher—type of risk. In this situation, if the stock price rises, the danger is that intrinsic value may outpace time decay.

The higher the time value when you open the short option, the better your chances for a profitable outcome. A rich premium level is quite likely to experience rapid time decay in the last few weeks of the option's life. However, if you enter the final month with an ITM position, the nonintrinsic portion will have evaporated. In this phase, your greatest risk is that the underlying price will rise and the short option will gain point for point with the underlying, with each point representing more risk.

When this occurs, you have several choices for avoiding loss. First, the position can be closed before it becomes a large loss. You're better off with a small loss than a bigger one later, especially once time value has been used up. Second, you can cover the short option by buying a long option that expires later. This provides you with the ability to satisfy assignment, but it will cost money. Third, you can roll forward to a later-expiring option or, preferably, to a later-expiring and short position with higher strike. The problem in rolling is that it extends the period the short position is left open. The ideal swing trade is a fast in-and-out move using options to maximize leverage. Rolling forward is contrary to that goal; the most practical strategy is to close out a position once price begins moving against you, take the loss, and move capital to a different position.

Avoiding Early Exercise

In theory, a short option can be exercised at any time up to the last trading day. In practice, only ITM options are at risk of exercise, but using short positions as part of the swing trading strategy involves either ITM or ATM positions, and with at least one month (perhaps more) before expiration. So the chances of early exercise have to be considered in devising a swing trading strategy that includes short options.

The risk is very real. As long as your short calls are uncovered, if the underlying rises instead of falling, the potential loss is a serious problem. This is one reason why many traders will avoid using uncovered calls as part of their strategy. However, if you find exceptionally strong reversal signals and call premium is attractive, these present one alternative to long puts.

There is one situation worth avoiding, and that is writing short calls ATM or ITM during the ex-dividend month. Chances of early exercise are highest right before ex-dividend date. In order for stockholders to earn the current dividend, they must have purchased shares before ex-dividend date. So any ITM calls are at risk of exercise up to this point. Because ex-dividend date normally occurs every three months (for underlying stocks paying quarterly dividends), it makes sense to avoid using short calls during that specific month.

Every swing trader should have a "bank" of favorite underlying stocks to use for swing trading. The selection of stocks included in this bank is based on volatility levels, recent short-term swing duration and momentum, and predictability of establishing trading ranges. Given that you may have several stocks available for swing trading, avoiding ex-dividend month is an easy matter. It makes sense to avoid the risk of exercise of a short, uncovered call, and to pass up one swing trading opportunity for another—on a stock that does not have an ex-dividend date between today and expiration date of the options.

OFFSETTING TIME AND COST PROBLEMS WITH A LONG/SHORT-CALL APPROACH

When you are trading long options, you maximize the swing trade by selecting ATM or slightly ITM contracts that expire as soon as possible. This ensures that nonintrinsic value is at a minimum and that movement in the option premium is most likely to track intrinsic price movement in the underlying point for point.

With short positions, the situation is quite different. Those low-premium long positions are unattractive as short-side plays.

For short options, you want time value to be as high as possible so that time decay favors your trade, and you also need to time the trade so that time decay is accelerated as much as possible. This "sweet spot" seems to be when the option will expire in one to two months. During this period, time value remains but time decay accelerates. If you select options much further out, time decay will not be rapid enough to justify the positions, and you may end up having to keep short calls open longer, which means exposure to more risk of unfavorable upside movement in the underlying and the potential risk of early exercise due to ex-dividend date occurring during the hold period.

A second question about how to select short calls is moneyness. Do you use ATM, OTM, or ITM positions? Each of these has different attributes in terms of time decay and exercise risk. In any situation, you have two methods for creating profits from swing trading with short calls: downward movement in the underlying or time decay.

With long options, profit is potentially unlimited. An option's value may rise to the extent that underlying prices rise. With a short option, there is a limit to the profit you can realize, and this is equal to the premium level at the time the call is sold. The most you can profit is the entire premium. So the first question is: What is the highest-premium option you can sell with the most advantageous position (moneyness) and timing?

An ITM short call offers the greatest profit potential, but it also has the greatest risk. As long as intrinsic value falls as the result of a decline in the underlying price, the threat of exercise disappears once your option moves from ITM to OTM. But if that does not occur, then you have to close at a loss, roll forward, or accept exercise. None of these are the goal of swing trading, in which you hope to move in and out of positions in a very narrow time frame. This is the advantage to using long options: As long as the direction of underlying price moves upward, it favors your long call position, so that ATM or ITM long calls become profitable immediately. And if the underlying moves down, your losses are capped. With short positions, ITM has great potential but also the highest risk.

An ATM short call is a mix between both profit potential and risk. It all depends on the direction the underlying price takes.

Still, an ATM short call probably represents the most reasonable choice, for two reasons. First, as soon as the underlying price moves downward, premium (which is all nonintrinsic) begins to decay rapidly, and a profitable result is most likely. Second, even if the underlying price does not move downward (remaining at the same approximate price or even moving modestly ITM), time decay may occur more rapidly than the accumulation of intrinsic value. As any long-option trader knows, the chances of turning a profit in the last month are remote. From a short-side perspective, this makes ATM short calls attractive. The key to reducing risk is to rely on exceptionally strong reversal signals and confirmation—and to be prepared to cut losses if the underlying price moves upward quickly enough to pose a threat.

The OTM short call is the safest of all because if and when the underlying begins moving toward the money, the short call can be closed at breakeven, a small profit, or a small loss. Given time decay as a major factor for the OTM call during the last month of its cycle, you have the best chance of a positive outcome with that call. However, profits will be limited as well because the premium level for the OTM call expiring in one to two months is going to be quite low. Thus, maximum profits are equally small. The balance between small maximum profit and the risk of unfavorable movement in the underlying can make the OTM short call impractical.

Short Calls to Solve Short Stock Risk

The discussion of long options for a swing trading program explored the advantage of the long put over short stock. Another alternative is to use short calls rather than either short stock or long calls as a means for a bearish swing trade.

The major differences between long puts and short calls involve debit versus credit (you pay for the long put but you receive cash for the short call), risk levels (the put's maximum risk is equal to its premium, but the risk of the short call is much greater), and profit potential (the long put may increase in value as long as the underlying continues to decline, but the short stock's maximum profit is limited to the premium you receive for selling the contract).

Comparing these attributes is the deciding factor in selecting either long calls or short puts. That is, cash credit or debit, risk, and profit potential are weighed in determining which way makes the most sense. This is a decision of risk tolerance, risk and opportunity, and margin collateral, all of which affect your choice. With the short call, you are required to deposit higher initial margin (equal to the exercise value) than for the long put (which has to be paid in full, but no additional maintenance is required). If you have collateral on deposit, these differences are not an issue; however, if you will need to deposit additional funds to open a short call, then the long put might make more sense. Considering that the directional potential of the two is identical, the collateral requirement tilts the balance in favor of the long put.

If you do decide to use short calls for bearish reversals, you should rely on exceptionally strong signals and confirmation. It might even be wise to require initial signals and *two* or more forms of confirmation, so that reversal is even more likely. Because you will be opening an uncovered call, your confidence level should be higher than average. Even with the likely rapid decline in time value and selection of an ATM call, it makes sense to proceed with caution any time you open an uncovered option.

Example # 1: Chart-Based Reversal Signals

The primary concern with using short calls at the top of the uptrend is ensuring that reversal signals are exceptionally strong *and* finding multiple ways of confirmation. This combined approach reduces the chances of a failed signal. This does not mean that signals will never fail, and so you should limit exposure by avoiding highly volatile stocks, ex-dividend month, and weak signals.

For example, the chart in figure 11.1 shows the trend for Chevron (CVX) over several months.

The initial signal of likely reversal was seen in RSI, which moved into overbought territory the month before other signals appeared. This was not a specific reversal signal but a warning of changes to come. The first clear reversal occurred with the

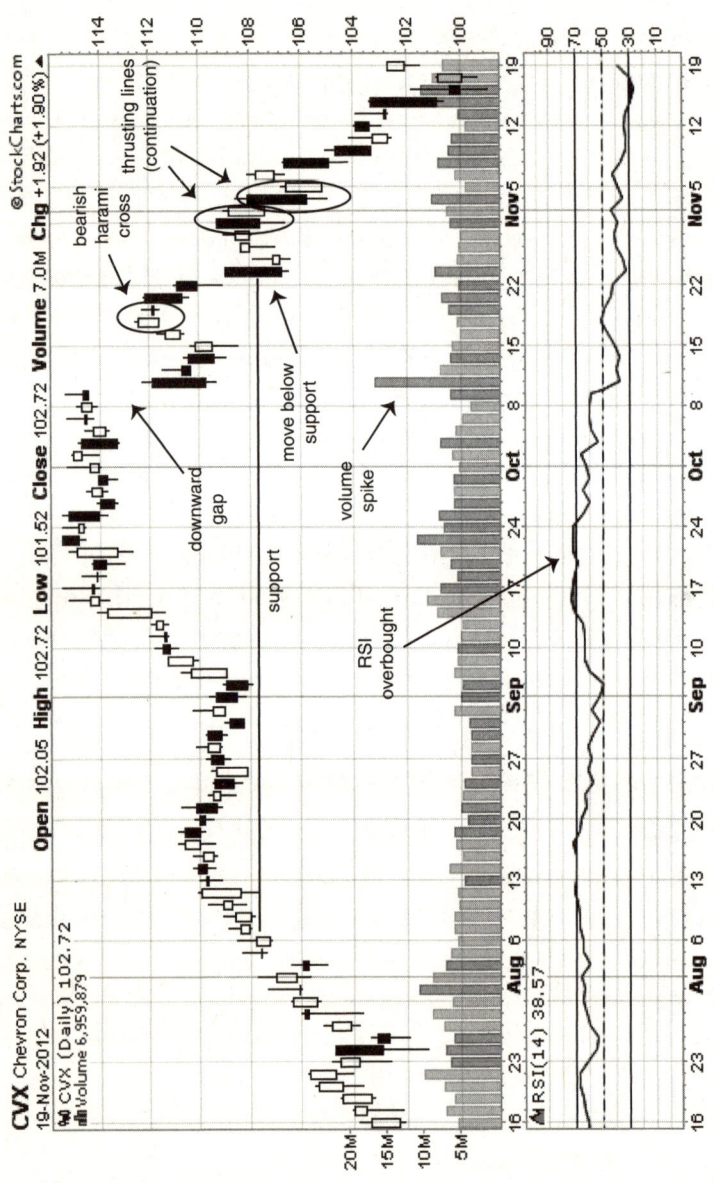

Figure 11.1 Swing trading with uncovered calls—example #1
Source: StockCharts.com.

combination of the downward gap and volume spike. This double signal was strong by itself, indicating a high likelihood of a new bearish trend.

A bearish harami cross quickly appeared and was confirmed once price moved below support. However, the question of whether price would remain there or not was a primary concern, especially since ex-dividend date was October 14, which was in the last week of the period shown. So if the bearish downtrend continued, exercise would not be likely as long as the strike price of the short call remained above the price trend. For example, if you had sold a short call during the second or third week of October with a November or December expiration, you would expect rapid time decay. Focusing on ATM calls, you would have been likely to select the 100 or 115 calls.

Still, the concern would be whether these would remain OTM. This concern was alleviated by an unusual double continuation pattern that soon followed. Two consecutive bearish thrusting lines signals appeared, providing exceptionally strong indication that the downtrend was firmly set and would continue. By the week before ex-dividend, these calls should have lost most of their value, since ex-dividend date occurred two sessions prior to the options' last trading day (November contracts)—that is, their value should have been close to zero as there would be no intrinsic value remaining. They could be closed or allowed to expire worthless. If you had selected December contracts, the decision to hold or close would depend on which ones were selected and how much their value had fallen and on whether or not the trend signals reversed and indicated a new uptrend. Based on the movement in the last two sessions on the chart, closing December short calls would have been a prudent decision.

Example # 2: Chart-Based Reversal Signals

Another example of exceptionally strong reversal at the top of a trend is seen in another chart, for Procter & Gamble (PG), shown in figure 11.2.

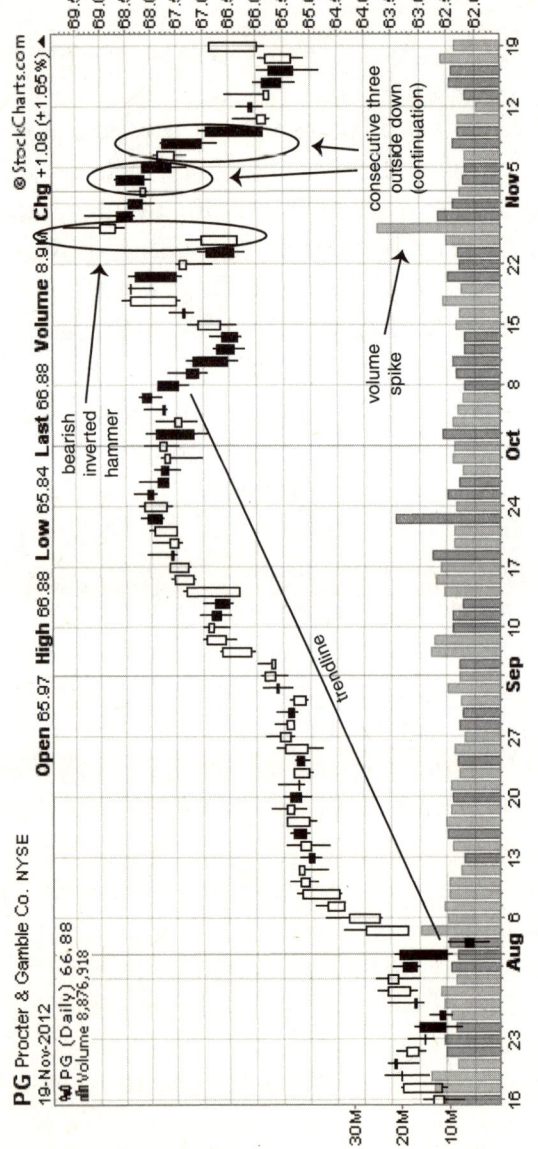

Figure 11.2 Swing trading with uncovered calls—example #2
Source: StockCharts.com.

The long trendline ended as price lost upward momentum and before an attempt to resume the previous direction. However, reversal was signaled strongly by the bearish inverted hammer and a volume spike. The inverted hammer included an especially long upside gap. While you would expect this to be a black session, the following day was black, which made the extension a confirmed bearish signal.

The ex-dividend date for PG was November 17, occurring near the end of this period. Before selling calls, you would want to decide that you need to exit if the short position had moved ITM or if the downtrend was not confirmed. So you probably would have focused on ATM positions such as the 70 strike. This was ideal as it occurred right at the inverted hammer.

That the downtrend was the real thing was confirmed by an unusual double continuation pattern, two outside down signals that occurred one after the other. One of these by itself indicates continuation; two of them provide a much stronger signal.

EXAMPLE # 3: CHART-BASED REVERSAL SIGNALS

A final example of exceptionally strong reversal to accompany a short call at the top of a trend was found in the chart of Exxon Mobil (XOM), shown in figure 11.3.

The two bearish engulfing signals were quite strong, reliable about 80% of the time. In this case, there were two, and the second one was confirmed by price moving below support and by the long black candle session. Together, these signals were very strong signs that the downtrend was reliable.

A potential problem with this case is that the ex-dividend date was November 7, the same day the long black candle appeared. If you had acted based on the second bearish engulfing signal and sold a call with a 90 strike (the closest strike to ATM), the trade would have worked out very well. Over the next few sessions, the price trended downward strongly, the ideal swing trade situation. The November contracts would have declined rapidly as well and ended up close to zero value.

* * *

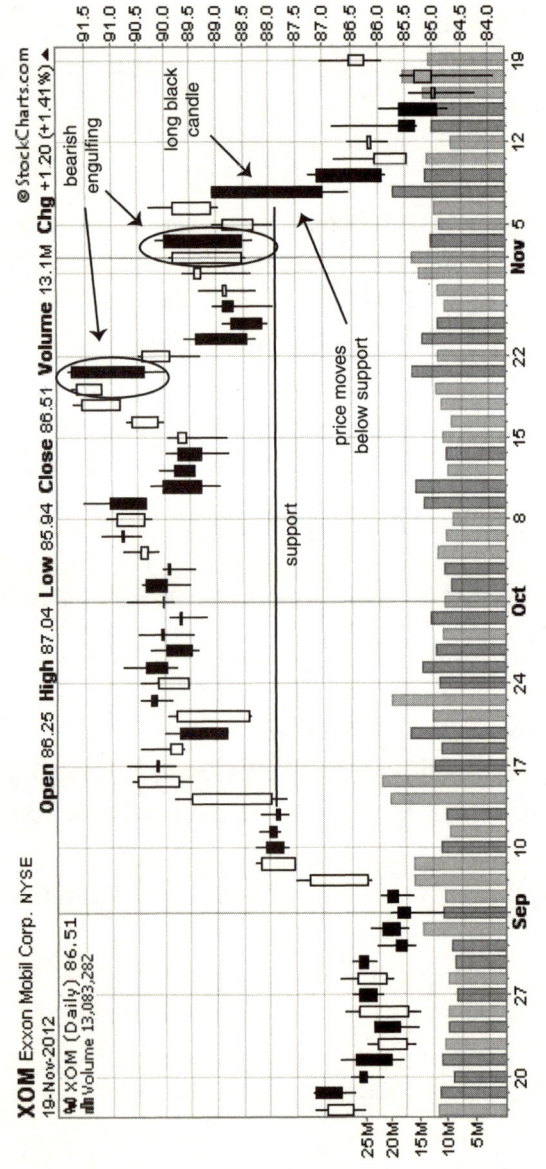

Figure 11.3 Swing trading with uncovered calls—example #3
Source: StockCharts.com.

When you combine long calls at the bottom of a swing with uncovered short calls at the top, you combine a relatively low-risk long position with a higher-risk short position. This disparity in level of risk supports the use of long calls over short puts. However, the credit of the short position is attractive as long as the reversal signals are exceptionally strong.

The next chapter expands on this idea with a method for reducing the short call risk by providing cover. However, this requires ownership of stock, but if and when the price declines, the value of the stock declines as well. This may be most appropriate when you intend to hold shares for the long term and when short-term price movement does not concern you. At the same time, selling covered calls generates current income, making the covered call a much lower risk and much more attractive than the uncovered variety.

CHAPTER 12

STRATEGY # 3: LONG/SHORT-CALL STRATEGY, COVERED SHORT SIDE

> A fool bolts pleasure, then complains of moral indigestion.
> Minna Thomas Antrim,
> *Naked Truth and Veiled Illusions*, 1901

THE COMBINATION OF LONG AND SHORT CALLS IS APPEALING IN many ways to traders, and it is risky when the short side is uncovered. However, does covering the short call reduce risks or does it only exchange one type of risk for another?

Any detailed analysis of covered call writing becomes controversial because it is widely believed to be a risk-free, high-yielding, and conservative strategy. It can be, but this is not always the case. Some believe covered call writing is foolproof because it generates current income with no risk beyond the risk of just owning stock; others see much more risk in the form of downside decline (below the net of stock cost less call premium) and upside lost opportunity (the difference between an exercised strike and current market value).

On the surface, a covered call strategy is aimed at generating consistent capital gains along with dividend yield and call premium to create low-risk returns. As long as the strike is higher than the cost of shares, this is an attractive basic strategy. However, it may be more appropriate for use with stocks held in your portfolio for the long term rather than as part of a swing trading strategy. In fact, the covered call, whether as a cash generator for a long portfolio or the basis of a swing trading program, may carry additional risks. Specifically, there are two. If the value of the underlying rises above the covered call's strike, shares will be called away at the strike, and you suffer the lost opportunity risk of further price appreciation. The second risk is that shares will fall below the adjusted basis (purchase price minus covered call premium), resulting in a net loss.

These kinds of risk should be considered if covered calls are to be used as part of a buy-and-hold strategy, but in a swing trading strategy the motivation is short term, and covered calls create the same options returns as uncovered calls, but with less market risk. The covered call has a place as a reduced risk version of short calls for bearish reversals. In fact, as long as you believe that the underlying is going to experience predictable price swings within a well-understood price range, you want to see price decline as long as the short call is open, so that it can be closed at a profit. This profit comes from two sources: reduced intrinsic value from the price dropping below the strike and rapid decline in nonintrinsic premium.

Beyond the question of risk, covered calls used at the top of the swing cycle offer limited profit potential. This is true of all short-side trades. The maximum profit from shorting options is the premium of the option. You hope for a rapid decline so that the short option can be closed at a profit or can be allowed to expire. The greater the nonintrinsic value (time and extrinsic), the higher the profit potential is going to be. For this reason, as with the uncovered call, a covered call is particularly ideal when it will expire in one to two months, the period when time decay is at its highest rate.

Writing covered calls is most appropriate when you hold shares of stock that you would prefer to hold on to for the long term but that you are willing to place at exercise risk as part of the swing trading strategy. The offset of short-term income and longer-term dividend income, especially on high-yielding stock, is a matter of balance and personal choice. You can avert early exercise related to dividends by avoiding writing covered calls during the ex-dividend month. That addresses one of the concerns about writing covered calls; even though exercise produces a profit, it may be more desirable to earn the dividend and hold on to shares for future growth and swing trading. By avoiding the ex-dividend date, you can enjoy the best of both worlds.

This exercise risk only becomes an issue if the short call moves in the money. So if your strategy is based on very strong reversal signals and if you avoid the ex-dividend month, your exposure to unexpected exercise is drastically reduced.

THE COVERED CALL ADVANTAGE

The market risks of uncovered calls are eliminated with the covered call, the ownership of 100 shares of the underlying stock for each call sold. One rationale when evaluating the strategy on its own merits is that the covered call reduces the risk of owning shares. This is true in the sense that the premium received reduces your net basis, forming a cushion against a price decline. However, writing a covered call also exchanges that market risk for two other types of risk.

The first risk is that the stock value may decline below the adjusted basis of stock and short call. Even though this is a mitigated risk in comparison to just holding stock, it is also a different version of market risk. If you own shares without a covered call, you can close out at any time and take a small profit or a small loss. With a covered call, selling shares converts the covered call into an uncovered call unless you also buy to close the option.

The second risk is that of lost opportunity. The greatest criticism of writing covered calls is that if and when the underlying price rises above the strike, exercise means you settle for the strike and lose out on potentially higher profits. Covered call writers counter this argument by noting that the consistency of regular returns from writing covered calls is advantageous even if the occasional bonanza is given up. Furthermore, exercise can be avoided by closing the position, by rolling forward (creating yet more income), or by rolling forward and up to a higher strike. The forward-and-up roll may create breakeven or a small debit but also sets up a higher exercise price in the future.

Covered call writing creates double-digit returns on an annualized basis. Writers understand that focusing on options expiring in one month or less is a great advantage because time decay is rapid. Thus, even if the stock price does not decline, profits are created because nonintrinsic value declines quickly. Even if the stock price moves above strike, the reduced nonintrinsic value may match or exceed intrinsic value and make the covered call strategy even more attractive. To annualize the return from covered calls, the return should be divided by the holding period and multiplied by one full year (for example, a 1.5-month holding period would create a calculation in which the return is divided by 1.56 months and then multiplied by 12 to arrive at the annualized rate).

Regarding return from covered calls, calculating the rate is not a simple matter. Do you divide income from the covered call by your original cost, the current value, or the strike? Using original value or current value may distort return and make the outcome inconsistent between different underlying stocks as well as between different strikes. Using the strike is rational since if the short call is exercised, that will be the exercise price. For swing trading, this is less of an issue than the benefits of reducing market risk.

Swing trading covered call writing is a lower-risk alternative to uncovered calls and can be used on stock held in your portfolio. If you want to use shares of stock for risk mitigation and you are willing to risk exercise, the trade-off is attractive returns from covered calls as well as timed reversion swings to create short-term profits without the uncovered call risk. Even a decline in time decay without much price movement in the underlying yields profits, pointing out the great advantage of short option positions over long ones.

COMBINING FUNDAMENTAL STRENGTH WITH TECHNICAL PREDICTABILITY

The selection of a company and its stock for a call-based swing strategy is critically important considering that it also involves ownership of shares. The best of all worlds is to write covered calls on an underlying stock with a historically small level of price volatility but with rich call premium. Since higher volatility normally translates to higher call premium, this combination is not easy to find. Consequently, it is tempting to select conservative stocks but write options deeper ITM in order to get a more favorable level of income. This might end up in higher profits as long as the stock moves in the desired direction, but the risks are greater as well.

The best method for picking an underlying is to focus on companies you want to hold in your portfolio before even considering whether or not covered call writing will be profitable. A conservative fundamental choice should include comparisons of the basics: revenue and earnings trend, dividend yield and history, P/E ratio and range, and the trend and level of the debt ratio. These are the basic fundamentals everyone needs to compare in stock selection; you might have additional tests you also apply to stock selection, but this short list is a good starting point.

On the technical side, it is desirable to select stocks that rise and fall within a narrow trading range but does not gyrate wildly above or below. These modest movements bouncing between resistance and support create desirable swing trading opportunities.

For example, the chart of General Mills (GIS) in figure 12.1 shows that the stock price has trended upward over six months but for the most part traded within a two-point range. Within that narrow range, prices rose and fell in a consistent manner, making this an excellent choice for swing trading. It is a candidate for covered call writing because the fundamentals (dividend yield, revenue and earnings, P/E ratio, and debt ratio) were also reasonable over time.

A competitor with very similar fundamentals was Kellogg (K), whose chart is shown in figure 12.2. Even though the fundamentals were similar, the technical record was much less consistent, making this less likely as a candidate for a covered call and swing trading. While GIS maintained its 2-point range for six months, K began with a 3-point range that gradually shrank to a 2-point range, much less desirable for both covered call writing and swing trading.

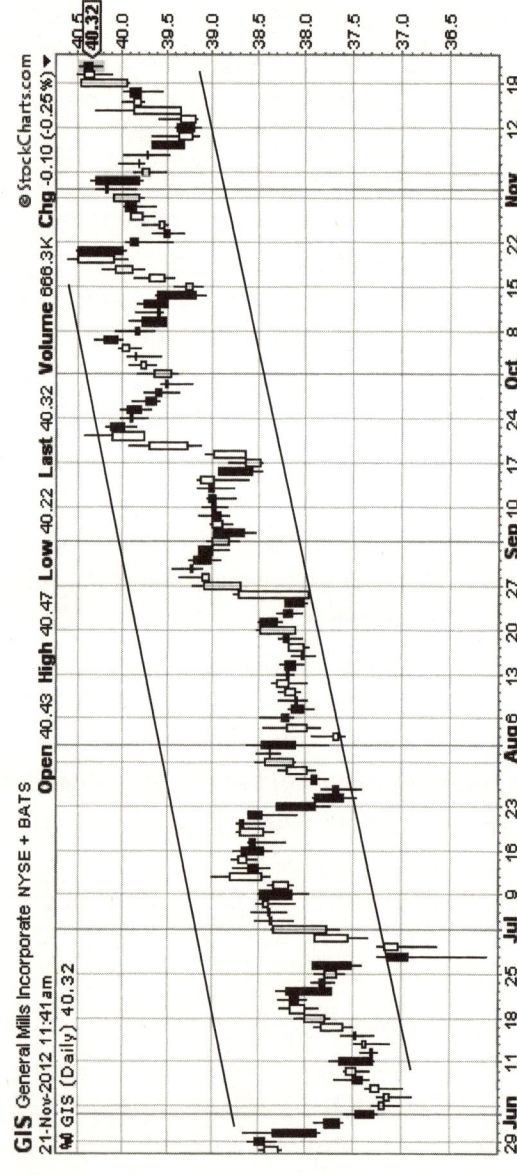

Figure 12.1 Trading range—consistent
Source: StockCharts.com.

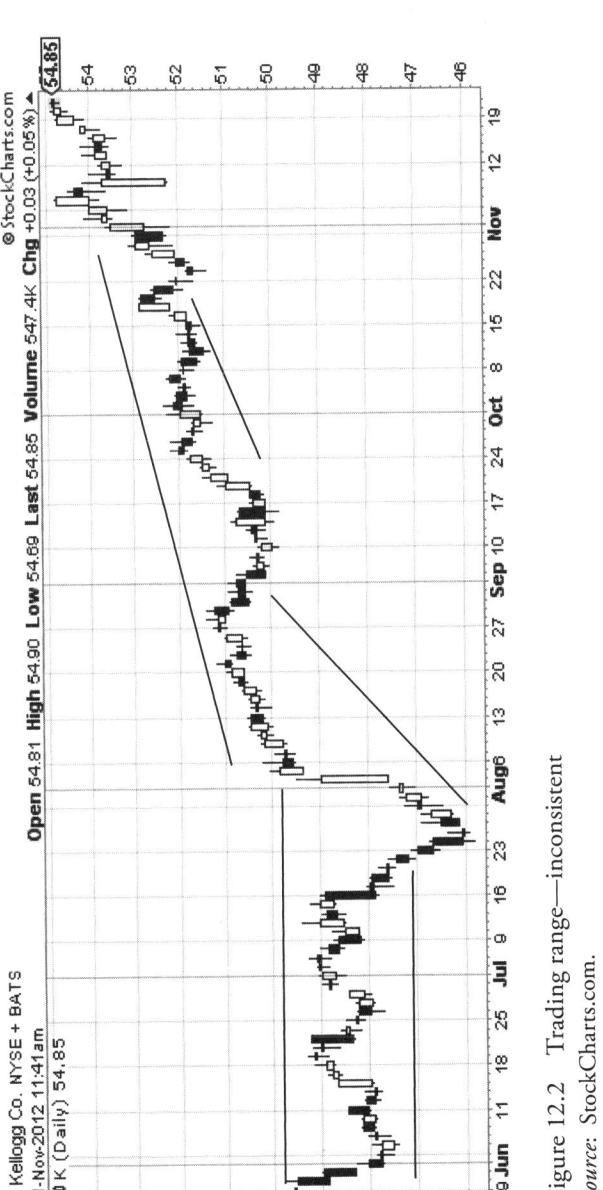

Figure 12.2 Trading range—inconsistent
Source: StockCharts.com.

The purpose in selecting one company over another has two aspects. First, if you are going to own stock, it should be qualified in terms of fundamental strength. Second, price volatility should be low enough so that you have a sense of its future predictability. This is not the same as price being predictable; rather, it refers to how you judge the technical aspects based on past performance. Among other things, you should test for how well resistance and support have held over time and how much price has moved within that established trading range. The range—the price area between resistance and support—serves as a test of price strength. As long as trading remains within that area, traders know what to expect. But if and when price begins moving above and below, without as much predictability, it is impossible to predict the near-term future

Comparing Covered Calls to Uncovered Puts

Another issue concerning covered calls: Are these better, safer, or more desirable than writing uncovered puts?

The risk profile of both is identical, and it is defined as changes in a position based on the changing price of the underlying. But there are also important differences between these risk profiles. These include:

1. *Trading level.* You will need a higher level of approval to sell uncovered options than to open covered calls. This should not apply to anyone intent on using a variety of options strategies in a swing trading program, but for the relative newcomer, the authorized level identifies what can and cannot be traded. Even experienced traders are probably restricted from uncovered options in accounts such as IRAs.
2. *Dividend income.* Covered call writers continue to earn dividends as long as they own stock. In comparison, selling uncovered puts excludes dividend yield. This becomes a major consideration for high-yielding stocks held for the long term.

3. *Cost of the trade.* An uncovered put is a single trade, generating one commission when sold and another when bought to close (none if it expires worthless)., If, instead of selling uncovered puts, you buy 100 shares and sell a covered call, this doubles the cost because they are two separate trades. This does not matter if you write calls against shares you already own, and the dividend yield might justify the double cost as well.
4. *Margin collateral.* Your broker is likely to require that you provide collateral equal to the strike of the uncovered put, but if you own stock and write a covered call, you will not be required to provide additional collateral.
5. *Rolling and closing flexibility.* There may or may not be a difference in your ability to avoid exercise between a covered call and an uncovered put. The call is more vulnerable to early exercise if it is ITM before the ex-dividend date. Either option can be rolled forward to avoid exercise. However, in the case of the put, you might have more flexibility because you do not need to be concerned about the comparison between original cost of shares and the strike of the short call. If you end up closing the put to reduce losses, you are out of the trade. If the same price decline occurs in stock, you may close the short call but you also have to decide whether to keep shares of stock or cut losses in a decline.

Given these offsetting attributes, the decision to use covered calls or uncovered puts is not so much a risk decision as it is a flexibility issue. If dividend income is important and you own shares of stock as a long-term investment, writing covered calls is a sensible idea for creating additional income without giving up dividend income (but avoid shorting calls in the ex-dividend month).

THE BEST STRIKE AND EXPIRATION

Covered calls are going to be most profitable when time value declines quickly. At the same time, the richest calls will be those in the money, but these calls also present exercise risk. So the balancing act between these two considerations is to stick with options ATM or only slightly ITM.

At the same time, there is a large difference between long expiration and short. With the use of long options, swing traders—relying on a three- to five-day turnaround time—will prefer options expiring very soon. The level of nonintrinsic value should be as low as possible. However, for trading covered calls, it is going to be much more desirable to focus on options expiring within one to two months. During this time frame, time value remains but will decline rapidly.

You will find the ideal swing trading covered calls expiring within 30 to 60 days and ATM. There is one additional factor, however. Avoid issues in which the ex-dividend date occurs before expiration of the short call. The ex-dividend month is the most likely time for early exercise, notably the week just before ex-dividend date. Exercise of any ITM short call is likely to occur in this period, but exercise may occur even earlier in that ex-dividend month. So ideally, if you want to avoid exercise, make sure that the one- to two-month options have passed an ex-dividend date, or that the company does not pay dividends at all.

Example # 1: Chart-Based Reversal Signals

The key points to remember about using long calls and covered short calls are that (1) the swing trading rules still apply, including the need for reversal signals *and* confirmation, and (2) it is best to avoid having short calls open before ex-dividend date if they are ITM and if you want to avoid exercise.

The first example of what a chart for this version of swing trading looks like is the case of Altria (MO), shown in figure 12.3. Its six-month chart included five bullish signals and four bearish signals. The chart began with a signal in the form of a bullish engulfing pattern, confirmed by a double volume spike. By June 11, you would expect to open long calls based on these reversal signals. But it would make sense to wait one session, since June 12 was the

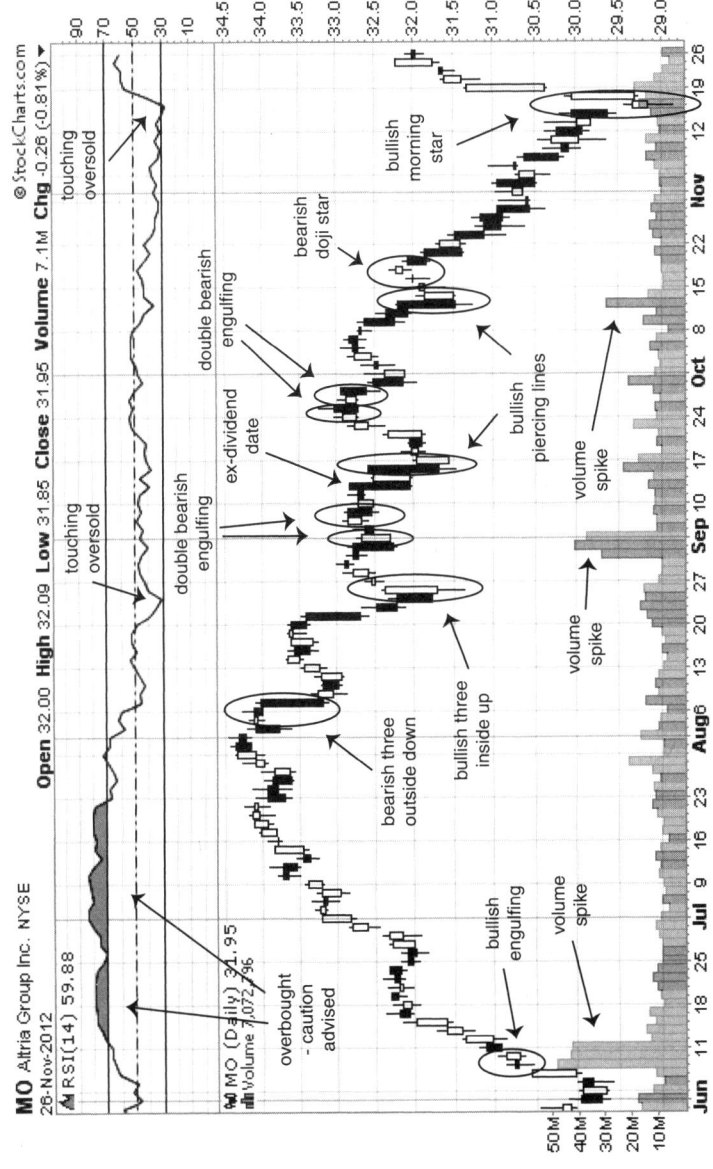

Figure 12.3 Swing trading with covered calls—example #1
Source: StockCharts.com.

ex-dividend date. In spite of the bullish signals, RSI quickly moved into overbought territory, so it would have made sense to close the long calls at any time after midmonth. Also note that the RSI level remained at overbought until the third week in July.

Prices paused and consolidated, and a clear bearish reversal appeared, starting on August 6, with a three-session bearish three outside down signal. The last of the three days was an exceptionally long black candle.

By the last week in August, a bullish three inside up signal appeared with mild confirmation as RSI touched (but did not move into) the oversold level of 30.

A very unusual double bearish engulfing pattern showed at the beginning of September's second week. At the same time, volume spikes in three sessions signaled a bearish turn. The double candlestick was confirmation enough, but the volume spikes added more strength.

It would have been wise to pay attention to these signals and close the long calls that should have been opened before August 27. However, it would not be wise to sell calls at this point since the ex-dividend date was September 12. So this bearish signal should be skipped unless you would be willing to risk exercise if and when the underlying price moves above strike.

A new bullish signal appeared by September 17 in the form of a piercing line, a three-session indicator. This was confirmed two sessions later by a nice upward price gap. The bullish trend did not last long. A double bearish engulfing pattern (second time on this chart) foreshadowed strong downside reversal, and prices did move down for the next three weeks.

On October 11, a bullish piercing line pattern signaled the end of the downtrend. This was confirmed by a volume spike at the same time.

The uptrend lasted only four sessions and was ended with the appearance of a bearish doji star. This was the beginning of a downtrend of nearly one full month. During this period, RSI also descended. This was weak confirmation since the oscillator was merely reflecting the downward trend in price; even so, RSI did not contradict the downtrend.

The last signal appeared mid-November, a bullish morning star. At the same time, RSI touched and briefly moved into oversold territory.

The Altria example was worth tracking since it demonstrated clear reversal signals ranging from a few days to several weeks, showed coordinated price and momentum trends, and avoided short selling right before the ex-dividend dates of June and September.

Example # 2: Chart-Based Reversal Signals

Another example of finding reversal with the use of covered calls can be seen in the chart of JPMorgan (JPM), shown in figure 12.4.

The chart begins with a strong bullish signal, piercing lines. At the same time, RSI had fallen into oversold condition, so the bullish trend was confirmed.

By the final week of June, the bullish trend had run its course. A reverse was signaled by the bearish engulfing pattern and a volume spike. However, while this was a good time to close out the long calls opened previously, it was not advisable to sell calls since the ex-dividend date was only a few days away. It was a good spot to wait out the trends.

On July 23, a new bullish engulfing signal appeared. While no obvious confirmation was found, this is an exceptionally strong bullish signal, leading to reversal about 80% of the time. Confirmation did appear over the next three sessions, each of which was separated by an upward price gap.

By the third week in August, a bearish harami cross marked the end of the uptrend. But the resulting downtrend was brief and not especially strong. It concluded with a rare reversal signal, three consecutive doji or near-doji days called the tri-star. This one was bullish because it came at the end of a short downtrend.

The final week in September saw yet another bearish engulfing pattern, this one confirmed by RSI moving into overbought range. This was yet another point at which to close out long calls

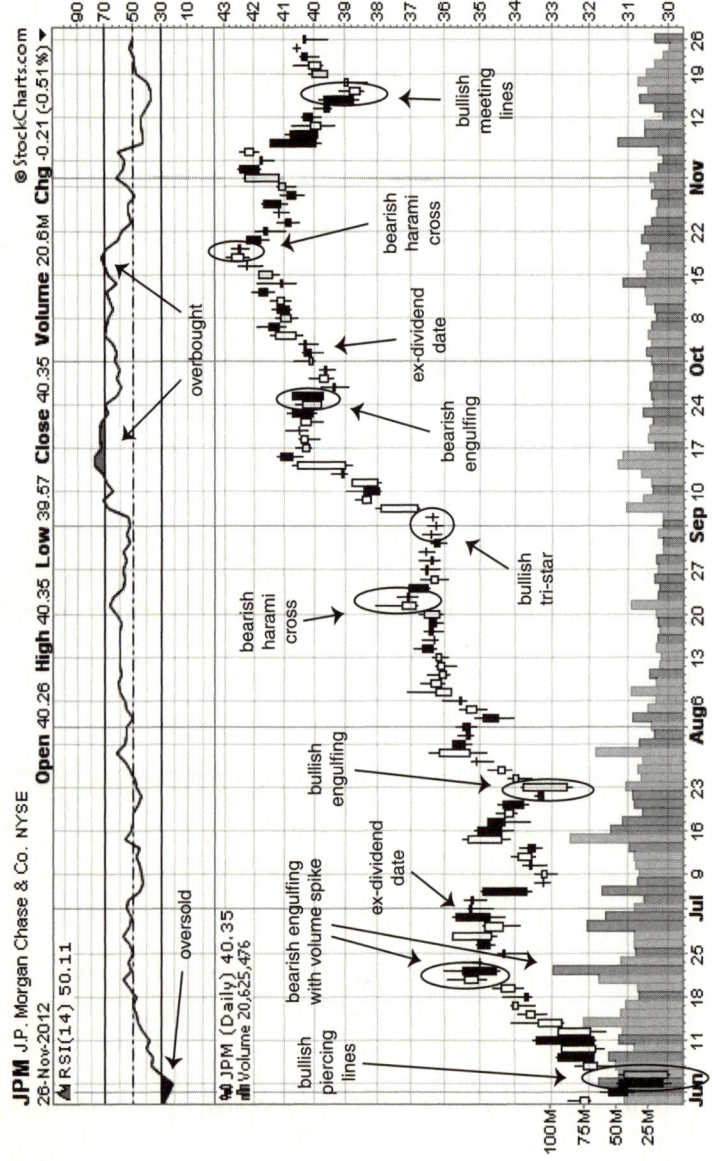

Figure 12.4 Swing trading with covered calls—example # 2
Source: StockCharts.com.

but to hold off selling calls. The ex-dividend date was October 3, only a few days away.

The next action point occurred in the third week of October in the form of a bearish harami cross, a white session followed by a doji within the trading range of the first day. This was confirmed by a brief move of RSI into overbought range.

The final entry on this chart was a bullish meeting lines signal, found halfway through November. This was not confirmed until two sessions later when a price gap strengthened the upward direction of price.

Example # 3: Chart-Based Reversal Signals

A third example of the swing trading system with long calls and short covered calls can be seen on the chart of Pfizer (PFE), shown in figure 12.5.

This chart contained many reversal signals useful in a call-based swing trading strategy. Near mid-July, a bullish engulfing indicator announced a likely reversal to the upside, a move that occurred immediately.

This ended with the appearance of a bearish harami cross, which was further confirmed by a triple-session volume spike. This was a good point to sell long calls, but not to open short calls. The ex-dividend date occurred on August 7, so it was wise to remain out of any trades on the bearish side for the moment (unless you were to employ the alternative of a long put in place of a short call right before ex-dividend).

After the ex-dividend date, prices moved sideways for a full month before a bullish piercing lines signal foreshadowed a new uptrend. This was confirmed by a volume spike that, while small, was twice the length of sessions over the preceding month.

The uptrend concluded as buyers began losing momentum, shown in the RSI move into overbought range in the first week of October. By the middle of the month, this was repeated when a bearish harami pattern appeared. The harami by itself is not a reliable reversal, but combined with the RSI move, it was enough to close long calls. However, the next ex-dividend date was coming

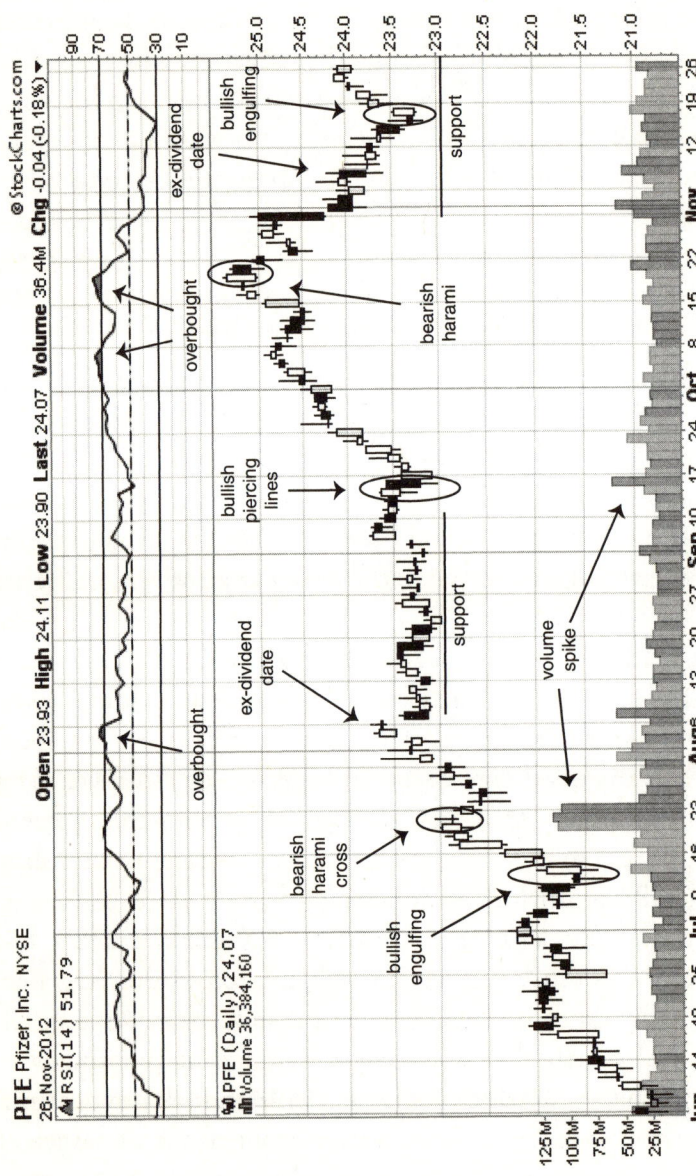

Figure 12.5 Swing trading with covered calls—example #3
Source: StockCharts.com.

up on November 7, so it would not have been wise to sell calls at this point (again, buying puts would have been a sensible alternative to avoid early exercise of a covered call).

Prices declined close to the established support level, where traders should have been looking for likely reversal. It appeared as a bullish engulfing pattern, signaling the final bullish move on the chart.

The covered call as a bearish move certainly provides many interesting possibilities in a swing trading strategy. The ideal timing is one to two months before expiration to set up conditions to exploit rapidly declining time value. The most desirable strike will be ATM or very slightly ITM but only with strong reversal signals and confirmation.

Avoiding the ex-dividend date can be frustrating for swing traders, but if you want to avoid early exercise, it is prudent not to open short calls in the period of one to two weeks prior to this key date. If you discover strong bearish reversal and confirmation, choose long puts in this one quarterly period to avoid exercise risk. If you would welcome exercise, sell the covered call in the knowledge that it will result in a capital gain on the stock but loss of the current quarterly dividend.

The plan using covered calls can be expanded and made even more interesting with the use of a ratio write when conditions turn bearish. This is appropriate only when the reversal indicator is exceptionally strong and you are aware of the added risks in the ratio write. You may also use a variable ratio write to reduce market risk. In either case, as with the one-to-one covered call, avoid opening ratio writes immediately before ex-dividend date and use this strategy only for the most compelling bearish reversals. And follow the rule of timing to maximize time decay. This makes the ratio write potentially a very profitable variety of swing trading.

The next chapter examines the risk profile and selection criteria for swing trading with covered calls in the form of ratio writes.

CHAPTER 13

STRATEGY # 4: LONG/SHORT-CALL STRATEGY, RATIO WRITING ON THE SHORT SIDE

> For there never was yet philosopher / That could endure the toothache patiently.
>   William Shakespeare, *Much Ado About Nothing*, 1598–99

THE USE OF LONG AND SHORT CALLS PROVIDES RISK REDUCTION if the short side is covered. However, this does not eliminate risk but only shifts from market risk to exercise risk and also limits the income potential of bearish moves. With any short option, your swing trading profit can never be greater than the premium paid for the call.

This does not mean that the strategy should be rejected. By accepting a degree of higher exercise risk, you can greatly improve income potential during bearish moves if you adjust the covered call. Using a ratio write accomplishes this. The ratio write involves writing more calls than you are able to cover. For example, if you own 300 shares and you write four short calls, you create a 4:3 ratio write. You can think of this as a 75% coverage strategy or as a strategy combining three covered calls and one uncovered call. Either way, the risk is higher than with a 1:1 covered call. However, that risk can be managed if you set up to (a) maximize potential income, (2) are prepared to close or roll, and (3) avoid ex-dividend date to minimize early exercise risk.

THE NATURE OF THE RATIO WRITE

The ratio write strategy has two sides. At the top of the swing and upon locating a bearish reversal, you close any existing long calls and open a ratio write. Assuming you already own shares in the underlying, the transaction is straightforward. However, you should ensure that the exercise price of the lower strike is higher than your initial cost per share. At the bottom of the swing, the short calls are all closed and replaced with long calls upon locating a bullish reversal.

For the most conservative trader, the 1:1 covered call often is perceived as having the lowest level of risk. However, the lost opportunity risk at the top of the price movement and the potential market risk at the bottom demonstrate that covered call writing is not foolproof. However, it is a profitable strategy, combining capital gains, dividends, and option premium. Selection of options expiring in one to two months maximizes time decay, leading to a profitable outcome in most instances.

Even if the underlying moves to or into the money, the call's market value may decline, and, in fact, time decay may even exceed the growth in intrinsic value. This makes covered call writing in a one- to two-month window very attractive. The strike should be selected at a level above the purchase price of stock, and for swing trading purposes an ATM contract is ideal. It has no intrinsic value, which means that the entire premium is going to decline if the underlying remains at the strike or below. However, the limitation on potential profits makes short options less attractive in a swing trading strategy. This problem is partially resolved with the ratio write. However, in exchange for higher income, you also need to be willing to accept higher market risk.

The risk does not have to be quantified in terms of the short call attributes alone. The true risk is going to vary based on how strong the reversal signals are at the time you enter the short call positions. The bearish move—closing any long calls and opening a ratio write—has to be timed with reversal, and that reversal signal and its confirmation should be exceptionally strong. This means an initial reversal should not be acted upon until another, independent reversal signal is discovered. These confirmation signals may be related to price patterns, volume, moving averages, or momentum. The key point to remember is that the risk of the ratio write is going to vary based on how likely reversal is and on how you time your decision based on spotting reversal signals and confirmation.

RISK ANALYSIS OF THE RATIO WRITE

The ratio write provides partial coverage because the number of short calls exceeds the increments of 100 shares. This represents a higher risk than matching 100 shares to each short call. However, this risk has to be quantified based on several aspects. These include:

1. *Moneyness of the calls.* The closer the strike is to current price of the underlying, the greater the chance that the call will move ITM. This becomes an exercise risk; with this in mind, selection of the ratio write strike is a compromise between value and risk.

   An ITM short call is the selection carrying the highest risk. An aggressive swing trading strategy may include selection of an ITM call in order to achieve maximum premium income, but it should be based on locating exceptionally strong reversal signals with confirmation, preferably multiple forms of confirmation.

   An ATM call is often the most likely choice since the entire premium is nonintrinsic. The rapid time decay likely to occur if your timing is good based on reversal signals will make an ATM short call profitable very quickly. As the price declines below strike, the entire premium remains nonintrinsic, and the risk is reduced as well. It is then a matter of waiting for time decay to occur so that profits may be taken or the call left open until expiration. Even if the underlying remains at the strike, time decay will occur; if the call moves ITM, time decay may still exceed the pace of intrinsic value. However, when ITM, it remains an exercise risk, and the position will have to be closed before ITM expiration. In this circumstance, closing at a profit as soon as possible is a prudent decision even if a buy-to-close signal does not appear.

An OTM short call offers the least amount of risk, but the premium will also be lower than the relative premium of ATM and ITM contracts. If expiration is due to occur in less than one month, premium value for an OTM call will be low, probably too low to justify risk exposure. Because the short call can produce profits no greater than the premium you receive, the initial premium has to be high enough to take that risk.

2. *Time to expiration.* Short calls expiring between one and two months will experience the most rapid time decay. This makes the time window ideal. Once you move into the period of one month or less, nonintrinsic value may have declined so much that the short call for a ratio write is difficult to justify. However, when the time is two months or more, the period of risk exposure is a problem since prices can and do change. The great advantage of the ratio write is that time decay makes it more likely that the short calls will be profitable and less likely that they will be exercised. Of course, moneyness is a crucial consideration, and this is why selecting the right expiration date is so important.

The above-mentioned "window" will provide you with rapid time decay plus maximum nonintrinsic premium. Analysis of call values when ATM makes this point. You will see that in the one- to two-month period, nonintrinsic premium is attractive, and once there is one month or less remaining, that same premium declines rapidly. With this is in mind, the best timing for ratio writes is likely to be between one to two months but closer to the shorter side of that period (4–6 weeks). The desirability of higher premium has to be balanced against the greater risk exposure of a longer time during which the position is open.

However, for swing trading purposes, you are less concerned with keeping the ratio write open for long and more concerned with generating a profit very quickly. This is entirely possible for short ATM calls in the 4–6 week time frame. Once nonintrinsic value begins to evaporate, it becomes very possible for a double-digit return to occur within only a few days. The nonintrinsic value may, in fact, match or even exceed the point loss in the underlying below strike. There is no consistent formula for this, but it is most likely to happen during this period. For example, an ATM call may lose two points in value when the underlying loses two points, moving below the strike just as the time approaches one month to expiration. For long traders, this is a very difficult situation, and recovery from the loss is remote. But for the short-side trader, the fast decline is very desirable. A two-point decline on a short call sold for 5 represents a 40% return.

3. *Ratio level.* The higher the ratio (number of options to increments of 100 shares), the lower the risk because the percentage of cover increases as well. A ratio write can involve any number of shares, even fewer than 100. For example, if you own 75 shares and sell one call, it sets up a 1/0.75 ratio. This is the same level of risk as owning 300 shares and selling 4 calls or a 4:3 ratio. This can also be expressed as percentage of cover or, in this example, as 75%.

Some ratio comparisons are shown in table 13.1.

Table 13.1   Comparison of ratio write – ratios and cover percentages

Number of options	Number of shares	Ratio	%
1	50	1:0.5	50%
1	75	1:0.75	75%
2	100	2:1	50%
2	150	2:1.5	75%
3	200	3:2	67%
4	200	4:2	50%
4	300	4:3	75%
5	300	5:3	60%
5	400	5:4	80%
6	400	6:4	67%
6	500	6:5	83%
7	500	7:5	71%
7	600	7:6	86%

Source: Created by the author.

The higher the percentage of coverage, the lower the risk. With 80% coverage, for example, only 20% of your uncovered positions are exposed to risk. In comparison, with 50% coverage, one-half of your short calls are exposed to risk.

4. *Strategy for avoiding exercise.* Risk also has to be defined by your strategies for fixing the situation if and when your short calls go ITM. With exercise risk, you will need to accept exercise, close one or more of the positions, or roll one or more forward to defer exercise.

Even if a short call goes ITM, it may be possible to close at a profit. This occurs when time decay outpaces the increase in intrinsic value. However, this possibility is likely to exist only temporarily, and when it appears, take the profit (or breakeven or a small loss) to avoid exercise.

Rolling forward is the second method for exercise deferral or avoidance. Replacing one short call with a later-expiring one results in a net credit, which is more income. This reduces the likelihood of exercise when you roll from the exercise month into the following month. You may also roll forward and up to a higher strike to move ATM or OTM or to at least reduce the lost value if and when exercise occurs. You can also add more risk by rolling forward *and* adding more short calls. For example, you close two ITM short calls this month and replace them with three ATM short calls expiring in the following month. As a swing trading strategy, this makes sense if you believe the price will decline but the reversal signal has been delayed.

Exercise is also avoided by not opening ratio writes in the ex-dividend month. If these short positions move ITM, exercise is possible immediately before ex-dividend date. This will occur only for those owners of long calls who can justify the cost of early exercise by the capital gain and dividend amount, which means not all ITM calls will be exercised, but many will.

The early exercise risk in the ex-dividend month may occur unintentionally if you open calls in the month before that month but then roll forward into the month in which the ex-dividend date occurs. You may be unaware of this if you focus only on the immediate problem of wanting to avoid exercise at or near expiration.

Example # 1: Chart-Based Reversal Signals

The first example of a chart with a worthwhile signal for ratio writing is that of Procter & Gamble (PG), shown in figure 13.1. The ex-dividend date in October is worth avoiding with short calls because of the threat it poses for early exercise. However, once that has passed, a bullish engulfing signal is a good initial entry point for a long call. This was followed by a very large price gap and volume spike. This sudden and strong rise in the price level was bearish.

Entering a ratio write in the session following the price gap would have made sense. The long upper shadow indicates lost momentum among buyers. If this signal was missed, the next session repeated the long shadow.

At the close of the charted period, a likely candidate for the ratio write was the January 70 call. The entire premium of 0.56 was nonintrinsic, and the sharp rise in price preceding that date is a clue that there may be another price reversal coming. However, no specific bearish reversal signal was found, and until that occurs, it would make sense to monitor price and be ready to move. The 0.56 premium of the 70 calls is less than 1%, so even doubling this up is not especially worth the risk unless a strong bearish signal can be located.

Example # 2: Chart-Based Reversal Signals

Home Depot (HD) displayed a more interesting series of signals in its chart, shown in figure 13.2. Ex-dividend date did not appear until late November, and in the period before that a lot of signaling appeared.

The RSI indicator showed overbought at the peak of the September-October uptrend, followed by a fast but brief decline. A buy signal was seen with the bullish harami. The harami

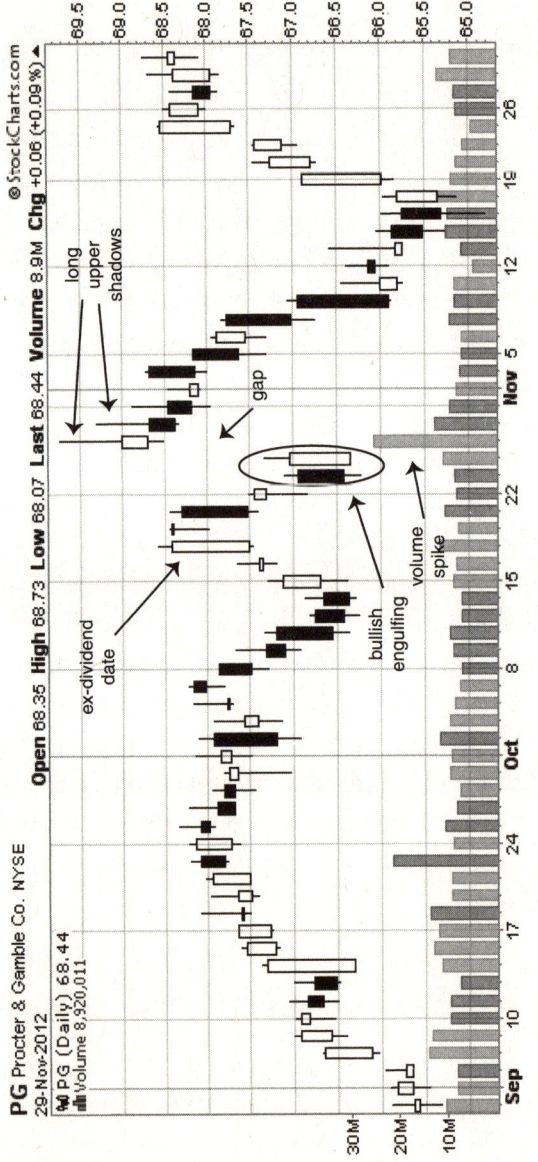

Figure 13.1 Swing trading with ratio writes—example # 1
Source: StockCharts.com.

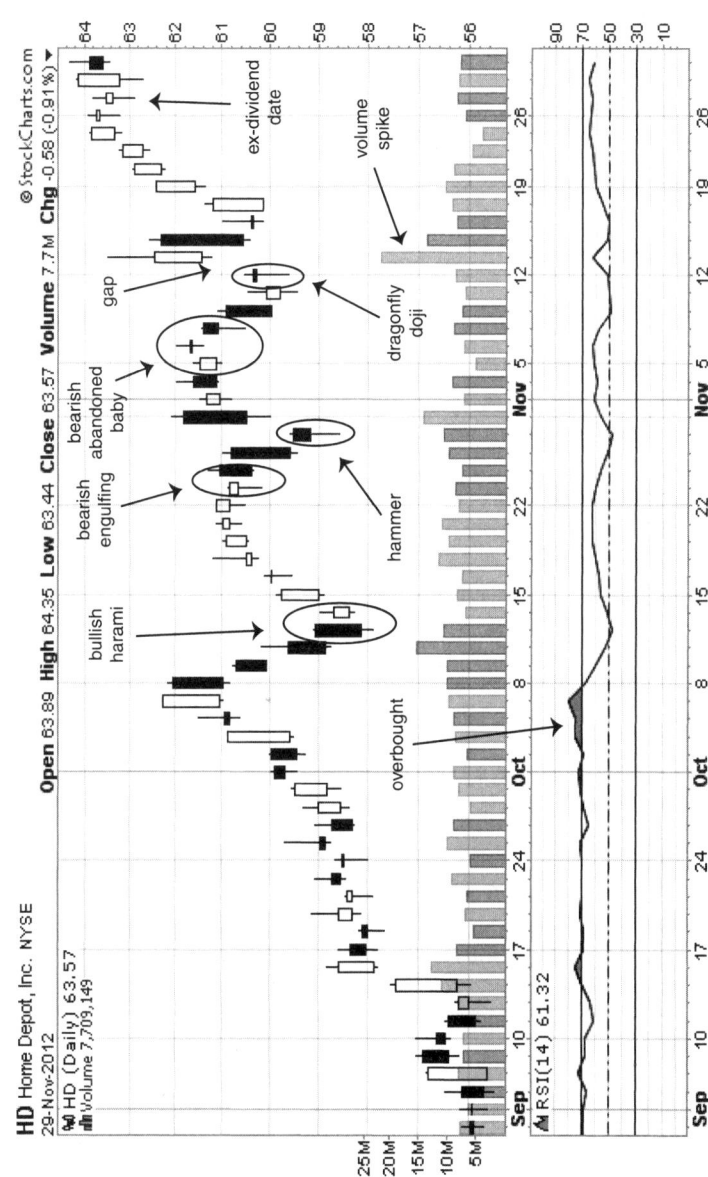

Figure 13.2 Swing trading with ratio writes—example #2
Source: StockCharts.com.

by itself is not a reliable indicator for action, but RSI had also retreated into its midrange, so this was a reasonable point to buy long calls.

Two weeks later, a stronger bearish signal appeared in the form of a bearish engulfing pattern. However, two sessions later, the hammer indicated yet another reversal, this time to the upside. A strong bearish signal appeared as the latest entry to these very fast reversal trends, namely, as a bearish abandoned baby.

The dragonfly doji can serve as a reversal signal in either direction, depending on where it is found. In this case, it was at the bottom of a three-session downtrend. It was confirmed immediately by the price gap and volume spike, two patterns that are very strong when they appear together. The last action point in this pattern might be the bearish white session with the long upper shadow, and with ex-dividend date approaching, it would be wise to close any outstanding short calls before that date.

As of the end of the charted period, the December 65 calls were at 0.79, a 1.2% return based on the ending price of $64.24 per share. A ratio write at this point makes sense as long as a clear bearish turn is located. The preceding action was to the upside, and prices then leveled out for the last week, but before acting you would need a more convincing signal of a bearish direction to follow.

EXAMPLE # 3: CHART-BASED REVERSAL SIGNALS

Yahoo (YHOO) provided a somewhat more interesting chart for swing trading with the ratio write. The three-month chart is shown in figure 13.3.

Yahoo does not pay a dividend, so there is little danger of early exercise. In this respect, Yahoo is an attractive underlying for the ratio write. The interesting price action began in the last week of October when the combined gap and volume spike provided a very compelling upside indicator. This was a sensible point to buy calls.

The question with any trend is, when will it end? Notice that RSI spent most of November in overbought territory, a signal that

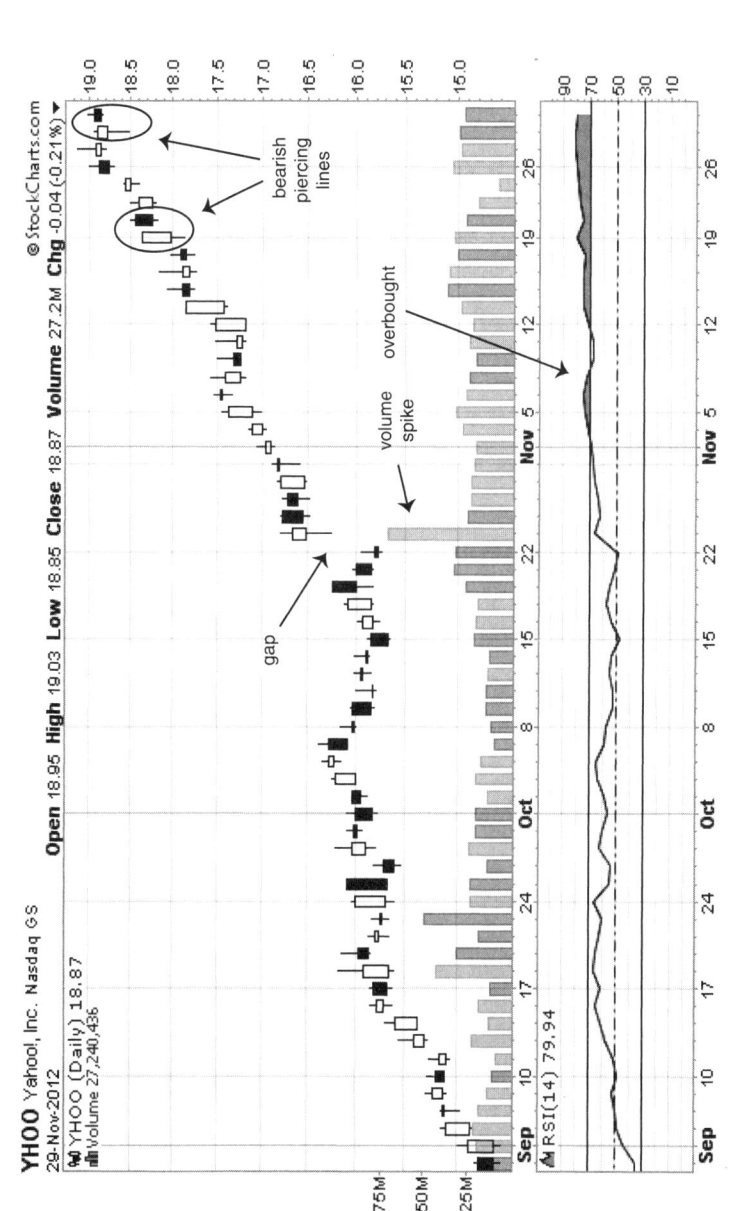

Figure 13.3 Swing trading with ratio writes—example #3
Source: StockCharts.com.

this gradual uptrend was becoming a likely candidate for reversal. But the oscillator by itself is not reliable enough to prompt action because its index reflects the upward movement without contradicting it. The end of the chart finally provided confirmation of a likely reversal with two bearish piercing lines. These occurred in close proximity. At the same time, it's noteworthy that RSI moved strongly up to nearly 80. The overbought line is 70, so this is a very strong sign that a bearish move is likely.

As of the end of the charted period, with the price at $18.87 per share, the December 19 calls were at 0.40, a 2.1% potential return. A ratio write at this point and with this strike would be entirely nonintrinsic and have only three weeks to expiration.

RISK REDUCTION: THE VARIABLE RATIO WRITE

The ratio write based on a single strike presents a specific risk. If the short calls move ITM, they are all at risk of exercise, which means that the uncovered portion has to be closed or rolled to avoid taking a net loss.

This risk is greater than in 1:1 covered call selling, and that risk has to be understood. For a conservative swing trader, even strong bearish signals and confirmation may not provide enough certainty to enter into a ratio write. However, the variable ratio write provides a lower-risk alternative that might be more acceptable for swing trading.

The variable ratio write involves more than one strike. So if one is ATM and the other OTM—or if both are OTM—the exercise risk is low, and the flexibility is greatly improved. Even if the lower strike moves ITM, the higher strike calls can be closed or rolled or the ratio can be equalized before exercise becomes a real possibility. As with the one-strike ratio write, the risk to the variable ratio write should be analyzed based on several attributes. These are:

1. *Moneyness of the calls.* The 1:1 ratio write is high-risk when the strike is close to the current price of the underlying. In the case of the variable ratio write, this is true for the lower

strikes. However, considered alone, these are covered even while the higher-strike calls are not (or are only partially covered). For example, if you own 300 shares and sell 4 calls (two ATM and two OTM), both lower-strike calls are covered and one of the two higher-strike calls is covered.

Using ITM strikes for the variable ratio write is aggressive, but the use of two strikes poses an interesting compromise for swing trading. Based on the assumption that you have found exceptionally strong bearish reversal and confirmation, you could employ a strategy of mixing the variable ratio write between ITM and OTM strikes. This is a high-risk approach due to the risk of exercise with writing ITM calls even in a ratio write; at the same time, it offers the potential for rapid profits as long as the underlying moves down, in which case the intrinsic value will disappear immediately.

2. *Time to expiration.* The ratio write is most advantageous when time to expiration is between one and two months, and the same applies to the variable ratio write. Contracts expiring in less than one month will not contain much nonintrinsic premium, so profit potential is small. The desirability of one- or two-month options is that nonintrinsic value can be found, but it will decline rapidly. Added to the safety of two strikes, this makes the window of one to two months ideal for swing trading.

3. *Ratio level.* The ratio write was described in terms of the ratio as a factor of risk; the higher the ratio, the lower the risk. Thus, a 5:4 ratio is 80% covered, whereas a 3:2 is only 67% covered. When it comes to the variable ratio write, a lower ratio continues to represent higher risk, but the use of two strikes offsets this risk. Accordingly, 67% coverage generates more income and might be equivalent to a higher coverage level due to the use of two strikes. The higher strikes sets up more "wiggle room" for the underlying price to move before going ITM, and this reduces the risk. For example, a single-strike ratio write at 67% will carry a higher risk if the calls move in the money. With the variable ratio write,

a portion of the short calls does not go ITM until the price moves higher.

This offsetting and mitigating factor cannot be defined precisely. Each situation will vary in terms of moneyness and time to expiration as well as in strength of reversal signals and confirmation. The point, however, is that with the variable ratio write, your perception of risk levels is altered because of the lower risk level in general due to including one strike OTM and the other either ATM or OTM (and in some cases even ITM).

4. *Strategy for avoiding exercise.* Whenever some of your short calls are uncovered, you need to set rules for yourself concerning the moneyness and timing of rolling or closing. With the variable ratio write, you create much greater flexibility for these than with the one-strike ratio write.

It is possible to close one or more of the short positions at a profit if and when the underlying price begins to approach the strike. Even if the short call moves ITM, it is still possible to close at a profit as long as time decay outpaces the increase in intrinsic value. However, this means running a high risk because you cannot control how rapidly price will change. If your strategy is to close, it makes sense to do so as soon as the price begins to trend against the short strike.

The variable ratio write is ideal for rolling. With two strikes, you can roll one or more positions forward or forward and up a strike. You can also decide whether to roll the lower strike or the higher strike. The decision might depend on (a) whether or not the lower strike has moved ITM and (b) on the level of premium income earned by rolling to a later expiration.

Since the goal of swing trading is to move in and out of positions with a two- to five-day schedule, rolling should be considered as a last resort. It is more prudent to close positions to avoid exercise of uncovered calls and to then accept the profits gained with exercise and move on to the next trade. Allowing open positions to be rolled forward converts what should be a short-term strategy into a longer-term holding pattern.

A final note on exercise avoidance: don't open variable ratio writes in the ex-dividend month. This is the same rule as that of the ratio write. Although not every ITM short call is exercised before ex-dividend date, the possibility is high, and this is worth avoiding except if you want to get exercised. In some situations, the underlying will be profitable at the strike, and exercise combines a capital gain with a 100% profit in the premium of the short call. As a means of escaping ownership of the underlying at a profit, ex-dividend exercise deprives you of the current dividend but creates profits well above the dividend level.

Example # 4: Chart-Based Reversal Signals

The first example of a chart appropriate for the variable ratio write is that of MMM. Its three-month chart is shown in figure 13.4.

The first point worth mentioning is support level just below the $92 level. The spinning top preceded a very strong downside gap, followed immediately by another strong bearish signal, the three black crows. At this point, it would seem that the trend was downward, but all of these were false signals.

This points out the fact that some signals, even strong ones with confirmation, are going to fail. The only slight contradicting signal was that RSI moved marginally into oversold levels, but this was easily explained away by the large price decline.

Another false signal appeared in the form of a bearish engulfing pattern. This is 80% reliable as a reversal, but in this case prices moved upward instead. Shortly after this, the ex-dividend date appeared. By the end of the chart, the last two sessions formed a bearish piercing lines signal. Although this is reliable for reversal about two-thirds of the time, there is no confirmation accompanying this signal, and given the multiple false signals appearing on this chart, reversal is not certain by any means.

If you were to rely on the chart for a likely reversal candidate at the ending price of $90.65, the December contracts offer a rich premium level. The December 90 call was priced at 1.68, of which 1.03 was nonintrinsic, a 1.1% yield on the current price

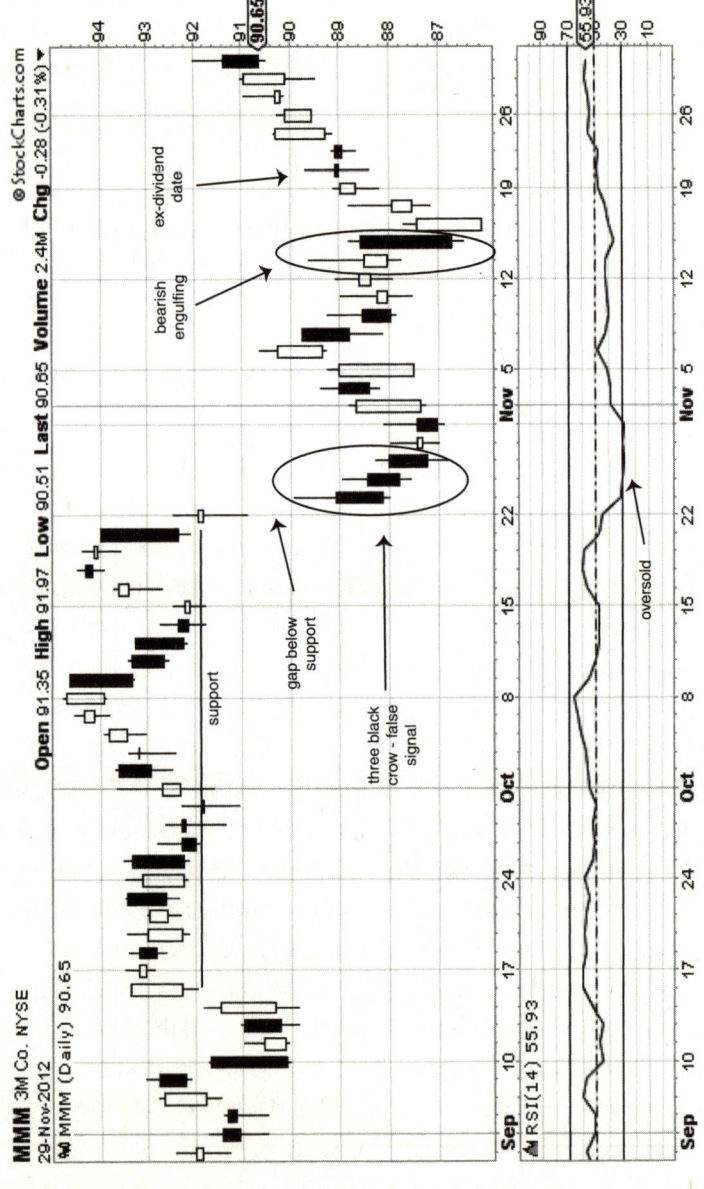

Figure 13.4 Swing trading with variable ratio writes—example #1
Source: StockCharts.com.

(1.03 ÷ 90.65). The 92.50 December calls were priced at 0.50. Purely on the basis of the premium with only three weeks until expiration, the combined 90 and 92.50 calls are an attractive swing trading candidate. However, price did not react to signals as you would expect.

Example # 5: Chart-Based Reversal Signals

The second variable ratio write candidate was United Technologies (UTX). A number of interesting signals developed in this three-month chart, which is shown in figure 13.5.

In mid-September, a bearish engulfing pattern appeared after a brief but strong price run-up. Four sessions later, a volume spike confirmed the bearish trend, and after three more sessions the bearish meeting lines again confirmed the downward trend. At any of these points, a variable ratio write at combined 80 and 82.50 strikes would have made sense.

The downtrend signaled its end by establishment of four sessions failing to continue moving downward, the last one a doji day followed by an upward price gap. This could have been viewed as a bullish reversal or only as a point to close the short calls opened previously.

The bearish engulfing pattern appeared at a point when daily trading was also extended into long days. This would have been another point to open a variable ratio write. The downtrend continued until a brief fall below support followed by white sessions. Once again, closing the short calls makes sense here, especially in view of the ex-dividend date rapidly approaching.

The decline below support failed with the spinning top and price gaps, leading to a strong upward move. At the end of the charted period, the single black session could be viewed as an initial bearish reversal signal, as swing traders define a reversal day. However, additional confirmation should be found before once again entering a bearish move such as a variable ratio write. However, given the two strikes and potential for rolling or closing positions, swing traders at this point might be tempted to enter a new position. If so, the January 80 calls were worth 1.97 (2.5% of

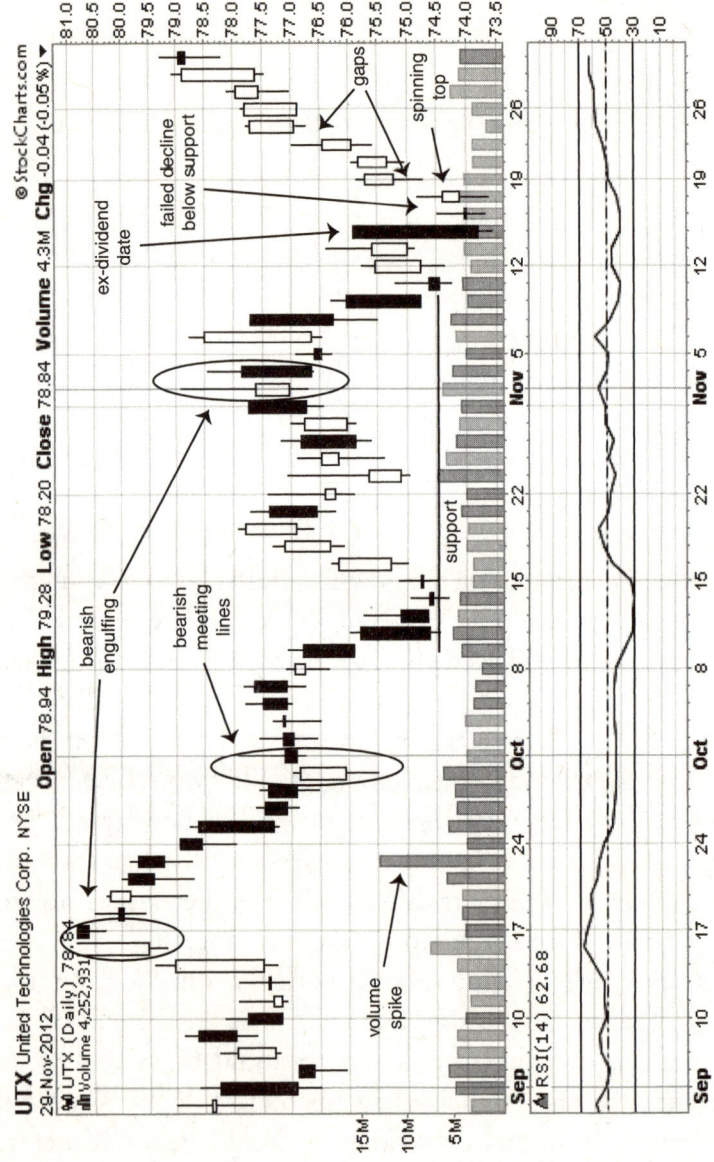

Figure 13.5 Swing trading with variable ratio writes—example # 2
Source: StockCharts.com.

current value), and the 82.50 calls were worth 0.89 (1.1% of current price). Both of these were entirely nonintrinsic, making the timing and return very attractive.

EXAMPLE # 6: CHART-BASED REVERSAL SIGNALS

Perhaps the most interesting chart of these three is that of Wells Fargo (WFC). The three-month chart is shown in figure 13.6.

The chart is interesting for the high volume of signals, with little or no substantial movement for the first two months. It all began with a bullish abandoned baby, a very strong signal that led to a two-session uptrend.

Next, a very unusual series of four signals appeared, one after the other. The first three were bearish engulfing patterns, a pattern that leads to reversal 80% of the time. The price was trending downward until the fourth signal, a bullish engulfing pattern (also reliable about 80% of the time). This preceded a six-session uptrend that concluded with another unusual example of two consecutive bearish signs: a piercing lines signal and then another bearish engulfing pattern.

All of this price action took place within a three-point range, or about 8.5% of the price. After the bearish engulfing pattern, a downward gap confirmed the downside trend, but the downtrend then stopped and a three-week period of uncertainty followed. The six weeks from the beginning of September to the middle of October included a lot of indicators but little result. The price movements did not go below support either.

During the period of uncertainty, a wait-and-see attitude was wise since the ex-dividend date was approaching. In fact, right after this date, price did finally trend below support, perhaps a timely signal for opening a new variable ratio write. The bullish three inside up was a strong signal of reversal, confirmed by a brief and marginal dip of RSI into the oversold area.

By the end of the session, direction was as uncertain as ever. However, if you were to open a variable ratio write at this point on the chart, the December 33 calls were valued at 0.67 (2.0% of current value), and the December 34 calls were valued at 0.25

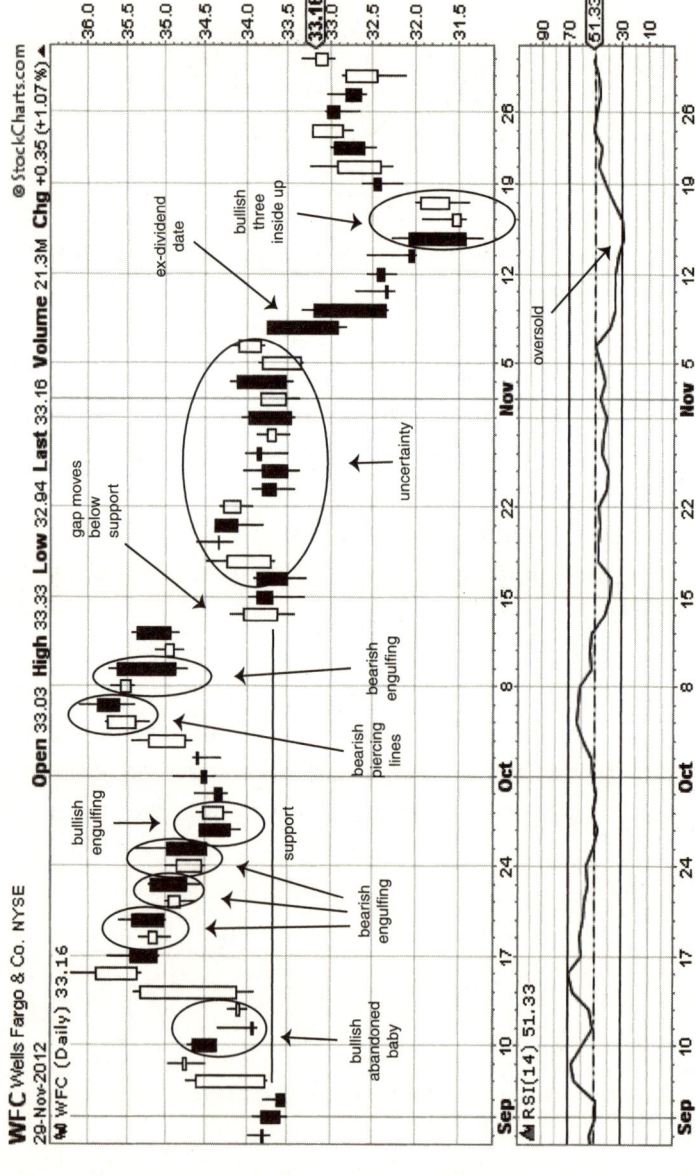

Figure 13.6 Swing trading with variable ratio writes—example #3
Source: StockCharts.com.

(0.8% of current price). These were both marginally accepted as a variable ratio write, but a bearish reversal signal and confirmation should be located before making such a move.

The use of long and short calls is one of the two ways to swing trade. However, looming ex-dividend date presents a constant problem for any swing trader hoping to avoid exercise. Using puts instead avoids this problems altogether. The next chapter examines the use of long and short puts as the basic for a swing trading strategy.

CHAPTER 14

Strategy # 5: Long/Short-Put Strategy

> I have always fought for ideas—until I learned that it isn't ideas but grief, struggle, and flashes of vision which enlighten.
> Margaret Anderson, *The Strange Necessity*, 1969

THE DECISION TO USE PUTS IN PLACE OF CALLS FOR SWING TRADING involves several advantages and, as you might expect, a few disadvantages as well.

Put premium value, as in the case of calls, is affected by dividends, so in ex-dividend months you may discover a benefit (for long call positions) in having positions open—and a cost for short puts. However, short calls come with associated early exercise risk, but when you use long and short puts, you do not have to be concerned about timing based on that particular risk.

Another important difference is that with short puts market risk is much lower than with short calls. A short call can be very risky because, in theory, the underlying price can rise without limit. Realistically, the risk is much lower than that infinite potential risk, but even so it cannot be ignored. A short put is a safer bet because a stock's price can only fall so far. Many think the maximum decline is to zero, but realistically the floor is going to be the tangible book value per share. Market activity also reveals that changes in put valuation based on price decline in the underlying are not likely to be so extreme. Most price movement conforms to resistance and support levels, so true market risk is not usually so extreme.

Even so, anyone trading with uncovered short puts should be aware of the risk levels involved. The desirability of receiving premium over paying it and the advantage of time decay are offset by the risk of holding the short put if and when the underlying price does decline.

Many variations of put trading mitigate market risk, including more complex configurations and combinations. This chapter examines how puts fit into a swing trading strategy. It's a mistake to ignore one type of option in favor of another, and your swing trading program is enriched when you are comfortable with strategies based on both calls and puts or on the use of both in either long or short positions.

Puts Used in Place of Calls

The first observation any swing trader will make is that, in general, put premiums for ATM contracts are going to be slightly higher than call premiums. Puts are more expensive than calls, and this means that you have an advantage using short puts in bullish conditions over using short calls in bearish conditions. The higher put premium is often only marginally worthwhile. A comparison of seven underlying stocks as of December 13, 2012, and their ATM call and put values closest to expiration demonstrates this point in table 14.1.

The dollar value of put premiums over call premiums at the next-expiring ATM strike is quite small, but the percentage this represents ranges widely. This will be further affected by the proximity of the actual price to the strike. But what is the purpose in comparing premium levels between calls and puts? You gain an advantage in using short puts for this reason (compared to long calls), because of the higher cost of the puts.

For example, Wells Fargo's price is 10 cents below the strike, and the put is 29% higher than the call. The difference in premium is also 10 cents, representing the intrinsic value of the put. The same observation applies to Microsoft with its 28% higher put premium. The stock is 8 cents below the strike, and the difference in premium is also 8 cents. In both cases, if adjustment

Table 14.1 Stock prices, expiration months, strikes, and call and put values, 7 companies

Underlying	Price	Month	Strike	Call	Put	%
Wells Fargo (WFC)	$33.40	DEC	33.50	0.34	0.44	29%
Boeing (BA)	75.02	DEC	75	0.82	0.83	1
Facebook (FB)	28.47	DEC	28.50	0.85	0.90	6
Firstenergy (FE)	40.99	DEC	41	0.45	0.50	11
Potash (POT)	40.92	DEC	41	0.49	0.56	14
Yahoo (YHOO)	19.50	DEC	19.50	0.25	0.26	4
Microsoft (MSFT)	27.42	DEC	27.50	0.29	0.37	28

Source: Table constructed by author based on quotations on Charles Schwab & Co., at www.schwab.com.

is taken for the intrinsic value of the put, the two options are at parity.

The remaining positions should also be judged by comparing proximity to intrinsic value of the put. Once these adjustments are made, the outcome will demonstrate that the often-cited put advantage is quite small, and when the underlying price is truly ATM, the difference will be small indeed. For example, Yahoo was the only company in this group whose price was exactly ATM, and yet the difference between put and call was only $0.01.

One way to analyze relative value of put versus call is to consider the typical market interest rate compared to future dividends. This is similar to the attempt of arriving at a fair price under Black-Scholes and similar pricing models. The result, accurately described as the price for future delivery of a share of stock, is approximately equal to the current stock price plus assumed risk-free interest and minus dividend. The problem with this model is that it ignores volatility of the options as well as market demand for the stock, both of which have an effect on the value of stock and options.

While proximity and time have an effect on the pricing of options, and dividends also affect both calls and puts, the probable advantage is quite small. Swing traders will be likely to view the short-term advantage or disadvantage of put pricing based not on pricing and volatility models but on clearly observed reversal signals and confirmation.

The Dividend Effect

A stock's price is expected to fall around the time of ex-dividend date due to the impact of dividend declaration. Right before the ex-dividend date, a stockholder of record is entitled to earn the current dividend, and the value of that dividend comes out of the stock. The effect is not always visible since many other forces may offset the dividend's impact on the stock's price.

For swing traders, a somewhat different perspective is applied to the dividend effect. For a stockholder not engaged in swing trading, the expected price decline is merely an offset. The dividend is income and the decline in price reduces the value of shares, in theory, to an equal degree. However, for swing traders, knowledge of this provides an incentive for both long-side and short-side trading.

You will use long puts at the top of a swing since the put increases in value as the underlying price declines. And so just as a short call may be a risky swing trade right before ex-dividend date due to the risk of early exercise, the opposite is true for the long-put trade. The short call and long put are used at the same point in the swing, but the disadvantage of the short call is converted to an advantage for the long put.

The expected decline in stock price due to the impending ex-dividend date may cause the stock to decline, and this means that the long put will increase in value. In addition to the normal reversal signal and confirmation, the ex-dividend date itself thus provides an extra timing advantage for a bearish entry. Short-call swing traders are likely to avoid the ex-dividend month, but long-put traders may want to seek opportunities, assuming the bearish reversal also appears at an advantageous moment in the month—ideally, within a week before ex-dividend date.

The opposite applies to short-put trading. Short puts are going to be used at the bottom of the swing as a form of bullish reversal. The richer the premium, the more benefit you gain when the underlying price rises. Any intrinsic value will evaporate when the underlying price rises, and nonintrinsic premium also declines when the puts move OTM. However, when the short put is close to the money, a decline in value will increase the put's premium as it is forced ITM, and the value of the put then increases while you want it to decrease. Although the short put is used for the same reversal point as a long call, its timing in the ex-dividend month is potentially counterproductive.

Given the effect of the ex-dividend month on the value of both short calls (for bearish reversal) and short puts (for bullish reversal), both may be avoided in the ex-dividend month. It is a safer play to revert to long puts (for bearish reversals) and long calls (for bullish reversals) in the ex-dividend month. The alternative, if the reversal does not appear at the desired point, is to simply avoid swing trading in any company during its ex-dividend month.

THE SHORT-PUT RISK

Many traders hesitate to use short uncovered options under any circumstances. If you rely on strong reversal signals and equally strong confirmation, this risk is mitigated. Even so, a conservative trader may want to use only long options or covered calls.

The short-put risk is not as high as that of the short call. But even beyond this, the risk profile of the short put is identical to that of the covered call. This is interesting for several reasons. First, it enables you to swing trade at the bottom of the swing with a short put without needing to also own shares of stock. In contrast, using covered calls at the top of the swing requires that you own 100 shares of stock. The short put requires you to provide margin collateral equal to the strike of the put, so the advantage is not as pure as that of the difference between owning shares and not owning shares. However, if you have adequate capital in your trading account consisting of a variety of equity positions, the short put could be a good alternative to having to buy shares just to create a covered call.

Second, closing the short put is far more flexible than closing a covered call and the underlying 100 shares. When a call's value has declined so that the short position is profitable, the stock is likely to have depreciated, which means that you have to take a loss if you sell or wait in the hope that the price will rise again. With a short put, however, closing is a relatively simple matter. If it has become profitable, it can be closed no matter what the stock price has moved to.

Third, you can avoid exercise of the short put by rolling forward. However, rolling is not necessary just because the stock has declined and the short put has become ITM. In many instances, even an ITM put loses value since the nonintrinsic premium declines more than the points of intrinsic value in the put. The "nonintrinsic premium" refers to those portions of the overall premium beyond intrinsic premium. When you add intrinsic and nonintrinsic premium total, you get the total value of the option.

The risk of the short put is very real due to the potential for exercise and the threat of loss if the stock price falls far below the strike. However, by managing the put and focusing on the typical two- to five-day swing and relying on strong reversal signals and confirmation, you reduce exercise risk. If you also limit swing trading to less volatile underlying stocks, you further reduce the risk of a large and unexpected price drop.

Ratio Put Spreads

The plain use of long puts for bearish entry at the top of the swing and of short puts for bullish entry at the bottom is very similar to the relative use of long and short calls at opposite points in the swing. However, there is more. Just as the use of short calls can be expanded through ratio writes, you can make swing trading with puts more interesting and varied with the ratio put spread.

This is a strategy that spreads the risk while offsetting long and short positions. In the typical ratio put spread, you adopt a bearish position (thus, this would be entered at the top of the swing upon identifying reversal and confirmation). The strategy consists of opening long-strike puts and selling a higher number of lower-strike puts. The configuration of each side is quite flexible. The ratio may consist of 2:1 or of 3:2, for example. Two different cases demonstrate how this works:

U.S. Steel (X)

Midway on December 13, 2012, the stock price was $22.34. The following December puts were available:

strike	premiuum
21.50	0.20
22	0.37
22.50	0.63

One form of ratio put spread would be to buy two of the 22 puts at 0.37, paying $74, and sell three of the 21.50 contracts at 0.20, gaining $60. The net debit of $14 is a minimal cost, but this sets up a reduction of the short positions. All of the options in this example were OTM. A second approach would be to sell the 22.50 contract at 0.63 and receive $63 and offset that with two long 22 contracts at 0.37. This creates a credit of 0.11 and also involves an ITM long position, which is more desirable than the 3:2 OTM ratio put spread if the price declines.

In the event the stock price rises, the potential loss in this overall position will be minimal. If the price falls as expected, the long puts will become profitable and will be partly or completely paid for by the short puts with lower strike. Because these were all OTM, nonintrinsic value in the short puts falls more rapidly.

Travelers (TRV)
This stock price was $73.61 at halfway point on December 13, 2012. The following December puts were available at the same time:

72.50	0.35
75	1.53

In this circumstance, you would buy a 75 at 1.53, paying $153, and would then need to sell four or more of the lower-strike puts to cover the cost. Given the disparity in price, this situation is less feasible than the U.S. Steel example. From this, you can see that selecting the right moment for a ratio put spread is a matter of pricing.

A variation on this idea is called the ratio put calendar spread. It's the same idea, but the long positions expire later than the short positions. The idea here is that with accelerated time decay, short puts will lose value more rapidly than the later-expiring long puts. The same strike is employed, and instead of the vertical construction of the ratio put spread, this variation involves a horizontal construction. It presents the potential for cover and perhaps even greater profits, but for swing trading it does not always make sense to employ such complex configurations when simple long and short options are just as likely to lead to profits—especially when they are timed for reversal and confirmation at the top of the swing. Because both the ratio put spread and its calendar variety work best as a bearish play, a corresponding bullish version is not practical.

Example # 1: Chart-Based Reversal Signals

The purpose in using puts for swing trading is to mark reversal opportunities while paying attention to the ex-dividend date. If a bearish reversal is signaled right before ex-dividend date, that is an advantage because a drop in price will increase the value of the long put. However, if the signal is bullish right before ex-dividend date, opening a short put could prevent or delay development of the desired two- to five-day trend.

The chart of American Express (AXP) in figure 14.1 demonstrates how a range of different reversal signals and confirmation can help time opening put positions.

The first noteworthy date is the ex-dividend date, but no bearish signal was present. That did not show up until after an uptrend finished about one week later. Another bearish trend started after a short-term price decline in the form of a piercing lines pattern. This set up a strong downtrend, which ended with the bullish meeting lines, followed two weeks later by a bullish engulfing pattern confirmed by volume spikes. Price did not trend lower until this later appearance of a bearish signal along with confirming volume spikes. This reveals that even with a clear signal, the convincing turn in direction may be delayed.

This chart lacked strong confirmation in some instances, and it demonstrates that even strong reversal signals often suffer a delayed reaction before the price moves as expected. The pattern seen with the unconfirmed bearish signal was repeated in the opposite direction in the bullish turn toward the end of the period. The bullish meeting lines pattern was not confirmed.

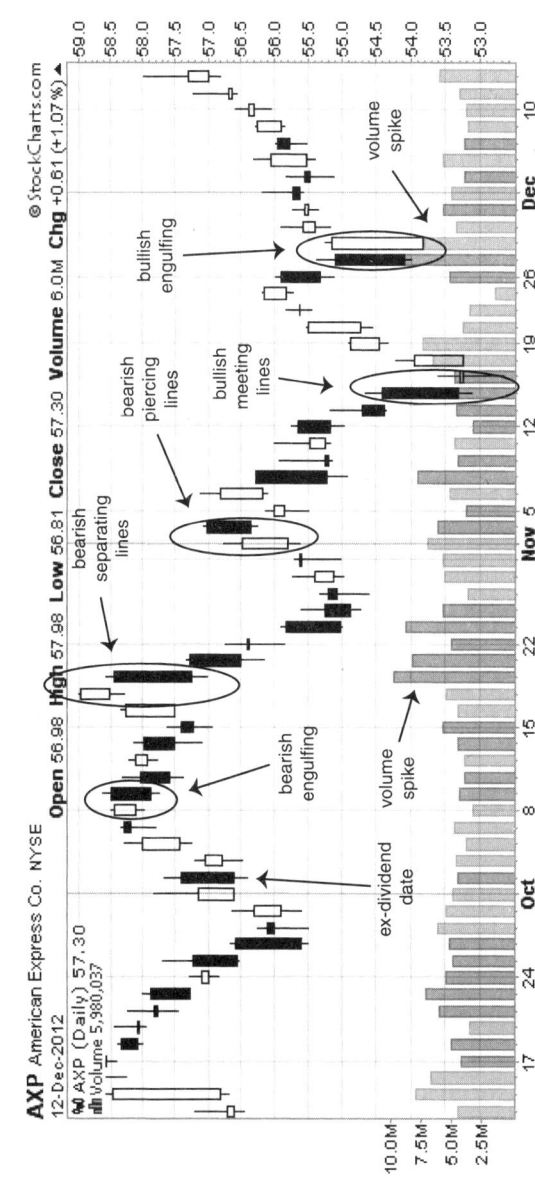

Figure 14.1 Swing trading with puts—example #1
Source: StockCharts.com.

Only when the bullish engulfing pattern showed up with volume spikes was it clear that the trend had turned.

Example # 2: Chart-Based Reversal Signals

Another chart presents a more interesting combination of signals and confirmation. The chart of General Electric (GE) in figure 14.2 begins with its ex-dividend date.

The turn was first signaled in a bearish engulfing pattern confirmed by an overbought signal from RSI, a pause, and a bearish harami cross. The strength of the following downtrend consisted of confirmation in the form of repetitive price gaps and volume spikes.

A bullish engulfing pattern led to a very brief uptrend, followed by an evening star, a strongly bearish signal. These fast turns in direction are typical for swing trading where you expect to see short-term trends of two to five days duration. When such activity is high, you need to pay close attention and be ready to move quickly.

Finally, an exceptionally strong reversal was signaled by the double reversal patterns, an inverted hammer and a piercing lines signal. At the same time RSI moved down to oversold, signaling a coming uptrend. RSI is somewhat troubling, however. As a confirming signal, it adds some weight to other reversal signals—in this case, to the consecutive candlestick bullish signs. However, when RSI moves into overbought or oversold territory, this is often simply the result of average price movement. On this chart, the early overbought and later oversold conditions were exactly this, a reflection of strong price movement. So RSI is not necessarily a valuable signal unless it contradicts price indicators; however, it is useful if it confirms a separate, strong reversal signal in candlesticks, volume, or traditional Western indicators.

This busy chart is characterized by a long-term bearish trend in the middle, consisting of several short-term bullish reversals. However, a busy chart is not always an easy chart to read. The delayed reaction in reversals adds to difficulty in timing both entry and exit, and swing traders will find charts like this difficult to use unless stronger price movement and stronger confirmation develop.

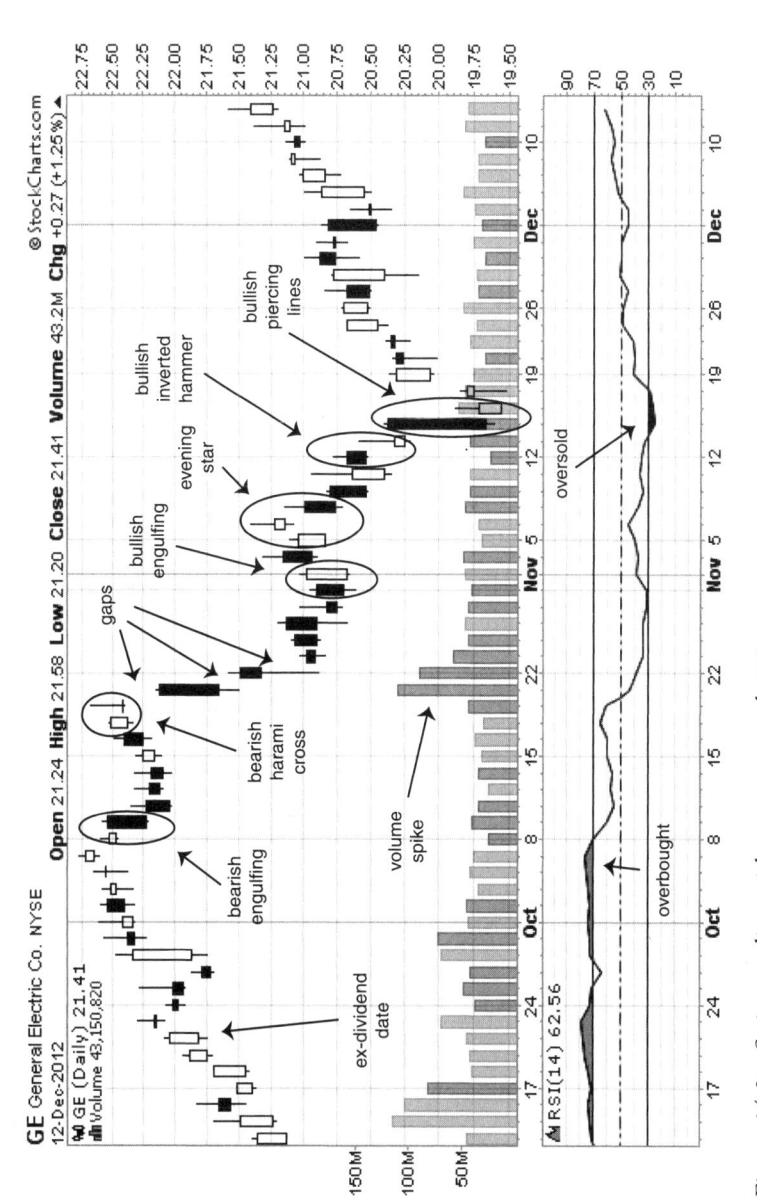

Figure 14.2 Swing trading with puts—example #2
Source: StockCharts.com.

Example # 3: Chart-Based Reversal Signals

The third chart is that of Johnson & Johnson (JNJ) in figure 14.3; here, the first interesting signal is a price gap to the downside, leading to a failed test of support in the form of a double bottom. This is a subtle but powerful signal. Traders have a tendency to focus on one type of signal, but if you seek candlestick-based reversals, you can easily miss a strong signal in Western price patterns. This double bottom that tests support is a good example.

Typically, when support is tested with signals like the double bottom, the resulting turn is exceptionally strong. The strength of the double bottom in this case was demonstrated by the very strong uptrend in this situation. This offsetting movement included price gaps and a strong upward move for four sessions, all white candlesticks, and the last two long days as well. But even a strong move like this is going to come to an end. The signal that the uptrend was about to end abruptly was seen in the bearish harami, which was confirmed with volume spikes and overbought in RSI. The harami by itself is one of those fifty-fifty signals. It is not useful as a reversal sign. After a strong uptrend, a black session is a reversal day. Also note the distinctive long-legged doji session appearing immediately after the bearish harami. This is the doji with long upper and lower shadows. As with the harami, the doji's significance depends on where it appears. The combined harami and doji serve as confirmation that the uptrend is done; in this case both were further confirmed by what happened next.

After a pause, the downtrend resumed with the appearance of a bearish engulfing pattern. Although signals for a bullish turn were evident, it would not make sense to take up a bullish entry due to the impending ex-dividend date. However, open bearish positions could have been closed around the middle of November when the downtrend had stalled.

Right after the ex-dividend date, the price resumed a strong uptrend and was characterized by unusual triple bullish engulfing patterns. The occurrences of several bullish patterns confirm one another.

* * *

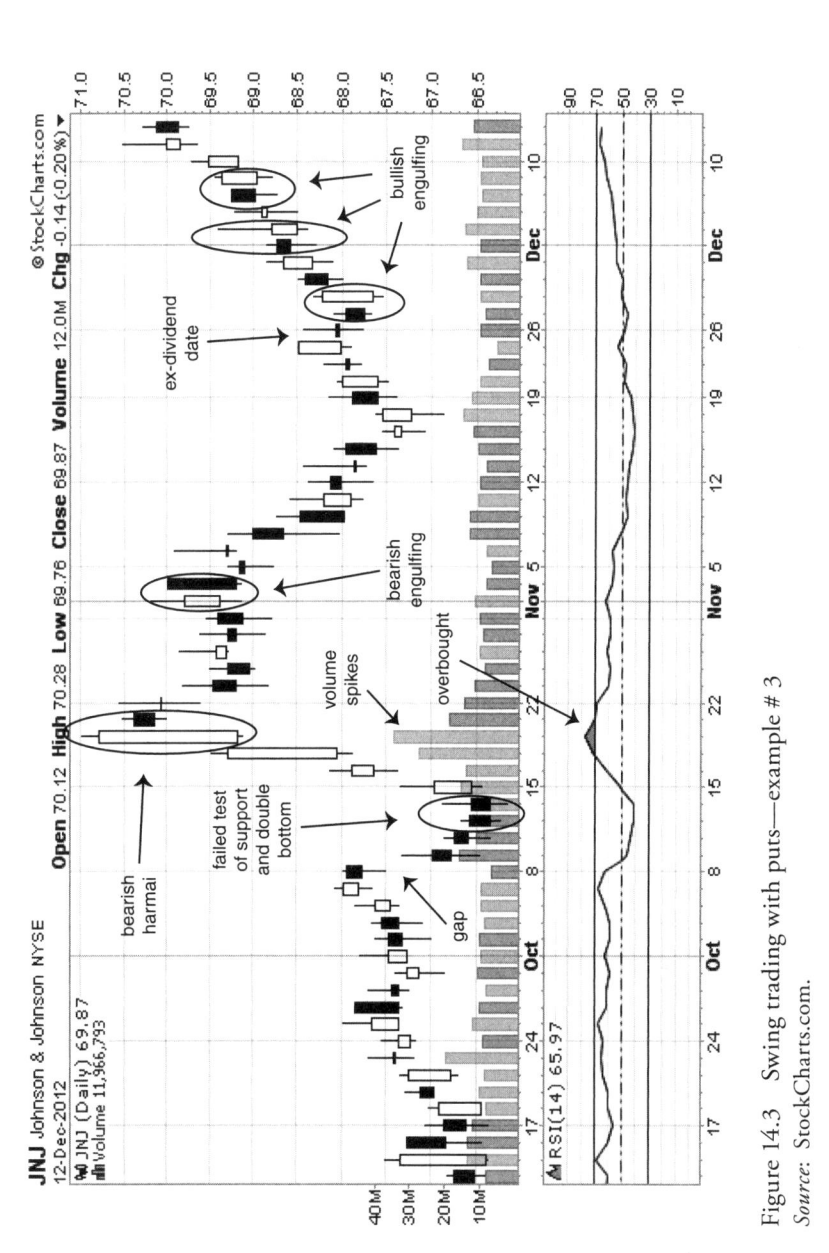

Figure 14.3   Swing trading with puts—example #3
Source: StockCharts.com.

The use of puts adds great variety to a swing trading program. However, just like calls, puts are affected, favorably or unfavorably, by the timing of the ex-dividend date. The long put tends to benefit whereas the short put does not. If you seek the typical very short trend for swing trading, it is wise to avoid ex-dividend date for those bullish short puts and to seek confirmation of entry timing for long puts. The reversal signals do not always occur at the perfect moment to suit your swing trading needs, and therefore great patience is required.

Given the difficulty in finding the right timing for advantageous long put (bearish) entry, puts can be as challenging as calls around and immediately before ex-dividend date. For this reason, it could make sense to just avoid the ex-dividend month altogether. Price action during the ex-dividend month adds an element of uncertainty that many swing traders prefer to avoid.

An alternative to the decision to use either calls or puts is to focus on a more aggressive strategy, namely, the use of short options only. This involves entering short calls at the top of the swing in anticipation of a bearish turn and short puts at the bottom in anticipation of a bullish price movement. This is a higher-risk approach, but swing traders may justify the decision by relying on exceptionally strong reversal signals and confirmation. However, both short calls and short puts present significant problems during the ex-dividend month. The short call exposes you to the risk of early exercise, and the short put could increase in value due to the ex-dividend when you want it to lose value. If you use short options on both sides, avoiding the ex-dividend month is smart.

The challenge of the short-option strategy is that potential profits are limited. The best outcome is that value declines in the option due to its move to OTM status and loss of nonintrinsic premium. The ideal timing for selling options will be one to two months prior to expiration, in order to maximize time decay; this may also mean that the holding period for the swing will have to extend beyond the usual two- to five-day holding period as well. The market risk of short uncovered positions is offset by the ability to close or roll to avoid exercise. The short-option strategy is the topic of the next chapter.

CHAPTER 15

STRATEGY # 6: SHORT-OPTION STRATEGY

> Every great advance in science has issued from a new audacity of imagination.
> John Dewey, *The Quest for Certainty*, 1929

THE COMBINATION OF LONG AND SHORT OPTIONS PROVIDES AN endless array of opportunity and risk, and anyone using options to trade needs to be constantly aware of those risk levels. It is even possible that a strategy starting out as a low-risk one may evolve into a high-risk exposure. For this reason, any time you open short positions, you need to track them for as long as they are open.

In this chapter, comparisons are made between the use of short calls at the top of the swing and short puts at the bottom of the swing. This approach requires analysis of risks, timing, proximity of strikes to current value of the underlying, and awareness of risk and reward potential.

The two key elements defining risk and value—proximity and time—apply to all positions, but when your swing trading program consists solely of short calls and short puts, you also have to be aware of the following additional risks:

1. Ex-dividend and the risk of early exercise affect the timing of short calls, and the value of short puts can also be adversely affected. With both of these problems in mind, it makes

sense to avoid opening short-option swing trades of both calls and puts in the ex-dividend month.
2. The time element is different for short options than it is for long options. With long calls or puts, you are in the best possible position with ATM options expiring within less than one month because nonintrinsic premium is a minor element, and you can focus on intrinsic movement with little or no time decay or extrinsic value offset. But for short options, profits are limited to the premium value of the option, at best. As a result, you will realize the best profits with options expiring in one to two months, and the higher the nonintrinsic premium, the greater your profit potential (and the lower your risk). Even if the price of the underlying moves against you, it is possible that the premium value of the short option will rise because nonintrinsic decline may outpace intrinsic growth.
3. Moneyness is always an issue for swing trading. The ideal for swing trading with options is ATM status because a move in the desired direction creates profits most rapidly. That direction is going to be:
   - upward for long calls
   - downward for long puts
   - upward for short puts
   - downward for short calls

All of these elements affect the selection and timing of short options for swing trading. For many, the most persistent problem is the cost of an option. If you use long calls or puts, you need to create well-timed reversal-based strategies so that the intrinsic value will grow as quickly as possible, not only creating profitable change but exceeding the original option cost. Options traders in long-side positions struggle with time and cost continually. However, short-side traders benefit from the same issues that create problems for long-side traders. The more rapidly time decay occurs and, in fact, the higher the nonintrinsic premium at entry, the greater the advantage. So short-side swing traders accept higher risk of exercise, but in exchange their chances for generating profits are also greater.

It comes down to the offset between profits and risk, which is true for all trading. Short-option profits are limited to the premium itself, whereas long-option traders have potentially higher profits, all based on speed and extent of favorable price movement. On the other hand, short options generate a credit, and long options cost money to enter. Each trader must decide what combination and focus to use in swing trading. The decision to focus on short calls and short puts should be made with complete awareness of the risks involved as well as with a focus on how profits are generated.

Short Calls: Risks and Benefits

Uncovered short calls are considered one of the option positions with the highest risk. However, the level of risk is also affected by other questions. For example, what is the moneyness of the option? When does ex-dividend date occur? How long is it to expiration? And how much confidence do you have in the reversal signal and confirmation prompting entry?

The risk of an ITM call is clearly higher than that of an ATM call, and the farther OTM the position is moved, the lower the risk. In terms of moneyness, it is not reasonable to just assign an uncovered call the status of high risk. For example, an OTM short call can be closed or rolled if the underlying makes an unfavorable move toward the strike; the risk of exercise can be avoided by monitoring the position. However, the premium you received for an OTM call will be much lower than that for an ATM or ITM call. So in swing trading with uncovered calls, the decision of which call to choose may depend on weighing ITM and OTM positions.

Writing uncovered calls should be avoided when the ex-dividend date will arrive in the near future. This is the time period when early exercise is most likely. It does not always occur, even for ITM calls, but the risk is present, and it is easily evaded by avoiding that one month of the quarterly cycle. With awareness of ex-dividend timing you will be able to sidestep early exercise risk and the losses that could accompany it.

Timing for time to expiration is vastly different for short options. If you are long with a call, you expect to generate a short-term trend profit in three to five days, so selecting calls expiring in two weeks or less is rational. However, when you are short, you want higher nonintrinsic value, but you also want that nonintrinsic value to decline as rapidly as possible. So the best window for short calls is one to two months before expiration. Depending on how much nonintrinsic premium is available in the short call, you might be able to further narrow down the "ideal" time to between four and five weeks.

The uncovered call risk is further mitigated when you time your entry based on strong bearish reversal signals *and* equally strong confirmation. Even the best reversal and confirmation signals do not provide a 100% assurance about reversal, but they certainly improve your chances for good timing of entry. This reduces the overall risk because the odds of favorable reversal are improved when you time your decision based on observed reversal signals in traditional Western chart patterns (double top or bottom, head and shoulders, gapping price movement, failed tests of resistance and support), candlestick patterns (engulfing patterns, white soldiers and black crows, or piercing lines, for example), volume indicators and spikes, and momentum oscillators.

In comparison, a covered call is considered a low-risk strategy. With 100 shares available in the event the call is exercised, you remove the potential loss when exercise does occur in exchange for lost opportunity of owning the stock. Many proponents of uncovered calls point out that owning the stock actually increases market risk. This is true in the sense that a price decline below net basis (cost of the stock minus call premium received) creates a net paper loss. In addition, it is relatively easy to close out an uncovered call, but with a covered call, you might also need to sell stock, and that could mean taking a loss. There is no capital advantage to owning shares, given that margin collateral requirements for an uncovered call are the exercise value of that call. So you either need to have assets on deposit (for an uncovered call) or own shares at the equivalent value (for a covered call).

SHORT PUTS: RISKS AND BENEFITS

Though many features of the short put are similar to those of the short call, there are also many important differences. Writers of short calls and those writing short puts are both well-advised to avoid opening positions in the ex-dividend month. As a writer of short puts, you time entry for anticipated increases in the stock price. However, as soon as dividends are earned, you expect the underlying price to decline. This increases the value of the short put, which is the opposite of your goal of seeing that value fall. When you are holding the short put, you want its value to fall, and that only occurs when the underlying rises. So an increase in the put's value is not desirable.

The short put writer relies on the decline in the put's value due to both intrinsic loss (if applicable) and nonintrinsic decline. This decline occurs most rapidly during the last month, so timing of the short put is the same as that of the short call. The most likely timing for profits will be between four and five weeks before expiration.

The market risk is also quite different for short puts than for short calls. In theory, the risk of an uncovered short call is unlimited since the underlying price may rise indefinitely. (In practical terms, this unlimited risk is actually limited, but you cannot easily quantify how limited.) A short put, in comparison, is limited because the underlying price can only fall so far. This raises the point that a low-priced underlying is less risky than a higher-priced one; the maximum decline is fewer points. This is so because a lower-priced stock has fewer maximum points it can fall. A $20 stock can never decline more than $20. In comparison, an $80 stock could fall four times more to the same zero point. However, the premium for lower-priced underlyings will also be lower, so selecting a lower-priced underlying to limit market risk also limits profit potential. (This is offset when your focus is on percentage rather than dollar amounts of premium. For example, 400 shares and four options on a $20 stock are the same position as 100 shares and one option on an $80 stock, assuming the option value is the same percentage for both.)

The downside risk in short puts is not actually the underlying's going to zero as many traders assume. It is actually the tangible book value per share, adjusted by the premium received for selling the put. For example, if book value currently is $8 per share and you receive 1.50 for selling a put, your true floor is $9.50 per share. It is possible but unlikely for share value to fall below tangible book value per share.

Another analysis point is to compare uncovered puts to covered calls. The risk profile for each of these positions is identical. Some traders assume that the uncovered put is preferable because it is not necessary to buy 100 shares (as it is to create a covered call). However, the margin collateral requirement for uncovered puts is equal to the strike, so on the basis of capital demands there is no difference. The major difference is found in the greater flexibility of the short put.

When you open a covered call, a decline in price makes it possible to close the call at a net profit. However, the underlying price will also have declined. So if the current price is close to the basis price, it is possible to create a small profit in the covered call but to see it offset by a small loss in the underlying. A trader is not always able to write a new covered call without risking a capital loss upon exercise, so this leads to a wait-and-see position with depreciated stock in the portfolio.

You overcome this problem with the short put. You can close a declined put profitably no matter how the stock price has changed. This profit may result from the stock price rising, so that the short put loses value, and it can also come from an unchanged stock price when nonintrinsic value falls over time. Rolling a short put forward is also easier, considering that no stock ownership is involved. For example, if your short put has risen in value, you can close it at a loss and open a later-expiring put at breakeven or a credit. You can also afford to open a lower-strike short put to create a more desirable net credit; however, this may also involve taking higher risks since the new put may be deeper ITM. In theory, you can roll indefinitely, but in practice keeping short puts open over a lengthy period prolongs the exposure to market risk and ties up capital. This is contrary to the purpose of swing trading.

If you employ short puts in your swing trading strategy, it makes sense to require exceptionally strong reversal and confirmation, just as for short calls. The short put serves as the bullish reversal in the swing, and opening a position at the right moment leads to declining value in the position. As the underlying price rises, the short put loses value and can be closed profitably. However, timing is of critical importance, so you need to rely on strong reversal and confirmation signals, perhaps on much stronger ones than for any long option strategy.

Limited Profits in Exchange for Credit Entry

The major advantage of using short options is the credit they create. This cushion brings about profits more easily because time decay works for you rather than against you.

The major disadvantage is that profits are limited. The amount of premium is the maximum profit you can earn, and realistically, it's more likely that you will close the short position within a few days and take relatively limited profits. This is not a pure disadvantage, however. You are likely to do the same thing with long options and take profit when they are available. Swing trades are opened and closed when reversal signals appear and are confirmed and not always just on the basis of profit or loss.

Even so, with short options you are going to acquire profits even without movement in the underlying. As time decay sets in, the nonintrinsic premium will drop, especially time value (extrinsic value, or implied volatility, is going to change as well, but not just due to the passage of time). So if the underlying price remains within a point or two of the option's strike, that option will become profitable as expiration approaches. As a short seller, you are not going to be willing to wait several weeks for this to occur and will prefer to take profits very quickly.

Short options are more likely to become profitable, but their risks are also greater. There is a trade-off between these two attributes. You reduce risk by avoiding the ex-dividend month, relying on exceptionally strong reversal and confirmation, and focusing on ATM calls and puts rather than on the rich but risky ITM or on safe but low-priced OTM alternatives.

EXAMPLE # 1: CHART-BASED REVERSAL SIGNALS

The first chart used to demonstrate a short-option strategy is the three-month chart of General Electric (GE), shown in figure 15.1.

The first noteworthy event on this chart is the ex-dividend date of September 20. In a wise short-option swing trade, you would want to have all positions closed prior to this date to avoid the risk of early exercise associated with events surrounding this quarterly period.

After the ex-dividend date, many good swing trading signals appeared. First was a bearish doji star, confirmed by the overbought condition in the RSI momentum indicator. This signal preceded a three-day downtrend. That trend ended with a morning star, a bullish three-day indicator.

Six more sessions passed before the next bearish signal, an engulfing pattern. The engulfing pattern is one of the strongest signals, leading to reversal 80% of the time. It was further confirmed by RIS remaining above the overbought line. Even so, price paused in uncertainty for the next five sessions. Then a bearish harami cross appeared and was confirmed by volume spikes. This was followed by a very strong downtrend complete with downside price gaps.

Although price paused and appeared ready to move upward once again, the bearish piercing lines signaled that the downtrend was about to resume. It continued downward strongly, finally ending with the appearance of a bullish inverted hammer. The subsequent uptrend was confirmed with a bullish neck line, a continuation pattern.

All open option positions should have been closed some time during the last week on the chart. Prices had risen nicely and no clear reversal was found; however, the next ex-dividend date arrived on December 20, so a prudent measure would have been to close down any short positions well in advance of that date.

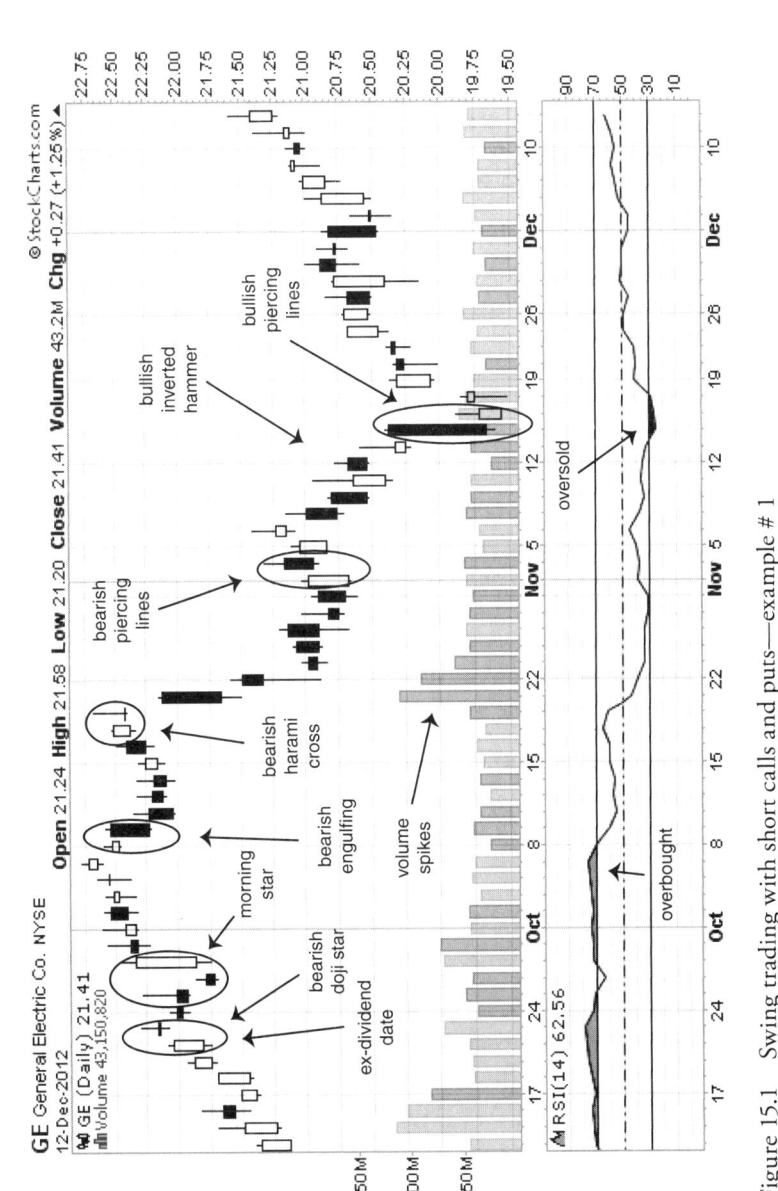

Figure 15.1 Swing trading with short calls and puts—example # 1
Source: StockCharts.com.

This chart shows many strong reversal signals and good opportunities for swing trading. You may also mix in long positions with the indicated entry and exit of short positions, especially if you are concerned about signals that may not be as strong as you wish or when the ex-dividend date is approaching.

Example # 2: Chart-Based Reversal Signals

The next example in figure 15.2 is the chart of American Express (AXP). Like the GE chart, this one begins with the ex-dividend date, so prior to this all short-option positions should have been closed.

Right after the ex-dividend date, a short uptrend was marked by the bullish harami. This is not an especially strong signal and leads to uptrend reversal only 50% of the time, and since it came right after the ex-dividend date, it was also dubious. The very long upper shadow on the ex-dividend date further confused the bullish possibilities.

The weak bullish signals might have led swing traders to not act on this signal. However, only three days later, a bearish engulfing pattern appeared, and this pattern leads to reversal 80% of the time. Even so, the price moved sideways for another week before finally starting a serious downtrend. This trend paused but was confirmed with continuation in the form of a bearish piercing lines pattern.

Thus far on the chart, the swing trading signals were fairly weak. A swing trader would tend to rely on time decay to create profits, but the chart does not display any strong signals until the bottom of the downtrend. Here a three inside up pattern provided very strong bullish signals. A few sessions later, the bearish reversal ended the uptrend in the form of a doji star, another three-session indicator.

The last signal on the chart is the bullish engulfing pattern, which like its bearish counterpart, reliably predicts an uptrend 80% of the time. Traders would want to close out all short options by the end of the charted period since the December ex-dividend date was due to arrive within a week. This chart provides many

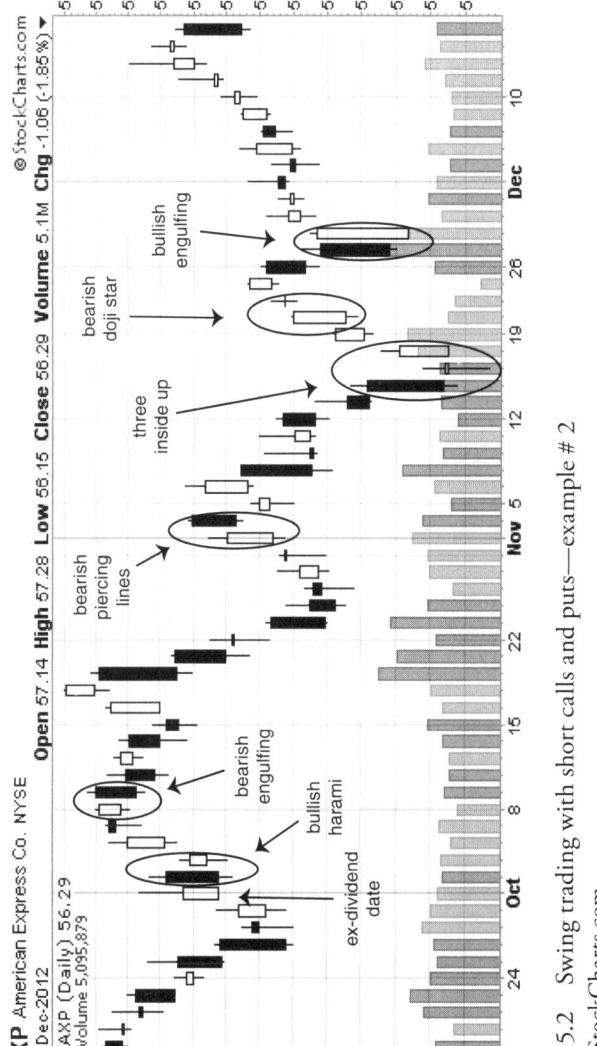

Figure 15.2 Swing trading with short calls and puts—example # 2
Source: StockCharts.com.

unconfirmed indicators and not always very strong ones either. It is a good example of a chart that is not easy to read.

Example # 3: Chart-Based Reversal Signals

The final example of a chart for short calls and puts is the chart for Johnson & Johnson (JNJ), shown in figure 15.3.

The first two signals were very reliable, even without confirmation. The bullish engulfing pattern preceded a brief uptrend, and this reversed with the bearish engulfing pattern. Both of these are very strong reversal signals, reliable about 80% of the time.

The downtrend was characterized by a large downside gap and a double bottom. These strong traditional technical signals also marked the turning point and an exceptionally strong uptrend that moved price 4.5 points or about 15% in only four sessions.

The top of the uptrend was marked by a bearish harami marked by consecutive long white candlesticks. The gapping price action in the uptrend indicated possible fast loss of momentum, and the harami by itself is reliable only 50% of the time. However, it was confirmed not only by the fast rise in the price of the underlying, but also by volume spikes at the uptrend's top. At the same time, RSI moved into overbought conditions, but this signal is questionable even as confirmation of the bearish reversal. Given the fast rise in the underlying price, this RSI move probably reflects the recent price averages rather than being a clear momentum signal.

After the reversal, price paused and moved sideways for a week. Then a new bearish engulfing pattern appeared, a strong signal that the downtrend would resume. By mid-November, it was time to close all open short positions since the ex-dividend date was about to occur. Once this date passed, a new bullish engulfing signal marked the continuation of the uptrend. As it turned out, the underlying price declined less than half a point after the ex-dividend date. This very small ex-dividend effect reveals strength in the price and favors the bullish trend.

* * *

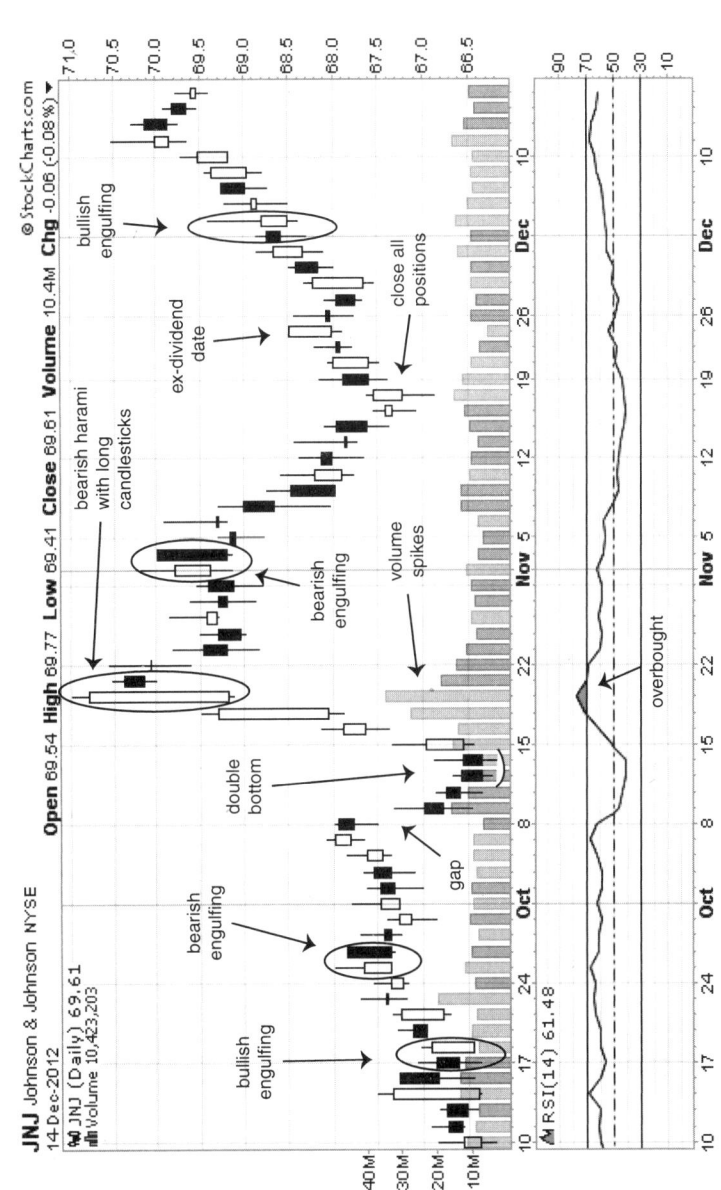

Figure 15.3 Swing trading with short calls and puts—example #3
Source: StockCharts.com.

Short options allow you to enter swing trades with a net credit. Properly timed, you can take advantage of rapid time decay, often creating profits even when the underlying price does not move very much at all. However, short options are risky and demand collateral in the form of equity or cash equal to the strike. They are expensive forms of swing trading equal to using shares of stock, but with stock you are likely to accumulate some losses that could have been avoided with short options.

Both short calls and short puts have their positive attributes, but both should be closed before ex-dividend date. Short calls expose you to early exercise risk, and short puts will increase in value if the stock price falls around the time of the ex-dividend, resulting in a loss (since you want the short put's value to fall). With a short put open, you benefit from an increase in the underlying price. The higher the underlying price moves, the more the short put declines in value and the higher your profits.

Profits are limited to the premium you receive, so short options have a disadvantage over the theoretically unlimited profit potential of long options. However, many swing traders prefer net credit received for selling options over net debits you have to pay for long options.

The next chapter explains how long and short positions are combined in a different way to create low-cost, no-cost, or net credit positions in which both a call and a put are opened at the same time. The synthetic stock strategy will require margin collateral equal to the value of the short option, but the synthetic position mirrors price movement in the underlying. In this respect, synthetic stock is an intriguing swing trading strategy that combines long and short at both sides of the swing.

CHAPTER 16

STRATEGY # 7: SYNTHETIC OPTION POSITIONS STRATEGY

> There are strange flowers of reason to match each error of the senses.
>
> Louis Aragon, *Paris Peasant*, 1926

SWING TRADING WITH STRAIGHTFORWARD LONG OR SHORT OPTIONS presents many opportunities as well as risks. One variation that solves the collateral problem and yet allows you to enter positions with effective and low-risk leverage is the *synthetic stock* position.

This position consists of opening one long and one short position at the same strike and on the same expiration. A synthetic long-stock position is a combination of a long call and a short put. If the underlying price rises, the overall net synthetic position will also rise, mirroring the movement in the underlying point for point. This occurs because the long call is paid for by the short put, especially when the positions were opened at the money, and as the stock price rises, the short put loses value and the long call moves ITM.

Synthetic long stock is not a high-risk strategy since a short put has the same risk profile as a covered call. It can be managed in the event the underlying price declines by closing, covering, or rolling. It can also be closed at breakeven or a profit, converting the synthetic to a long call. The net cost of the long call would be the original premium paid minus any profit generated by transacting the short put, and this means that the remaining open call is discounted from what it would have cost originally to just open the long call by itself.

A synthetic short stock is the opposite. It consists of one long put and one short call. The short-call income pays the cost of the long put. As long as the underlying price declines, the short call loses value and the long put tracks price intrinsically, point for point.

Unlike its long stock cousin, the synthetic short stock potentially carries very high risk due to the short call. If it is uncovered, the risk is significant if the underlying price moves up instead of down, as you hope. Awareness of this risk may lead some traders to avoid synthetic short stock, but the risk can be eliminated by also owning 100 shares of the underlying stock. This coverts the synthetic short-stock position into a modified collar. Even though the strikes of both options are normally the same (and with a collar two strikes are used), the result is the same: a combination of long stock, a covered call, and a long put. This provides a cost-free form of downside protection in the insurance put. However, one remaining risk is that of exercise. As long as call exercise will generate a net capital gain, this may be viewed as an acceptable risk.

As a swing trade, both synthetic long and short offer clear advantages over long-only or short-only strategies. The synthetic option is not likely to be kept open up to expiration but will more likely be subjected to the same swing trading decisions as other strategies. That is, short positions that become profitable are closed at a profit and may be replaced with different strikes or with later-expiring short options. Synthetics allow you to generate profits in legs, and as long as you keep track of the overall net credit or debit, an original position can be expanded and modified indefinitely. This allows you to get the best of both worlds and take swing trading profits as they materialize on either side of the trade while opening positions at close to zero cost.

THE COLLATERAL ISSUE

A synthetic stock position requires margin collateral but only a relatively smaller amount that is necessary for uncovered short options. The synthetic long-stock collateral requirement is 10%

of the short-put strike value. The requirement on the long side is 20% of the call's strike value plus premium received and minus any credit generated.

For example, you open a synthetic long-stock position at a 50 strike. You get a net credit of $125, and the call premium is $600. The margin requirement is:

20% of strike of 50 = $500
Less: credit earned = $125
Plus: premium for short call = $600
Net collateral requirement = $975

This is much less than the equivalent margin for borrowing against a stock purchase, in which you accrue a debt of $2,500 (50%) and have to pay interest on it. If you want to compare the margin requirement to the cash purchase of stock without using margin, the synthetic long stock costs $975 versus the stock cost of $5,000. The synthetic costs less than 20% of the cash purchase price of the stock—this is excellent leverage.

THE LEVERAGE GAINED WITH SYNTHETICS

The great swing trading advantage to synthetics is leverage. The fact that the long position is paid for by premium from the short positions sets you up with control over 100 shares of stock at zero cost—and for very small margin requirements. This makes synthetics one of the most attractive of all options-based swing trading strategies.

As in all options trades, risk awareness has to be at the top of your list when picking a strategy, and you should only proceed with complete knowledge about the risks, especially for the short side of the synthetic position. But is that risk really so severe? The short put is equivalent to a covered call in terms of risk, and even that risk is smaller than that of stock ownership. Owning stock carries a downside risk as far as the price falls. (Realistically, the true risk is equal to the tangible book value per share plus premium earned for selling the put.)

The short synthetic risk is much greater. The short call is an exercise risk of considerable weight if uncovered. This is managed by ownership of stock, avoidance of ex-dividend month, and close monitoring to roll forward if necessary as a risk-avoidance strategy. As with all swing trading strategies, you also need to rely on exceptionally strong reversal signals and confirmation.

Leverage is a difficult balance to maintain, however. For example, if the long side of your synthetic stock position becomes profitable and you close it, you should also close the short side. If you leave the short side open—perhaps hoping for more time decay and profits—you will also have to post more collateral on margin. Once you have only a short uncovered option left, your collateral has to match the strike price.

The leverage rule should therefore be that both sides are left open until both can be closed profitably. This depends on the underlying price moving in the direction desired or no movement at all but rapid time decay for the short side. As long as the time decay of the short side exceeds that of the long side, a small profit is possible. However, because both options are at the same strike and expiration, time decay is likely to be close on both sides. A solution may be to close the short side at a profit and hope the long side also turns profitable before expiration. If it does not, then the short side can be replaced with another short option—the synthetic position can be modified in many ways to take profits on time decay shorts while offsetting the net cost of the long option with another short—same expiration and different strike, later expiration and same strike, or even short puts or calls offsetting either long puts or calls. The flexibility in how these changes can be offset makes synthetic positions very appealing.

Synthetic Long Stock

A synthetic long-stock position—a long call and a short put, both with the same expiration—is ideally opened when the underlying is ATM or within 10 to 15 cents of it. Otherwise, the relationship will be potentially distorted by one side being ITM and the other OTM. If you pick your reversals carefully and then confirm them, the leveraged advantage of the synthetic long stock opened ATM is significant.

The synthetic long-stock strategy combines unlimited profits (on the long side) with limited losses (on the short side). The potential maximum loss is limited because an underlying price cannot fall indefinitely. Its true floor is the tangible book value per share, adjusted by the put premium paid. For example, if the underlying price is $30 per share and you sell a put for 3 ($300) and the tangible book value per share is $14, your floor, or maximum loss, is $13 per share or $1,300 per 100 shares:

Current price per share $30
Less: tangible book value per share - 14
    Net risk $16
Less: premium received from short put 3
    Adjusted maximum risk $13

On the other side, the long call could in theory rise to an indefinite price based on how high the underlying price moves. Once the long call is ITM, intrinsic value matches the underlying point for point. As expiration nears, nonintrinsic offsets diminish, and intrinsic value then represents most of the overall value. Of course, the risk assessment involves several additional elements, in particular, timing with ex-dividend date in mind and the importance of strong reversal signals and confirmation.

For example, if you open a synthetic long-stock position on Merck (MRK) based on strong bullish signals on the chart and equally strong confirmation, and the ex-dividend date will not again occur until March 2013, you have no reason for concern on this point. The chart for MRK is shown in figure 16.1.

The prior support at approximately $44.80 flipped to the new resistance level, at least for the moment. This level was not established long enough as of this chart's date of December 18, 2012. However, in November the price dipped far below prior support and then came back, stopping at the prior support level.

This normally might indicate that the new resistance level would hold. But a very unusual candlestick signal appeared in the

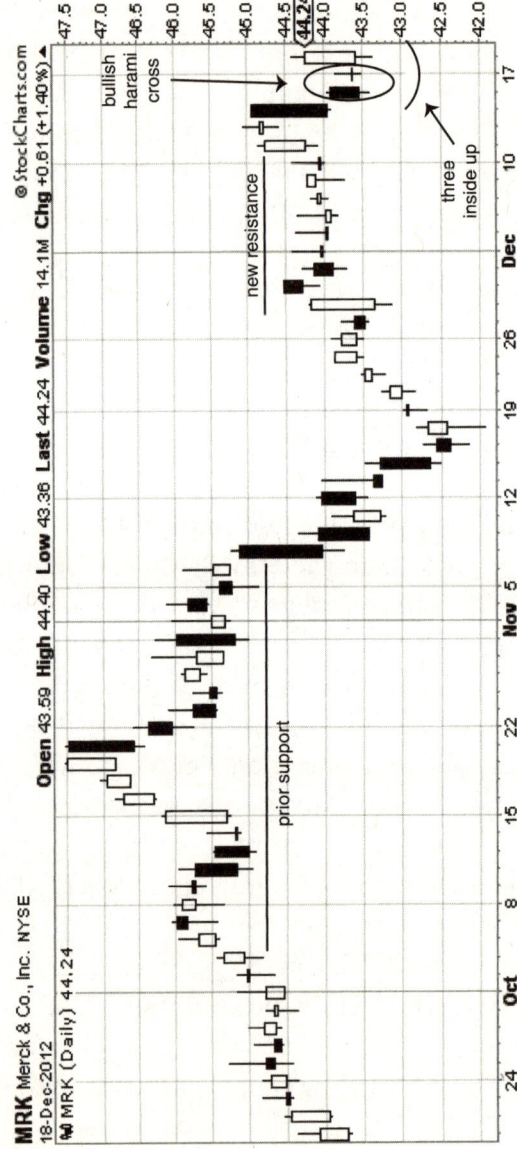

Figure 16.1 Swing trading with synthetic long stock
Source: StockCharts.com.

form of a bullish harami cross. This is strongly bullish, but it is even more so when the same two sessions are extended to the last session on the chart. Now the last three formed a three inside up pattern, a three-session bullish signal.

With these three signals, testing resistance, and the two candlestick signals, the signs overall appear very bullish. With that in mind, the following synthetic long stock could have been opened at this point when the stock was at exactly $44 per share (and synthetics do not have to be limited to single contracts as in the example but can also involve several contracts):

Buy 1 JAN call @ 0.87
Sell 1 JAN put @ 0.86
   Net credit before trading costs: 0.01

How will this synthetic long-stock position change in value compared to 100 shares of stock? If timing is correct and an upward movement follows, the long call will appreciate point for point with the stock, and the short put will become worthless or can be closed at a profit, as shown in table 16.1.

At expiration, the net of option trades would have mirrored movement in the underlying stock exactly (the $1 offset reflects the net difference in the original opening of the options).

Table 16.1   Merck: Example of a synthetic position compared to underlying price movement

Price	long call	short put	net options	100 shares of stock
$40	$−87	$−314	$−401	$−400
41	−87	−214	−301	−300
42	−87	−114	−201	−200
43	−87	−14	−101	−100
44	−87	86	−1	0
45	13	86	99	100
46	113	86	199	200
47	213	86	299	300
48	313	86	399	400

Source: Quotations listed on Charles Schwab & Co., at www.schwab.com.

Synthetic Short Stock

The synthetic long stock's risk is restricted to the limited risk of the short put. This is easily managed compared to the risk of a short call in the synthetic short stock position.

Synthetic short stock is the combination of a long put and a short call, both opened at the same strike and expiration. The short-call risk can be mitigated if you also own 100 shares of stock but just reviewing the synthetics without stock, the short-call risk should not be overlooked. So the two alternatives—synthetic short stock based on uncovered short calls and ownership of 100 shares combined with synthetic short stock based on covered calls —are vastly different strategies with very different risk profiles.

The strength of reversal signals is the key to improving entry and exit for all swing trades, and synthetic short stock is no exception. For example, the chart of Facebook, shown in figure 16.2, is interesting as a candidate for this strategy.

The evening star appearing toward the end of the chart is a very strong bullish indicator. It is bolstered by the overbought condition of RSI shown at the bottom of the chart. Not only did RSI move into this range as the uptrend evolved, it remained at or near the 70 index value even while price leveled out. This demonstrates lost momentum among buyers. It also reveals that the price will not be able to break much higher than its current point of $27.71.

Considering developments over the previous three months, the most recent uptrend moving from a low of under $19 per share to nearly $28, a move of 47% from the low, makes any further upside movement doubtful. The general trading range appears to properly reside between $19 and $24 per share. With this in mind, a synthetic short-stock swing trading strategy makes sense. The following positions involving weekly options could have been opened on December 19, 2001, at a point when Facebook's share value was $27.91. The company pays no dividend, so the threat of ex-dividend early exercise does not exist:

Buy 1 DEC 28 put @ 0.80
Sell 1 DEC 28 call @ 0.80
Net before trading costs: 0.00

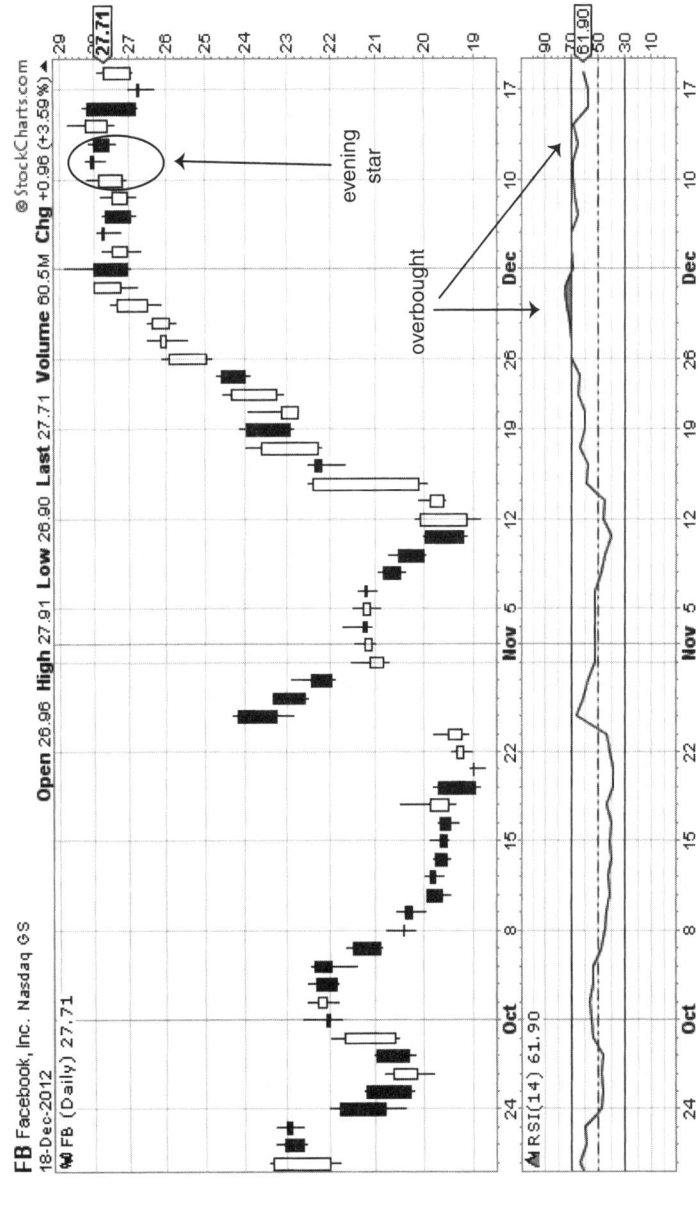

Figure 16.2 Swing trading with synthetic short stock
Source: StockCharts.com.

Table 16.2   Facebook: Example of a synthetic position compared to underlying price movement

Price	long put	short call	net options	100 shares of stock
$24	$320	$80	$ 400	$−381
25	220	80	300	−281
26	120	80	200	−181
27	20	80	100	−81
28	−80	80	0	09
29	−80	−20	−100	109
30	−80	−120	−200	209
31	−80	−220	−300	309
32	−80	−320	−400	409

Source: Quotations listed on Charles Schwab & Co., at www.schwab.com.

How will this synthetic long-stock position change in value compared to 100 shares of stock? If timing is correct and a downward movement follows, the long put will appreciate point for point as the stock declines, and the short call will become worthless or can be closed at a profit as shown in table 16.2.

This synthetic short-stock position tracks the stock just like the long version did, with the exception that the options increase in value as the stock declines, and they decrease in net value as the stock price rises. The intrinsic value of the long put will equal stock profit at expiration (adjusted by 0.09 for the difference between stock price and option strike). However, if the stock rises, the short call creates losses equal to the stock gains (also adjusted by 0.09).

THE RISK ELEMENTS OF SYNTHETICS

Studying stock charts of companies with ATM options priced closer together makes the point that synthetic long and short stocks work as leveraged forms of swing trades. However, the theoretical unlimited profits of these are invariably offset by losses that are, in theory, equally unlimited.

These potential losses can be controlled, mitigated, and avoided in several ways. With short options, time works for you, and time decay helps maintain ATM or OTM option declines favorable to the swing trade. Time decay works equally well on short calls and short puts, so whether the underlying price moves in your favor or not, this is a great advantage.

The risk to be aware of most in synthetic stock trades is that of exercise on the short side. If the underlying stock price moves up (when you have opened short calls) or down (with your short puts), exercise risk and potential loss grow with every ITM point. Offsetting strategies include closing to take small profits or small losses, rolling forward, and covering. The strategy of closing may prove to be advantageous when both sides are closed at the same time. It often occurs in synthetic positions that a loss on one side is offset by a profit on the other, which enables you to control losses rather than waiting them out.

A second risk is easily avoided, and that is the risk of early exercise around the time of ex-dividend date. Avoid this month for synthetic positions, as both short calls and short puts are at greater risk during this period. Short calls may move in the money and get early exercise, and short puts may increase in value while you are hoping for a decline. By avoiding the ex-dividend month or by opening synthetics on stock positions that don't pay dividends (such Facebook used as an example in this chapter), you eliminate this risk of early exercise.

The third form of risk is the well-known market risk of the underlying stock. Ultimately, you open a long synthetic stock position as an alternative to buying stock because you expect the price to rise. The risk is that the price will decline. In that case, either ownership of stock or opening of a synthetic long-stock position will suffer the same loss. The same is true for synthetic short stock, with one exception. You expect the price to decline, in which case the long put increases in value. A long put matches every point of decline in the underlying by one point in increase of the put. This is preferable to shorting stock, which is expensive and carries higher risk. You can close and take losses on synthetics with partial offset by closing both options; you can also roll losing short positions forward to avoid exercise. But if you short stock, you have to pay interest on the stock, and you cannot just roll out of the loss position if the stock price rises. In this respect, synthetic short stock makes more sense than shorting stock. On a point basis, however, the comparison of market risk between shorted stock and synthetic short stock is the same. The synthetic is cheaper to enter and exit and easier to control.

Recognizing strong reversal signals is the key to swing trading success. Synthetics are no exception. You want to time entry of a long synthetic at the bottom of a downtrend and upon recognizing reversal signals plus confirmation, and you want to enter a synthetic short at the top of an uptrend also based on clear reversal signals and confirmation.

The examples in this chapter met these tests. The Merck chart concluded with a very strong double candlestick bullish signal as well as indication that price could easily move above the newly established resistance price. The Facebook chart betrayed a suspiciously rapid price increase to the point of lost buyer momentum (seen in the leveling out of price as well as the RSI overbought condition). The bearish evening star appeared right at the point where price began moving sideways, making it most likely that the next move would be downward.

If you decide to pursue synthetic long or short stock as a swing trading strategy, another test you need to apply is that of risk versus cost. Long options by themselves require you to take the risk equal to the cost of the option, and short options by themselves involve specific but manageable risks. These are manageable through moneyness selection, time to expiration, and your ability to roll or close. Time decay vastly diminishes the exercise risk during the last month or so before expiration. Compared to the use of single long or short options, synthetic risk is not at all the same. This unlimited risk can be mitigated through cover (especially of short calls), rolling forward, or early closing of positions moving into risk (that is, moving toward the money or even moving ITM).

Synthetic stock strategies add an interesting dimension to swing trading. Taking the creative variations even further, you may discover that a number of advanced combinations based on options are good candidates for swing trading. The next chapter examines a few of combinations, analyzing the swing trading potential of weighting one side of the swing more than the other (when you believe a prevailing bullish or bearish sentiment dominates), swings on retracements, recognition of the retracement move as part of the swing trade strategy, and the use of ratio calendar spreads to expand the swing trade's duration and profit potential while managing and mitigating risks.

CHAPTER 17

STRATEGY # 8: MULTIPLE CONTRACTS AND WEIGHTING WITH RATIO CALENDAR SPREADS

> Every society honors its live conformists and its dead troublemakers.
>
> Mignon McLaughlin, *The Neurotic's Notebook*, 1963

THE MANY VARIATIONS OF SWING TRADING WITH OPTIONS HAVE mainly involved one type of option and equal balance: long or short, put or call, and the same number of contracts in both bullish and bearish conditions. This chapter examines a variation of this approach.

Even though options trading may take advantage of both bullish and bearish markets, the reality is that one side often dominates. As a result, a particular underlying security may be predominantly bullish even as it goes through interim bearish swings and vice versa. With this in mind, once you recognize an overall tendency favoring one direction, it also makes sense to expand and fine-tune your swing trading strategy so that it also emphasizes this directional bias.

This is accomplished by using multiple options, weighting positions on one side or the other, recognizing and taking advantage of retracements, and using advanced strategies such as ratio calendar spreads.

SWING TRADING WITH MULTIPLE OPTIONS: A MATTER OF FLEXIBILITY

Previous examples have been based on using single options in the swing. This makes the arguments clearer but certainly does not limit how you can construct your own swing trades. You can open as many contracts as you wish and are limited only by your risk tolerance and by being able to meet collateral requirements.

When you use multiple options, you add to the flexibility of your swing. Some possible secondary strategies to remember in support of using multiple options:

1. You can experience a level of profits adequate to close only a portion of the overall position, leaving remaining contracts open. If the profitable trend continues, these remaining contracts increase overall profitability. If the direction does not continue, profits were locked in with partial closure, and remaining contracts can be closed at any time. This flexibility fixes a degree of profits, freeing up the outcome for the remaining options.
2. If profits have not accrued in the position, some of the contracts can be rolled forward, especially for short positions and others left in place. For long-side contracts, greater numbers enable you to offset losses by replacement with later-expiring short options. In this way, rather than accepting losses on long trades, you absorb those losses with profits gained with short contracts. However, this recovery method also involves undertaking additional risks as well as increased collateral requirements. However, considering that short puts have the same risk profile as covered calls, the true market risk, while higher than that of long options, may be acceptable to create swing trading profits while managing that risk.
3. You may decide to employ more than one strike. In either long or short positions, spreading contracts among two or

more strikes spreads risks while adding to potential profitability. This is especially true for underlying securities whose options are available in $1 increments.

MULTIPLE OPTION RISKS

The risks of using multiple options are the same as those with single options, but the dollar amount of risk is greater, just as the profit potential is greater. Because of this, any use of multiple options may be structured with hedged positions to mitigate the higher dollar value at risk. But beyond this market risk, additional forms of risk also need to be considered.

Collateral risk refers to the higher amount of collateral required to be on deposit. This is especially significant for uncovered short options. Collateral requirements are equal to the strike value of the option, so opening a short 50 strike options requires that you have $5,000 (minus premium received) on deposit. If you open 10 contracts, you must have $50,000 on hand.

Long-option risks are widely understood as a struggle between time and value. This is further complicated by proximity. OTM options are cheaper but present difficulty in becoming profitable before expiration. ITM options are expensive but more likely to be profitable as long as the underlying moves in the desired direction. With swing trading, focusing on ATM options expiring in the near future (one to two weeks, for example) provides the most likely scenario for fast and considerable profits. This potential profit is even greater when the premium level is quite small.

For example, an ATM option expiring in one week might cost less than 1.00 ($100). If your reversal signals are strong and confirmation is also strong, buying multiple contracts may create very fast profits. A 0.50 option can be bought for $50 each or five options for $250. A ½ point move ITM at this point in the cycle (when non-intrinsic value is minimal) may create a very fast profit of between 50% and 100% in a matter of only a few days. This might be the most advantageous timing for multiple contracts. The market risk is low ($250), proximity is well established for a profitable move, and little nonintrinsic value remains.

The chart of Kellogg (K) in figure 17.1 reveals numerous important signals leading to strong reversal signal and confirmation. The chart set up a strong uptrend with a bullish continuation pattern, the ascending triangle. This continued into channel lines, a pattern in which the breadth of trading remains the same but the range moves—in this instance, upward.

As the channel lines moved toward conclusion, RSI advanced into overbought territory. This initial advance by itself was not significant since it may have reflected the averages of steadily rising prices. However, as prices then began moving sideways, RSI remained in overbought condition and actually advanced up to around the 80 level, far above the 70 line marking overbought conditions.

At the same point, two bearish signals appeared: a piercing lines and a bearish engulfing pattern. At this time, the JAN 55 puts (slightly OTM), which were to expire in approximately one month, were priced at only 0.30 each. At this price, as detailed in this book's epilogue, a purchase of five contracts at a cost of $150 turned profitable very quickly. They were closed on December 22 at 0.45, a profit of 50% in only four days.

This example shows that options with one month or less until expiration often are priced very low even when close to the money. The Kellogg puts appreciated even with very little price movement. That movement occurred due to numerous signals and confirmation. The two bearish candlesticks provided a strong initial forecast of reversal. The leveling out of price after an extended uptrend indicated falling momentum. Finally, RSI moving above 70 and remaining there (even extending up to 80) made a convincing case to buy these puts.

Short-option risks are quite different from long-option risks, but a time window of only a few weeks until expiration is the most likely point at which to sell ATM options—assuming the required collateral is on hand. At this point in the cycle, time decay will be at its fastest rate. This means that ATM options expiring in only a few weeks have a very slight chance of appreciating. For example, if there are three points of nonintrinsic value in an ATM option, a three-point move in the *wrong* direction will be a wash.

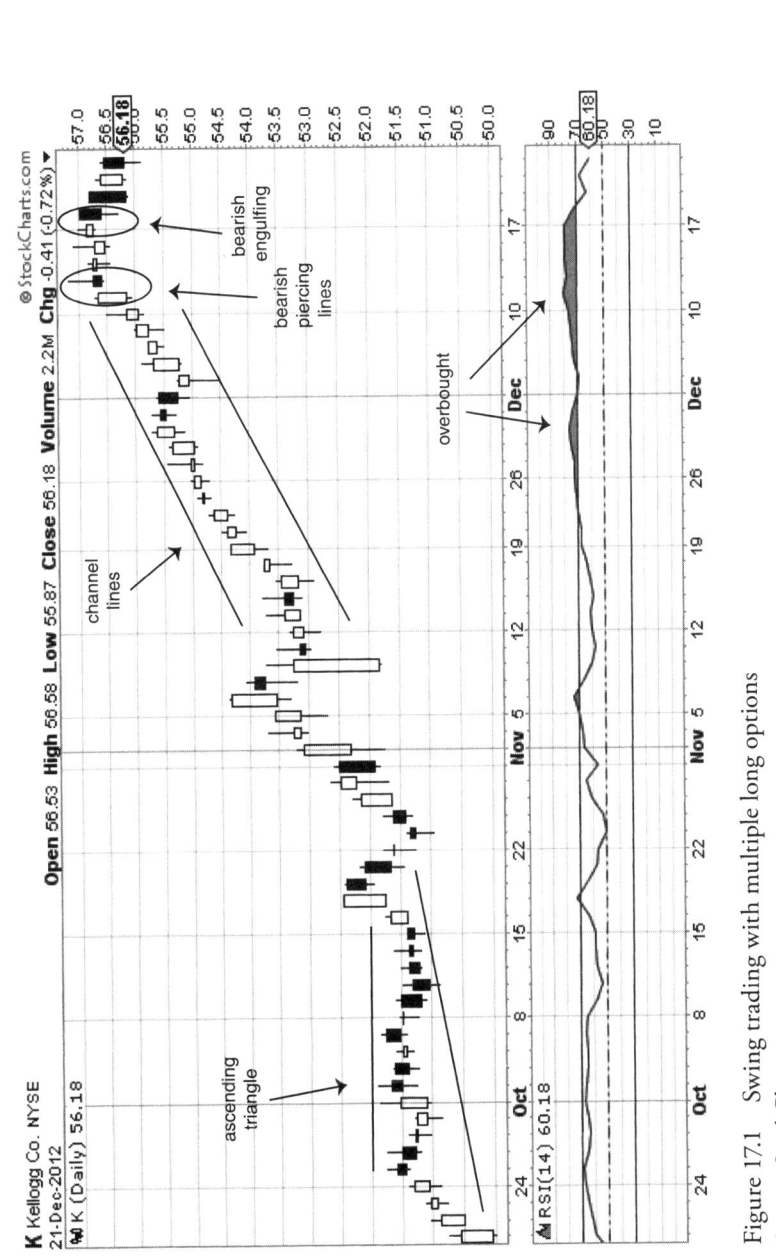

Figure 17.1 Swing trading with multiple long options
Source: StockCharts.com.

The option's value will not change. The nonintrinsic premium is simply converted into intrinsic premium, and the position can be closed before expiration.

Short-option risks are mitigated when, during these last few weeks of the option's life cycle, you are able to identify very strong reversal and confirmation. In that case, multiple contracts increase profits even when the holding period is short. An ATM option that moves OTM after you sell to open is going to lose value. This is a reflection of change in volatility that favors your short position and of time decay. The option price is not going to decline point for point, but in the marginal swing trading universe, a few points of reduced value in a short position translate to high-percentage profits. The dollar value might not justify a marginal profit with a single short contract, but with multiple contracts, trading costs are cheaper on a per-option basis, and net profits after transaction cost are more achievable.

For example, the chart of Chevron (CVX) show in figure 17.2 includes numerous bearish signals in a one-month period located midway on the three-month chart. The company's ex-dividend date occurred at the very end of that period, which marked the timing for exit from any short options.

The pattern was interesting because it was signaled early by a two-point downward gap. The usual rationale after this would be that prices should turn and move upward to fill that gap. Instead, a bearish harami cross appeared in the third month of October. This particular signal is not the most reliable bear indicator; in fact, about half the time it turns out to be a bullish continuation signal. Without further confirmation, this signal is not enough to take up a position in multiple contracts.

After a strong downward-moving three sessions, three very strong bearish signals emerged. First, there was a bearish engulfing pattern, which is reliable as a downward indicator about 80% of the time. Next, there were two continuation signals, the thrusting lines and then separating lines. Although the configuration of these two signals is opposite (black session followed by white and then white followed by black), both predict the same continued downward move.

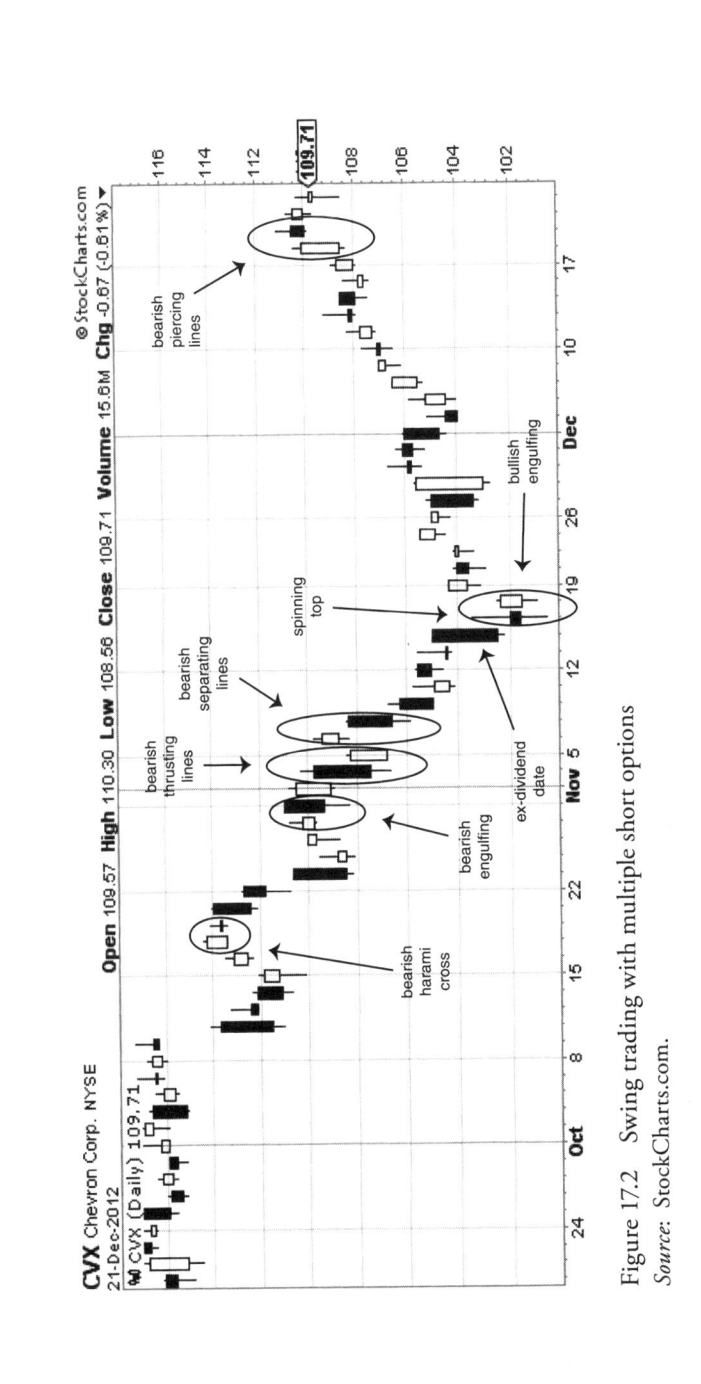

Figure 17.2 Swing trading with multiple short options
Source: StockCharts.com.

Price did continue to slide; however, at some point within the two to three days after these signals, any open short positions should have been closed. If reaction to the downward indicators had been to buy puts, those contracts should be kept open as the downtrend continued to move. Ex-dividend date appeared five sessions after the last bearish continuation pattern.

Immediately after ex-dividend date, an exceptionally strong reversal signal and confirmation appeared. The single-session spinning top—a relatively small real body with extended upper and lower shadows—appeared. This is a signal whose meaning depends on where it is found. In this case, it shows up at the bottom of an extended downtrend. Even so, it could act as a continuation signal. However, that same session formed up as a bullish engulfing pattern when combined with the session that followed. This is an 80% reliable signal for reversal, and it also confirmed the likely significance of the spinning top.

At this point, a swing trader who had closed multiple short calls only a few days earlier would want to open multiple long calls or short puts. In a short-contract strategy, the strength of this reversal and confirmation was enough to justify a short put entry. The CVX chart provided one of the clearest examples of strong signal and reversal, first on the continuation of a downtrend and then on reversal and confirmation of an uptrend.

WEIGHTING METHODS

The weighting of one side of a swing over the other should rely on your perception of the underlying's long-term trend direction. An analysis of every chart in this book reveals the nature of the trend history. Some stocks cycle back and forth and are difficult to predict beyond the immediate swing signals— and for short-term timing of entry and exit these charts are excellent as swing trading candidates. However, many other charts display a tendency toward either a strong upward growth or a strong downward slide.

When short-term trends appear, they tend to favor movement toward that longer-term trend. An uptrending stock is likely to have bigger upside moves than downside moves, and those trends may also last longer. The same is true on the downside.

When you conclude that the longer-term trend clearly favors one direction over the other, you can weight one side of the swing to take advantage of that tendency. For upside trends, at the bottom of swings, you would want more long calls expiring within less than one month or short puts expiring in one to two months. You can also weight one side by opening positions in both long calls and short puts. In this bullish synthetic position, the short puts pay for the long calls, and the risks of the short side are managed by favoring ATM or slightly OTM contracts and by being ready to close or roll if the price moves down instead of up.

The same approach can be used for stocks you believe favor a long-term downward move. At the top of upswings, upon locating bearish reversal signals and confirmation, a weighted entry can consist of short calls or long puts in larger numbers than on the opposite, bullish side. You may also combine both. This bearish synthetic stock strategy consists of short calls paying for long puts, so your overall entry cost will be close to zero. When the underlying price moves favorably, the short calls lose value and can be closed profitably or allowed to expire worthless, and the long puts gain value and can be closed at a profit.

Weighting one side over the other increases risk exposure, and this strategy should be used only in those situations where you have studied the trend and believe that it will continue. You also need to make sure you appreciate the level of added risk that comes with a weighted strategy.

Risk Analysis of Weighting Swings

All swing trading with options has to involve a risk analysis. In the case of a weighting swing strategy, it would be quite easy to take more risk than you intend. Swing trading, like any technical approach to trading options, requires appreciation of the dangers in making trades. No indicators, even strongly confirmed ones, provide you with 100% guarantee of price direction. If you can accomplish a 60% to 70% track record of well-timed entry and exit, you can strongly increase your profits with one-side weighting strategies. But you have to be willing to assume the added levels of risk.

These risks are mitigated, however, in several ways:

1. *Contrarian thinking has to prevail.* A contrarian is not just a trader who acts against the majority, but one who uses rational analysis and logic when most traders are reacting emotionally (greed and panic being the dominant emotions of the market). The contrarian recognizes that emotion-based decisions are ill-timed in most cases. Consequently, bullish decisions are made closest to the top of a price swing or spike and bearish decisions at or near the bottom. A contrarian swing trader observes irrational price swings in overreaction to current news or rumors, including earnings surprises, takeover rumors, or product announcements, as examples. When these announcements occur, prices tend to move too far and too quickly. A negative earnings announcement missing estimates by mere pennies of earnings may cause the stock price to drop four points in half a day. The crowd mentality tells the majority to sell and to sell quickly. The contrarian, knowing this is overreaction, calmly sees it as a swing trading opportunity, and the bigger the overreaction, the more weight may be placed in that short-term trade. The swing trade based on a contrarian point of view requires that you buy low and sell high—the majority does just the opposite.
2. *Risks have to be diversified.* As you weight entry into a position based on solid reversal signals, equally strong confirmation, and perhaps the added signal from overreaction to news, be sure to avoid "contrarian greed" as part of this move. The contrarian sells when others are buying out of greed, and buys when others are selling out of panic. But be aware of the dangers in hubris, a tendency to accept more risk than you should because the opportunity is there. The majority may be right some of the time, so your swing trading risks should be diversified. This means that executing a series of weighted trades based on observed overreaction is an

effective strategy. However, keep the dollars at risk the same among many trades made in this manner. For example, if your weighting strategy focuses on trading in low-premium options and placing up to $1,000 per trade, don't exceed that level. You might find one "sure thing" that has all of the right elements in place, and you may decide that just one time, you are going to "go for it" and trade $5,000. That might just be the trade that fails, and the resulting loss will be disastrous. Even if it turns out profitable and you double your money in two sessions, what does that mean? Should you double up to a $10,000 trade next time? The wise course is to find the formula of risk levels you can accept. You will lose on some of your trades, so go for the percentage of wins and not for the fast killing.

3. *Combine strong signals with short-term profit targets.* The weighted swing trade is exposed to risk, that is, the longer it remains open, the greater the risk of loss. With this in mind, an offset to weighting the trade may be to aim at a shorter profit target. If your swing trades tend to mature within four to six days, perhaps a weighted swing trade should be set up with a profit target of two to four days, for example. This offsets the higher risk of weighting by accepting a lower percentage of profit, but because more options are opened, the dollar value of profits will be greater. This means you may have a few bonanza trades of exceptionally high percentage yields but also a few high percentage losses. The short-term profit target mitigates the exposure. If your initial goal is a 30% return, tripling the number of contracts and cutting the goal to 20% will produce higher dollar profits. Even with setting targets, however, exit from swing trades may be based on reversal signals to a greater extent. The purpose of the advice to set shorter-term profit targets is to set up the potential to take an exit when profits occur, whether reversal signals show up or not.

4. *Continue seeking exceptional confirmation.* The stronger the confirmation, the more confidence you may have in timing of both entry and exit. With weighted swings on one

side, you will want to be certain that reversal is accompanied by very clear and strong confirmation. Check not only price-related confirmation (Western signals like double tops or bottoms, breakouts, or gapping price movement or Eastern candlestick reversals) but volume and momentum signs as well. Also remember to quantify the value of confirmation. For example, a momentum signal might reflect strong recent movement and not a true overbought or oversold condition, so this is not always the best confirmation (unless the condition remains after a period of flat prices or movement in the opposite direction).

5. *Remember to focus on moneyness to control risks.* The ideal moneyness for swing trading is ATM. For long positions, this means a favorable price move going ITM immediately becomes intrinsic, so that appreciation of the long option is at its most likely placement. For short positions, favorable movement going OTM tends to cause decline in the short position, often reflecting not only the expected time decay but also a decline due to extrinsic changes. The further OTM a short position becomes, the less likely it is that it will end up ITM. This means that the decline in reaction to movement away from the money is going to be strongest when you start out with an ATM position.

6. *Expiration timing.* The basic rule of thumb for swing trading options is that time to expiration is not the same for long and for short. Long positions should expire very soon, preferably in two weeks or less. During this time, nonintrinsic value is at its low, and so remaining premium will be most responsive to ITM change. For short positions, you need to have nonintrinsic premium within the contract, and profits accumulate from time decay more than from any other factors. If you sell options ITM, a favorable move will create profits from declines in intrinsic value, but ITM short positions also carry higher risk. Assuming you decide to focus on ATM short options, the best timing will be more than one month until expiration but less than 1.5 months. During this half-month period, nonintrinsic premium will evaporate

at an accelerated rate, and as expiration approaches, the position will lose value. This applies even if the underlying move creates an ITM move in the option. During this period, time decay may exceed the rate of increase in intrinsic value. However, any time the short option does move toward the money, it makes sense to close rather than to risk exercise.

7. *Be aware of ex-dividend date whenever opening short-options.* It is easy to overlook the risk of early exercise. Any weighted strategy involving short options should be set up to avoid ex-dividend date within the next two to four weeks. This applies to short calls and the related early exercise risk and also to short puts and the risk of losses resulting from price decline due to dividends. However, this brings up the possibility of opening short-option weighted positions with expiration two months away when ex-dividend date occurs within the next four to six weeks. Referring back to figure 17.2, the chart period ended with a bearish piercing lines pattern. If this were confirmed, it would serve as an entry signal for a bearish price reversal. The next ex-dividend date was scheduled for February 14. The following options could be opened in weighted multiples as of the close of December 14:

	calls	puts
JAN 110	1.77	2.46
MAR 110	3.20	4.70

Both of these were close to the money as the underlying closed at $109.71. The calls were thus 0.29 OTM, and the puts were 0.29 ITM. Either of the short-option positions were reasonable candidates for a weighted entry, and either expiration month would work as well. The January contracts had 28 days to expiration and the March options had 84 days. Even though ex-dividend date was scheduled before the March expiration, early exercise was unlikely. With high time value (for the calls, all of the premium except 0.29), a 0.90 dividend would not be justified given the value of these calls at 3.20. It would be possible, but the long-option holder considering exercise would need to have a very low basis in the position just to make the numbers work, and with a lengthy time to expiration that is not possible. For the short puts with their considerably higher premium, either the January or March contracts make even more sense than the short calls; with 84 days to go before expiration, these short positions would be manageable and have the same risk profile as a covered call.

8. *Pay attention to signals for exit as well as for entry.* Much emphasis in swing trading is placed on entry at a point of reversal and confirmation and then uncertainty about the timing of exit. Considering the added risks from weighting one side of the swing, a two-pronged exit strategy makes sense. First, an exit goal should be established based on either a percentage profit or loss or a dollar amount of profit or loss. If the profit or bail-out points are reached, the weighted position should be closed, without exception. On the profit side, this does away with continuing risk. On the loss bailout side, cutting the loss makes sense because with a weighted position, losses accelerate at the same rate as profits. However, the second prong is a reversal signal. Regardless of profit or loss at the time, if a reversal signal and confirmation appear, close the position. The rule for exit should be the same as the rule for entry: Take action when the signals appear.

SWINGS ON RETRACEMENTS

Within even a short-term trend, retracements occur and are found often. They present additional opportunities for swing trading.

A retracement is a contrary move against the prevailing trend. It does not indicate a reversal but only a temporary move in the opposite direction and is of short duration. The distinction between reversal and retracement depends on whether the change represents a new trend or merely an adjustment in the momentum of the trend already underway. It may be caused by buyer and seller conflicts or attempts by one side to create reversal, but it succeeds in becoming reversal only if enough sentiment is present to turn the price trend around.

Spotting a retracement is not an easy matter. In the moment, you need to study resistance and support and the role of the trading range. For example, when price changes direction at the borders of the trading range after failing to break through, this often represents a strong reversal signal. However, when the direction changes midrange for no apparent reason, this could be a retracement. This is especially the case when a signal appears without confirmation. A true reversal should be marked by both a reversal signal and confirmation, and if the turn in direction is not confirmed—or if confirmation appears but immediately loses momentum—it could be a retracement.

How long should retracement last? This is another difficult question. It could extend from only three sessions all the way to several weeks. Once a month has passed, it probably means the change in direction was a reversal, even if signals and confirmation were not present. Fortunately for swing traders, the action points remain the same whether there is reversal or retracement, because you seek a three- to five-day trend and that includes both retracement and reversal. However, distinguishing one from the other also helps you to spot subsequent exit points when the prevailing trend is resumed.

Chartists may use additional techniques to make distinctions between retracement and reversal. For example, the Fibonacci sequence (in which each number is the sum of the previous two: 0, 1, 1, 2, 3, 5, 8, 13, 21, 34, 55, etc.) is applied as a test of retracement. The degree of price movement is observed to be close to specific percentages, based on calculated relationships between values. However, this is an after-the-fact method and not always easily spotted within the short-term swing trade. Other chartists point to the Elliott wave principle as a means for identifying retracement. This theory identifies ebb and flow of market behavior within a series of five-wave and three-wave movements.

Swing traders are more likely to succeed in timing of entry and exit by treating retracement moves in the same way as outright reversals. The distinction is that when retracement ends, the reversal often is clearly identified and the resulting move (back to the established trend) is quite strong.

A retracement of three weeks, for example, is seen in the chart of U.S. Steel (X) shown in figure 17.3. This is a long retracement and could be interpreted as a short-term downtrend in between two distinct uptrends. However, confirmation was questionable.

The uptrend that began at the beginning of October lasted three weeks, until a bearish engulfing pattern appeared. A swing trader would like to see a confirming signal at the same point, but there was none. This was the first clue that the subsequent downtrend was the beginning of a retracement.

The black crows pattern that followed was very strong, consisting not only of the minimum of three sessions but five. This would have worked as confirmation of a strong downtrend, but it ended abruptly with a reversal day and then a bullish piercing lines pattern. This contradicts the indicated downtrend but should not have led to any bullish reaction since ex-dividend date was about to occur. In fact, any short options should have been closed as soon as the bullish piercing lines signal was spotted.

After ex-dividend date, price continued downward for four sessions. And then a very strong three-session bullish indicator showed up, the abandoned baby. This is a reliable reversal signal seven out of 10 times it is seen, and as expected, it marked a return to the prevailing uptrend. The long-term trend is marked from beginning to end of the chart. Whether the interim downward price move is a short-term trend or a retracement, the treatment based on signals is the same for a swing trader. Confirmation has to consist of observation of the overall trend rather than focus on confirmation of short-term price direction. The lack of confirmation or confirmation leading to price contradiction (after the black crows, for example) gives strong evidence that this is a retracement and not a true reversal.

The retracement is effectively used to weight one side against the other if you recognize the change in direction as retracement. In that case, you look for the final stage, a reversal back to the prevailing trend, and then take up a weighted position. In the example of U.S. Steel, the bullish abandoned baby marked the

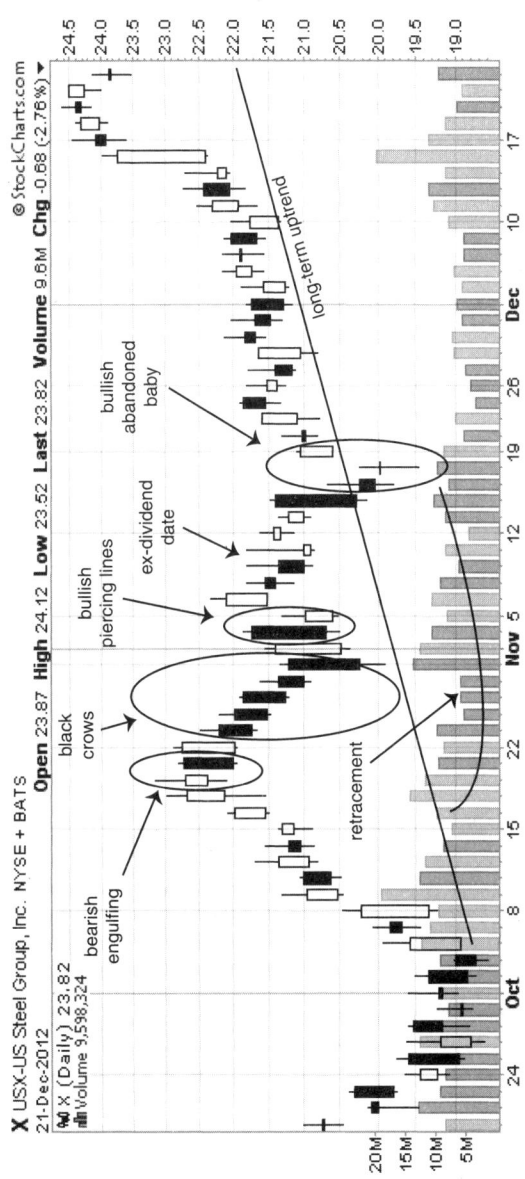

Figure 17.3 Swing trading on retracements
Source: StockCharts.com.

end of the retracement and accurately predicted a return to the uptrend. This signal marked the point for a weighted bullish entry with either long calls or short puts. With ex-dividend recently passed, early exercise was only a remote possibility.

SWING TRADING WITH RATIO CALENDAR SPREADS

Another system for weighting swing trades is with the ratio calendar spread. Under this strategy, you short two or more options against a smaller number of longer-term options. This may be done with both calls and puts.

This is an expansion of the well-known one-to-one calendar spread. One problem with using a calendar spread is that it creates a net debit because the expiration date of long positions is farther out. Using the ratio version solves this problem because more short options expire sooner and cover the cost of the long positions. However, this is also the opposite structure of the ideal swing trade, which prefers very short-term expiration of long positions over longer-term short expirations. Even so, the ratio calendar spread presents an alternative method of weighting with a hedging feature. If time decay creates a profitable outcome in the short options, then the remaining long positions were opened for "free" in the sense that the short-option profits covered their cost.

As with all ratio positions, the higher the ratio, the lower the risk. For example, a 2:1 ratio calendar spread (two short versus one later-expiring long) carries a 50% short risk; a 3:2 carries a 33% risk exposure versus a 67% cover ratio. If the underlying moves against the short positions, they can be closed or rolled to avoid exercise. Rolling forward creates additional income. They can also be closed along with a matching long position with later expiration, so that the loss in the short intrinsic option will be offset by the profit in the nonintrinsic long one.

For example, in table 17.1 the option values are based on closing values as of December 21, 2012:

All of these positions except the U.S. Steel 3:2 ratio with puts came out with a net credit. The exception was a $17 debit. This example based on the two stocks charted in this chapter makes the point that the ratio calendar spread is a swing trade designed not to create fast profits, but to set up cost-free long positions paid for by short positions expiring sooner. This is an appropriate strategy if the longer period of exposure is desired. In these examples,

Table 17.1 Chevron: Option premium and ratio write valuation examples

Chevron (CVX) – closed $109.71
Jan 110 calls 1.88
Feb 110 calls 2.61
   2:1 ratio = 2 short Jan 110 calls @ 1.88, $376
= 1 long Feb 110 call @ 2.61, $261
= net credit $115
   3:2 ratio = 3 short Jan 110 calls @ 1.88, $564
= 2 long Feb 110 calls @ 2.61, $522
= net credit $42

Jan 110 puts 2.88
Feb 110 puts 3.65
   2:1 ratio = 2 short Jan 110 puts @ 2.88, $576
= 1 long Feb 110 put @ 3.65, $365
= net credit $211
   3:2 ratio = 3 short Jan 110 puts @ 2.88, $864
= 2 long Feb 110 puts @ 3.65, $730
= net credit $134

U.S. Steel (X) – closed $23.94
Jan 24 calls 1.08
Feb 24 calls 1.58
   2:1 ratio = 2 short Jan 24 calls @ 1.08, $216
= 1 long Feb 24 call @ 1.58, $158
= net credit $58
   3:2 ratio = 3 short Jan 24 calls @ 1.08, $324
= 2 long Feb 24 calls @ 1.58, $316
= net credit $8

Jan 24 puts 1.15
Feb 24 puts 1.81
   2:1 ratio = 2 short Jan 24 puts @ 1.15, $230
= 1 long Feb 24 put @ 1.81, $181
= net credit $49
   3:2 ratio = 3 short Jan 24 puts @ 1.15, $345
= 2 long Feb 24 puts @ 1.81, $362
= net debit $17

Source: Based on price quotations at Charles Schwab & Company, at www.schwab.com.

the time value is not an issue since all of the long positions will end up with a net basis at or close to zero. This makes a future swing trade more likely to become profitable if the price direction turns favorably because the nonintrinsic value is eliminated with the premium from the short options.

There are many more ways to adjust your swing trades with weighting, whether offsetting in the same expiration period or using ratio calendar spreads and whether you use long or short or calls and puts or combinations.

The next chapter presents another interesting variation on the basic swing trade, the directionally neutral strategy. In this strategy, swings become profitable regardless of the direction of movement. Even a lack of movement creates profits in short positions, and the market risk of these is offset by corresponding long positions at the same strike and with a later expiration.

CHAPTER 18

STRATEGY # 9: EXPANDED IRON BUTTERFLY SWING TRADING

> It is better to fail in originality than to succeed in imitation.
> Herman Melville, in *The Literary World*, August, 1850

THE IRON BUTTERFLY IS A POPULAR STRATEGY DESIGNED TO provide limited maximum profit in exchange for limited maximum loss. This strategy may be viewed as acceptable for those willing to live with limitations on both sides; it may also be seen as unacceptable because profit can never exceed the limitations imposed by the strategy.

Swing traders would be inclined to avoid the butterfly for two reasons. First, it is set up as a hedge of these limitation levels, and swing traders seek to create very fast profits based on reversal signals. Second, the iron butterfly may need to remain open for more than the very short period of a trend in order to produce its outcome.

There is a solution, however, and this chapter explains how the iron butterfly can be modified to create a directionally neutral trade.

THE IRON BUTTERFLY AND ITS CONSTRUCTION

The iron butterfly has three strikes and four options—two calls and two puts—designed to limit both profit and loss. Because commissions can add up quickly, it makes sense to enter an iron butterfly only if it creates a large enough credit to (a) more than cover commission and (b) provide the opportunity for profits.

In the typical iron butterfly, you open an OTM long put and an OTM long call combined with an ATM short put and an ATM short call. Maximum profit occurs when the underlying is at the short strikes at expiration. Maximum loss occurs when price falls below the lower strike or rises above the higher strike, and that loss is equal to the difference between strikes minus the net credit earned.

For example, on November 14, 2012, ConocoPhillips (COP) had the following option values for its December expirations:

```
52.50 put = 0.60
55 put    = 1.55
55 call   = 1.29
57.50 call = 0.41
```

At the same time, COP closed at $54.77 per share, so the 55 options were closest to the money. An iron butterfly opened using these options consists of:

```
buy 1 52.50 put  =  0.60
sell 1 55 put    = −1.55
sell 1 55 call   = −1.29
buy 1 57.50 call =  0.41
net credit       =  1.83
```

The outcome is not accurately assessed on the last trading day because in practice traders are likely to close legs of this overall strategy as they become profitable. It is wise to emphasize closing short positions first or matching a short and a long position to close at the same time. Otherwise, two consequences have to be recognized. First, leaving a net short position outstanding sets up an uncovered short risk, whereas the iron butterfly is designed to limit loss potential. Second, that unexposed short leads to an immediate margin call equal to the strike of the exposed short option. Collateral in a butterfly with an equal number of long and short positions with the same expiration is equal to the net cost of long options at the most.

As a means for observing maximum profit and loss potential, the four options described in this example would be worth the values shown in table 18.1 as of the last trading day if all were kept open until that day.

This summary demonstrates how the iron butterfly works. On the upside, the short put profit is limited to the premium received, and the loss on the short put is offset by the gain on the long call. On the downside, both calls are fixed in outcome. The increasing losses in the short put are offset by equal value gains in the long put.

The maximum profit occurs when price ends up close to the short strikes; maximum loss is fixed at $17 (plus trading costs). However, for swing trading purposes, the iron butterfly may be too limited in potential and take too long to develop.

Another variation of the strategy is the *reverse* iron butterfly. This strategy uses the same options but consists of selling the OTM positions and buying the ATM call and put. In the example

Table 18.1 ConocoPhillips options used for the 1-2-3 butterfly

	Value of options at expiration				
Underlying Value	long 52.50 put	short 55 put	short 55 call	long 57.50 call	total
$50	$190	$−295	$ 129	$−41	$−17
51	90	−195	129	−41	−17
52	0	−95	129	−41	−7
53	0	5	129	−41	93
54	0	105	129	−41	193
55	0	155	129	−41	243
56	0	155	29	−41	143
57	0	155	−71	−41	43
58	0	155	−171	59	43
59	0	155	−271	159	43
60	0	155	−371	259	43

Source: Values derived for quotes at Charles Schwab & Co., at www.schwab.com.

above, this would set up an initial net debit of $183 instead of the net credit. The reverse iron butterfly has a place in some portfolios. It reverses the profit and loss zones.

EXPANDING THE STRATEGY: THE 1-2-3 IRON BUTTERFLY

The iron butterfly has both advantages and limitations. As a swing trading strategy, expanding it into the *1-2-3 iron butterfly* solves the problems by creating vastly greater profit potential. At the same time, it reduces risks with offsetting cover of short with long positions.

This is called the 1-2-3 for two reasons. First, an iron butterfly is opened in each of the next three expiration months. Ideally, these will be the next three calendar months as well although for some underlyings a gap appears between months two and three (for example, in December, you want to open an iron butterfly with expirations in January, February, and March, but instead of March, you might find the next available expiration occurs in April or May).

The second reason it is called a 1-2-3 is that the number of options opened at each position is increased each month. So in the first expiration you open one option at each of the strikes. In the second month, you open two. And in the third month, you open three. The number of options you open can also be weighted. For example, many sectors are cyclical based on the economy, such as transportation, energy, autos, housing, and leisure. Other sectors are cyclical based on time of the year, such as retail and construction. So if you believe a company's stock will rise or fall based on economic or calendar cyclical influence, the 1-2-3 can be weighted to time options positions in line with this belief.

Another aspect of the 1-2-3 iron butterfly is that the middle of the three expirations is a reverse iron butterfly. This creates an advantageous relationship in values between each month. Every short option is covered by a later-expiring long option at the same strike, and every long option is covered by a short one in the next

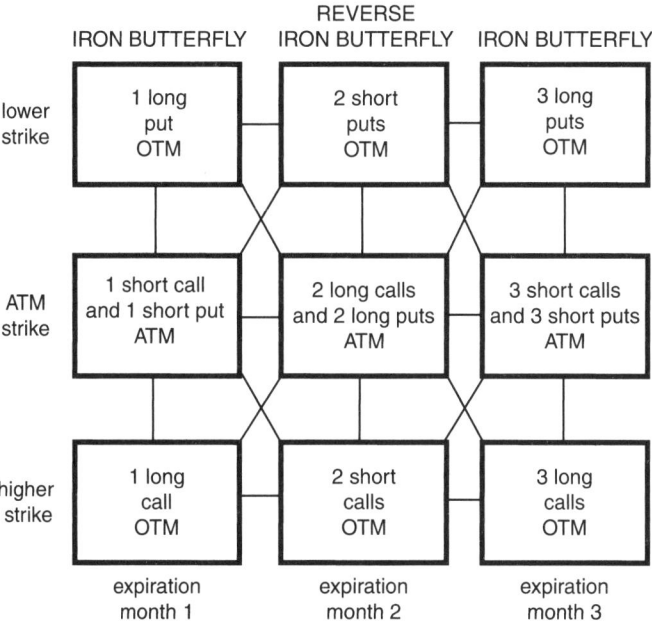

Figure 18.1 Construction of the 1-2-3 butterfly
Source: Figure created by author.

expiration month. The same rule applies to the reverse iron butterfly and the third expiration in the cycle. This is the "hedge matrix."

The 1-2-3 iron butterfly is shown in figure 18.1.

Creating the "Hedge Matrix"

The hedge matrix is so named because every open option is covered with an opposite one (long versus short or short versus long) that expires later. That is, every position you close should be offset with an opposite one (long versus short or short versus long), and this is why the system is called a hedge *matrix*. Matching can be accomplished in three ways. A vertical match is between a long and short option with the same expiration date but different strike. A horizontal match is between two positions with the same strike but different expiration dates. And finally, a diagonal match is set up between long and short options having different strikes and different expiration dates.

If you close single options, always select a short position, so that the remaining open options consist of more long than short options. This avoids unintended short exposure and also prevents margin calls. Ideally, you want to close long and short positions at the same time. And if you perform a horizontal or diagonal match, you also have to be aware of the mix of long and short contracts at each expiration date. Collateral requirements will be based on the matrix of long and short, so you need to maintain a balance between these or favor long over short.

One additional important aspect of the 1-2-3 iron matrix: You have to be aware of timing for the ex-dividend date. In the example of ConocoPhillips, ex-dividend occurred in January 2013. So any outstanding ITM calls would be closed at least a week before this date. If you have short calls ITM that expire later in the week prior to ex-dividend date, early expiration is only a remote possibility. The time value premium of these calls with longer expiration is likely to more than offset the dividend income a long-option holder would receive upon exercise. The most likely early exercise ITM calls are those expiring in the same month. In the example with December expirations, the iron butterfly should have been closed before expiration, and if any short positions were rolled forward, January expirations of ITM calls should be avoided. The December short calls could be rolled forward to February, for example. This creates additional income while avoiding early exercise.

Example of the Strategy

A 1-2-3 iron butterfly as of November 14 could be created for ConocoPhillips (COP) based on strikes in the previous example. This involves expirations in December, January, and February.

Because ex-dividend date was in January, any short ITM calls should be closed or rolled forward to avoid the risk of early exercise. In any strategy like the 1-2-3 iron butterfly, you have to be aware of the timing of the ex-dividend date or some positions may be exercised.

Table 18.2   ConocoPhillips 1-2-3 iron butterfly with opening values

December	
1 long 52.50 put @ 0.60 = 60	
1 short 55 put @ 1.55 = −155	
1 short 55 call @ 1.29 = −129	
1 long 57.50 call @ 0.41 = 41	net credit −183
January (reverse 1-2-3)	
2 short 52.50 puts @ 1.04 = −208	
2 long 55 puts @ 2.03 = 406	
2 long 55 calls @ 1.90 = 380	
2 short 57.50 calls @ 0.79 = −158	net debit 420
February	
3 long 52.50 puts @ 1.50 = 450	
3 short 55 puts @ 2.48 = −744	
3 short 55 calls @ 2.24 = −672	
3 long 57.50 calls @ 1.18 = 354	net credit −612
	overall net credit = −375

Source: Values derived for quotes at Charles Schwab & Co., at www.schwab.com.

As of November 14, 2012, a 1-2-3 iron butterfly could be set up on COP using the following positions shown in table 18.2.

These positions are summarized in figure 18.2, which shows the opened options for ConocoPhillips.

With ex-dividend due to occur around January 11, from the first of January forward any ITM short calls should be closed or rolled to avoid early exercise. This is the most likely timing of early exercise, and as part of your swing trading strategy this should be avoided. However, in the event that short calls are exercised, you can use long calls expiring at the same strikes but with later expiration dates (horizontal matching) to satisfy the assignment.

A test of this strategy in a virtual portfolio revealed that initial closings in the first three weeks all yielded double-digit returns. The hedge matrix enabled this while maintaining a careful balance between outstanding long and short positions. Closed positions between November 15 (one day holding period) and November 29 included opening and then closing additional positions. The outcomes for the first three weeks are shown in table 18.3.

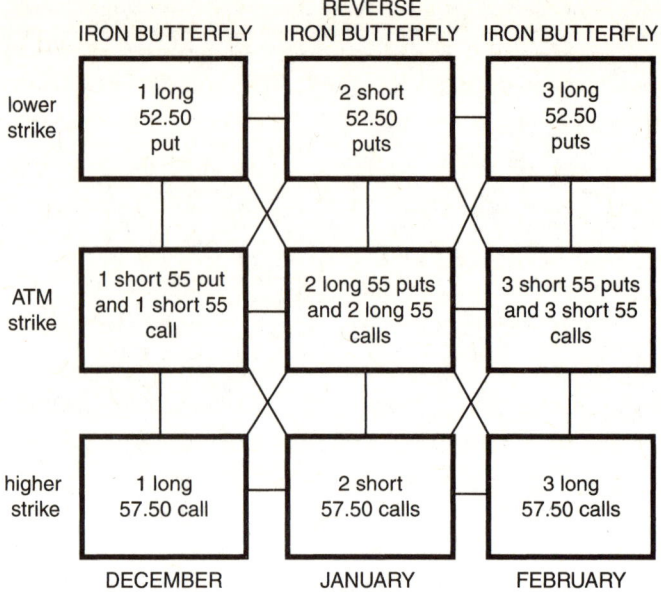

Figure 18.2   1-2-3 butterfly on ConocoPhillips (COP)
Source: Figure created by author.

Table 18.3   ConocoPhillips 1-2-3 iron butterfly, partial closings of options to take profits

	1-2-3 iron butterfly, closed positions:		
15-Nov	COP long puts	22%	1
15-Nov	COP short calls	12%	1
15-Nov	COP short put	41%	4
15-Nov	COP short puts	37%	4
15-Nov	COP long calls	21%	4
15-Nov	COP short puts	17%	4
15-Nov	COP long calls	19%	4
15-Nov	COP long puts	33%	12
29-Nov	COP short puts	17%	2
15-Nov	COP short call	78%	19

Source: Values derived for quotes at Charles Schwab & Co., at www.schwab.com.

The "Reconstituted Hedge" Matrix

After closing profitable positions as forms of swing trading within the 1-2-3 iron butterfly, you are going to end up with several "orphan" positions still open. These are long and short potions that were not closed and currently are at a net loss.

To resolve these, you can close at a loss and apply those losses against the accumulated profits from previously closed options. However, there is no need to take losses. You can just reconstitute the hedge matrix by adding new positions. This means filling in the gaps of long and short positions and perhaps extending the expiration months to another cycle. It also means moving to either a higher or lower range of strikes, based on how the underlying has moved since the positions were first opened.

This accomplished several goals, and provides new advantages. Those loss position orphans can be offset against newly opened positions so that, rather than taking losses, you create a net profit between a losing orphan and a winning newly reconstituted position.

For example, on December 6, 2012, the ConocoPhillips 1-2-3 iron butterfly was reconstituted with the following (newly added positions are in bold) positions shown in table 18.4:

Table 18.4 ConocoPhillips reconstituted 1-2-3 iron butterfly

	Dec expirations	
15-Nov	buy 1 52.50 put @ 0.60	60
6-Dec	**sell 1 55 call $ 2.4.7**	−247
15-Nov	buy 1 57.50 call @ 0.41	41
	Jan expirations	
15-Nov	buy 2 55 puts @ 2.03	406
6-Dec	**sell 2 57.50 puts @ 1.32**	−264
27-Nov	sell 2 57.50 calls @ 1.05	−210
27-Nov	sell 2 60puts @ 3.63	−728
27-Nov	buy 2 60 calls @ 0.29	58
	Feb expirations	
19-Nov	buy 3 52.50 puts @ 1.51	453
19-Nov	sell 3 55 calls @ 2.31	−693
19-Nov	buy 3 57.50 calls @ 1. 444	444
6-Dec	**buy 3 60 puts @ 3.80**	1,140
	May expirations	
6-Dec	**sell 4 52.50 puts @ 1.54**	−616
6-Dec	**buy 4 55 puts @ 2.30**	920
6-Dec	**buy 4 55 calls @ 3.97**	1,588
6-Dec	**sell 4 57.50 calls @ 2.58**	−1,032
6-Dec	**sell 4 60 puts @ 5.20**	−2,080
6-Dec	**sell 4 60 calls @ 1.37**	−548
	new net credit -1,308	

Source: Values derived for quotes at Charles Schwab & Co., at www.schwab.com.

One problem with this reconstituted hedge matrix is the out-of-balance condition in two of the three months. The January expirations include one short exposed position, and the May expirations have two exposed short positions. This will create an immediate margin call to cover the strike value of these positions and also increases risks. However, this situation can be remedied quickly by closing the needed number of short positions in each month or by opening additional long positions to equalize the balance of short and long.

Two important changes were made in this reconstituted version of the 1-2-3. First, the original strike range between 52.50 and 57.50 was expanded to a range between 55 and 60. Second, expiration date was extended one additional month to May 2013. These changes reflected the changing price range of the underlying as well as the need to provide cover for orphan positions.

THE OPPOSITE: A 3-2-1 IRON BUTTERFLY

It is also possible to vary the swing trading potential of the 1-2-3 by reversing the number of options opened in each expiration cycle. This variation, the 3-2-1, involves three contracts at each position in the first month, two in the second, and one at each position in the third.

The rationale for the 3-2-1 is that the time value of earlier short contracts will decline more rapidly than later ones, so opening more contracts takes advantage of this for the short positions. Meanwhile, the long positions in multiples of three have lower nonintrinsic value. These may appreciate well as long as the underlying moves in the desired direction. This is *either* direction since it includes both long calls and long puts. The long positions also serve as offsets to close short positions. For example, if a short option moves ITM and is due to expire within a matter of weeks or even days, offsetting these against profitable long options may create a net breakeven or small credit while avoiding a loss or exercise.

The 3-2-1 may be a more desirable swing trade for these reasons. The selection of 1-2-3 or 3-2-1 is a matter of personal choice. However, the 1-2-3 hedge matrix may offer better hedging because it combines later expiration (thus, more nonintrinsic premium) and a higher number of offsetting options. These two factors make it much easier to match and close at a profit. In the 3-2-1 matching is more difficult, but rapid decline in the time value of multiple contracts offsets this problem because short option values will fall rapidly, leading to faster profits.

The hedge matrix sets up an exceptionally effective swing trading system, in which profits are taken whether the underlying moves in a bullish or a bearish direction. In both directions the offset of long and short is effective since you match long calls and short puts (in an uptrend) or long puts and short calls (in a downtrend). If the underlying does not move out of a range-bound sideways trend, the short positions decay and offset losses in the long positions. For swing traders, the 1-2-3 and 3-2-1 iron butterfly strategies are highly leveraged and effective strategies to reduce risk and accumulate profits.

All swing trading strategies ultimately involve a balance between risk and profit. Some reversal indicators fail even when strongly confirmed; therefore, risks have to be managed by maintaining trade increments at a consistent dollar level. When timing does fail, cutting losses quickly is a wise management decision. Losses may also be offset by recovery strategies, but these usually involve increasing market risks.

The flexibility of using both calls and puts, alone or in long and short combinations, makes options ideal for swing trading. to s Options overcome the problem of shorting stock by replacing that bearish move with long puts or short calls. Options also provide enough flexibility with the use of combinations to hedge risk and to provide you with a desirable combination: mitigated risk with profits.

Epilogue—The Big Picture: Swing Trading and Your Portfolio

> We are all dangerous till our fears grow thoughtful.
> John Ciardi, *This Strangest Everything*, 1966

WHERE DOES SWING TRADING BELONG IN THE LARGER PICTURE of your portfolio?

Some traders are just that, traders. They have no interest in buy-and-hold or even in being invested in stock for any period of time. These traders use stock purchases primarily to facilitate options trades. Others combine investing and trading. These investors see options as a means for managing portfolio risks in two aspects: First, options offset long-position risks in equities, enabling investors to maintain a conservative risk profile at little or no added cost. Second, options create short-term income so that strategies like swing trading fit perfectly into the model.

Whether you are a swing trader or an equity investor seeking risk hedging, the many strategies involved with options-based swing trading deserve careful consideration. All trading is a balance of risk and profits, and a mistake all too often made is the pursuit of profits at the cost of added risk. It is easy to overlook risk altogether, especially when trades are going your way. However, to avoid expensive surprises, your swing trading strategies should be constructed based on solid risk management principles. Four suggestions:

1. *Keep increments of risk the same for all swing trades.* Some portion of swing trades are going to fail even with strong reversal signals and confirmation. This should always be in

your mind. The technical tests and signals you rely on in your swing trading program are not foolproof, so you need to be able to accept some losses. Using chart analysis of price, volume, and momentum reduces the odds of poorly timed trades, but those failed trades will occur. For this reason, avoid increasing your trade ante because you think the next trade will be just as profitable as the previous one. Avoid the common sequence of winning on several trades only to lose it all (and more) on one poorly timed trade. You avoid this by patiently and cautiously maintaining the same dollar amount at risk in all of your swings.

2. *Analyze worst-case outcomes rather than assuming the best-case scenario.* Traders tend to believe that they know a particular movement will occur based on a favorite reversal signal or a developed sense of rhythm in a trading pattern. The intuitive observations you make as a trader are valuable and should serve as a part of your strategy, but you should not ignore the risks. When you are about to enter a swing trade, analyze what will happen if the underlying moves in the *other* direction. Be aware of "zero base" thinking. This is a tendency for traders to consider their entry price the "zero base" and to expect prices to immediately move in a profitable direction. In reality, there is no zero base, and prices may easily remain in a narrow range or move in the wrong direction. Your decision of when to enter is best based on analysis of both profit and loss potential, the best-case and the worst-case outcomes.

3. *Be keenly aware of ex-dividend timing and its effect on all short positions.* The effect of the ex-dividend date on underlying price is expected to be negative, but this does not always occur. But for options-based swing trading, the momentary decline in price at or after ex-dividend date is not the biggest issue. Of greater concern is exercise risk for any uncovered ITM short calls and the potential for unfavorable price change in short puts. If you are going to use short options as part of your swing trading strategy, avoid ex-dividend date or close positions at least one week before it arrives. Early

exercise of calls and unfavorable price movement in puts makes this a smart timing decision.

4. *Set rules for yourself and stick to them, both for profit-taking and for loss mitigation.* The greatest risk for all traders is "discipline risk," the failure to follow self-imposed rules. Every trader knows what this means. You set rules for yourself about when to take profits and when to cut losses. But once the trade is entered, you suspend the rules, which is most often an expensive mistake. This is especially true with options, where today's value is likely to change rapidly in the near future. So when profits develop, the rationale is that more profits are possible if only you wait a few more days, but then the profits decline, and you lose the opportunity. When you reach your loss bailout point, you have set the rule for yourself that you will take the loss and close. But you become stubborn and decide to hold out a while longer, convinced that you can get back to your breakeven or better. Most of the time, this only ensures a 100% loss. A smart trading strategy is to set rules in advance for when to close positions and then to follow your own rules.

Testing the Swing Trading Strategies

All swing trading strategies with options present rational beliefs about building profit. But do these strategies work?

A note from the author: During the time I was researching and writing this book, I was also testing these strategies on my website, ThomsettOptions.com, where I managed a virtual portfolio. In this portfolio I tried all of the options-based swing trades based on actual stock and option prices. These strategic tests were quite successful, and this exercise made the point that swing trading with options does work. My strategy was to apply the same self-imposed rules to my virtual trades that I have explained in this book. Table E.1: The following is a summary of all the trades I made during this period. – MCT

Table E.1 Trades in ThomsettOptions.com virtual portfolio, Sep-Dec, 2012

Entry Date	Description	Open	Close	Profit or loss	%	days held
16-Sep	IBM short straddle					
	sell 1 Oct 215 call @ 1.31	131	0	109		
	sell 1 Oct 200 put @ 1.79	179	0	173	91%	19
25-Sep	Microsoft (MSFT) short puts	−100	152	52	52%	3
14-Sep	Verizon 1 short Oct 45 call	−37	36	−1	−3%	3
	Verizon 1 long Oct 44 put	94	−46	−48	−51%	3
12-Oct	Sprint short Nov 6 calls	−105	21	84	80%	3
29-Sep	SPDR Gold Trust (GLD) short Nov 172 calls	−802	300	502	63%	16
10-Oct	Johnson & Johnson (JNJ) short Nov 70 puts	−428	208	220	5%	6
9-Oct	McDonald's (MCD) short Oct 92.50 puts	−136	59	77	57%	7
11-Oct	U.S. Steel (X) Synthetic long stock ($20.78)					
5-Nov	buy 1 Nov 21 call @ 1.30	130	175			
5-Nov	sell 1 Nov 21 put @ 1.04	−104	76	73	281%	5
9-Oct	Kellogg (K) short Nov 52.50 put	−140	80	60	43%	9
2-Oct	GE—short Jan 22.50 call	−107	59	48	45%	17
2-Oct	GE—long Jan 22.50 put short Jan 22.50 call	95	125	30	32%	17
15-Oct	Verizon (VZ) 1 short call Nov 45	−81	40	41	51%	8
16-Oct	Altria (MO):sell 3 Dec 33 calls	−288	168	120	42%	7
	Altria (MO) buy 3 Dec 33 puts	291	426	135	46%	7
22-Oct	U.S. Steel (X) —buy 3 Nov 22 puts	267	363	96	36%	1
5-Nov	Verizon sell 1 call Dec 46 @ 0.75	−75	32	43	57%	4
6-Nov	Kellogg's 3 puts, Dec 55 @ 1.30	390	555	165	42%	1
6-Nov	Verizon sell 1 Dec 45 call @ 0.84	−84	46	38	45%	1
6-Nov	Altria sell 3 Dec 33 calls @ 0.30	−90	54	36	40%	1
3-Oct	Merck (MRK) long Nov 45 puts	132	178	46	35%	36
1-Nov	MCD—sell 2 Dec 90 calls @ 0.47	−94	38	56	60%	8
5-Nov	IBM—sell 1 call Dec 195 @ 3.95	−395	265	130	33%	4
	COP—buy 3 Feb 52.50 puts @ 1.50*	450	549	99	22%	1

Table E.1   Continued

Entry Date	Description	Open	Close	Profit or loss	%	days held
	COP—sell 3 Feb 55 calls @ 2.24*	−672	594	78	12%	1
12-Nov	Cisco (CSCO) 2 short Nov 16.50 puts	−86	0	86	100%	4
2-Nov	Yahoo Nov 17 put @ 0.21	21	0	−21		
2-Nov	Yahoo Jan 17.50 call @ 0.57	54	96	42	28%	14
15-Nov	COP sell 1 Dec 55 put @ 1.55*	−155	91	64	41%	4
15-Nov	COP sell 2 Jan 52.50 puts @ 1.04*	−208	132	76	37%	4
15-Nov	COP buy 2 Jan 55 calls @ 1.90*	380	458	78	21%	4
15-Nov	COP sell 3 Feb 55 puts @ 2.48*	−744	618	126	17%	4
15-Nov	COP buy 3 Feb 57.50 calls @ 1.18*	354	420	66	19%	4
14-Nov	SLV sell 2 Dec 32 puts @ 1.13	−226	158	68	30%	5
20-Nov	CAT buy 2 82.50 puts @ 3.02*	604	690	86	14%	1
20-Nov	CAT sell 2 87.50 calls @ 1.59*	−318	294	24	8%	1
20-Nov	CAT buy 3 80 puts @ 0.99*	297	336	39	13%	1
20-Nov	CAT sell 3 85 calls @ 1.56*	−468	381	87	19%	1
17-Sep	KO buy 2 40 calls @ 0.35	70	0	−70		
9-Nov	KO sell 2 Dec 35 puts @ 0.39	−78	6	72	0%	66
20-Nov	CAT sell 3 Dec 82.50 puts @ 1.72*	−516	408	108	21%	6
20-Nov	CAT sell 2 Jan 80 puts @ 2.08*	−416	340	76	18%	6
20-Nov	CAT sell 1 Feb 82.50 put @ 4.18*	−418	381	37	9%	6
15-Nov	COP buy 2 Jan 57.50 calls @ 0.79*	158	210	52	33%	12
26-Nov	IBM sell 1 Dec 195 call @ 2.25	−225	140	85	38%	1
28-Nov	M—sell 1 40 put @ 1.47*	−147	103	44	30%	1
28-Nov	M—sell 2 39 puts @ 1.35*	−270	234	36	13%	1
28-Nov	M—buy 2 40 calls @ 1.36*	272	332	60	22%	1
28-Nov	M—sell 3 41 puts @ 2.88*	−864	744	120	14%	1
28-Nov	M—sell 4 42 puts @ 4.85*	−1,940	1,740	200	10%	1
27-Nov	COP—sell 3 55 puts @ 1.44*	−432	357	75	17%	2
20-Nov	CAT—buy 3 87.50 calls @ 0.73*	219	348	129	59%	9
20-Nov	CAT—buy 2 85 calls @ 2.55*	510	700	190	37%	9
20-Nov	CAT—buy 1 87.50 call @ 2.46*	246	313	67	27%	9

continued

Table E.1   Continued

Entry Date	Description	Open	Close	Profit or loss	%	days held
28-Nov	M—buy 1 39 put @ 0.90*	90	118	28	31%	2
28-Nov	M—buy 2 40 puts @ 1.93*	386	432	46	12%	2
28-Nov	M—sell 2 41 calls @ 0.95*	−190	154	36	19%	2
28-Nov	M—buy 3 40 puts @ 2.12*	636	759	123	19%	2
28-Nov	M—sell 3 41 calls @ 1.32*	−396	324	72	18%	2
15-Nov	COP—sell 1 55 call @ 1.29*	−129	28	101	78%	19
28-Nov	M—sell 4 42 calls @ 2.11*	−844	584	260	31%	6
6-Dec	M—sell 3 37 puts @ 1.56*	−468	369	99	21%	1
8-Nov	GLD—long and short calls	810	924	114	14%	70
6-Dec	M—sell 2 38 puts @ 1.27*	−254	198	56	22%	1
6-Dec	M—buy 3 39 calls @ 1.79*	537	600	63	12%	1
15-Nov	COP—buy 1 57.50 call @ 0.41*	41	96	55	13%	22
6-Dec	COP—sell 2 57.50 puts @ 1.32*	−264	224	40	15%	1
27-Nov	COP—sell 2 60 puts @ 3.63*	−728	650	178	28%	10
27-Nov	COP— buy 2 60 calls @ 0.29*	58	90	32	55%	10
19-Nov	COP—buy 3 57.50 calls @ 1.48*	444	573	129	24%	17
6-Dec	COP—sell 4 60 puts @ 5.20*	−2,080	1,920	160	7%	1
15-Nov	COP—buy 1 52.50 put @ 0.60*	60	6	−58		
6-Dec	COP—sell 1 55 call $ 2.47*	−247	295	−48		
6-Dec	COP—buy 4 55 calls @ 3.97*	1,588	1,680	92		
6-Dec	COP sell 4 60 calls @ 1.37*	−548	604	56	5%	25
16-Oct	MO—sell 2 Jan 33 calls @ 0.83	−166	90	76	46%	57
16-Oct	MO—sell 2 Jan 34 calls @ 0.32	−64	30	34	53%	57
7-Nov	ED —sell 1 Dec 57.50 put @ 1.90	−190	145	45	24%	35
13-Dec	Western Union (WU)—collar					
	buy 300 shares @ 12.34	3,702				
	sell 2 Dec 12 calls @ 0.70	−140				
	Sell 2 Dec 13 calls @ 0.25	−50				
	Buy 3 Dec 12 puts @ 0.40	120	3,759	127	3%	39
14-Nov	Piedmont Office Realty Trust (PDM)—collar					
	BUY 400 shares @ 17.43	6,972				
	SELL 4 Dec 17.50 calls @ 0.90	−360				
	BUY 4 Dec 17.50 puts @ 0.75	300	6,988	76	1%	28
6-Dec	AT&T (T) collar					
	buy 400 shares @ $33.76	13,504				

Table E.1 Continued

Entry Date	Description	Open	Close	Profit or loss	%	days held
	sell 6 Jan 34 calls @ 0.58	−348				
	buy 3 Jan 34 puts @ 1.17	351	13,642	135	1%	6
6-Dec	CAT—sell 1 85 put @ 3.60*	−360	275	85	24%	7
6-Dec	CAT—buy 1 87.50 call @ 3.25*	325	375	50	13%	7
6-Dec	CAT—sell 2 80 puts @ 3.90*	−780	620	160	21%	7
6-Dec	CAT—buy 2 85 calls @ 6.55*	1,310	1,460	150	12%	7
6-Dec	CAT—sell 3 85 puts @ 10.52*	−3,156	2,862	294	9%	7
6-Dec	CAT—buy 3 87.50 calls @ 8.55*	2,565	2,802	237	9%	7
12-Dec	MCD—sell 2 Jan 90 calls @ 1.31	−262	224	38	15%	2
6-Dec	COP—sell 4 52.50 puts @ 1.54*	−616	556	60	10%	8
6-Dec	M—sell 2 39 calls @ 1.37*	−274	194	80	29%	8
6-Dec	M—sell 3 41 calls @ 1.08*	−324	243	81	25%	8
6-Dec	M—sell 4 39 calls @ 2.93*	−1,192	1,052	140	12%	8
12-Oct	Sprint (S)—buy 300 shares @ 5.76	1,728	1,665	−63	−4%	66
2-Nov	Yahoo buy 2 Dec 17 puts @ 0.47	94	0	−94	−100%	45
7-Nov	ED buy 1 Dec 55 call @ 1.70	170	85	−85	−50%	40
14-Dec	MO—sell 3 DEC 33 calls @ 0.40*	−120	54	66	55%	3
17-Oct	IBM—2 JAN 190 puts @ 2.64	−528	318	210	40%	62
5-Nov	AT&T (T) synthetic long stock:					
	buy two Dec 35 calls @ 0.64	128	6	−114	−89%	43
	sell 2 Dec 34 puts @ 0.57	−114	−58	94	82%	43
19-Dec	MCD—sell 2 JAN 90 calls @ 1.64	−328	250	78	24%	1
14-Dec	VZ—sell 1 DEC 44.50 call @ 0.44	−44	3	41	93%	5
17-Dec	K—buy 5 Jan 55 puts @ 0.30	150	225	**75**	50%	4
14-Dec	IBM—sell 1 JAN 195 call @ 2.98	−298	203	95	32%	10
	* All trades for ConocoPhillips (COP), Caterpillar (CAT) and Macy's (M) were portions of 1–2–3 iron butterfly strategies described in chapter 18.					

The purpose of all of these trades was to test swing trading strategies in a real environment and based on actual prices of stock and options on the dates indicated. Overall, the strategies succeeded, creating more profits than losses, mostly in a holding period of under one month. These outcomes exclude dividends earned, and all profits are without consideration of trading costs.

Notes

Introduction

1. "High-Frequency Trading," *New York Times*, October 10, 2011.
2. Securities and Exchange Commission (SEC) at *www.sec.gov/answers/pumpdump.htm*.

1 Options: Trading Basics

1. In future references to underlying stock, the term "underlying" will be used by itself as a noun, conforming to the industry usage (or jargon). When the term refers to price, that will be specified.

2 Swing Trading: The Basics

1. Josef Lakonishok, Andrei Shleifer, and Robert W. Vishny, "The impact of institutional trading on stock prices," *Journal of Financial Economics* 31(1992), 42.
2. Thomas Bulkowski, *Encyclopedia of Candlestick Charts* (Hoboken, NJ: Wiley, 2008). This book is the result of the author's study of thousands of candlestick trades, and Bulkowski concludes that the engulfing pattern is highly reliable. The bear engulfing pattern leads to reversal 79% of the time, and the bull engulfing pattern leads to reversal 63% of the time. Two additional signals of exceptional reliability are the bullish three white soldiers (82%) and the bearish three black crows (78%). Less reliable signals approximating fifty-fifty reliability include the bull and bear harami (both leading to reversal only 53% of the time) and the gravestone, dragonfly, and long-legged doji (51% average). Source: http://www.thepatternsite.com.

7 Powerful Timing Tools: Expanding Swing Signals with Candlestick Reversals

1. Jeff Augen, *Trading Options at Expiration: Strategies and Models for Winning the Endgame* (Upper Saddle River, NJ: FT Press, 2009), 4.

10 Strategy # 1: Long-Option Approach, a Basic Solution

1. Chicago Board Options Exchange (CBOE), link to *"Advisors"* and then to *"Advisor Knowledge Center,"* http://www.cboe.com/advisors/knowledge/myth1.aspx.

Bibliography

Ansbacher, Max. *The New Options Market*. 4th ed. Hoboken, NJ: Wiley, 2000.
Augen, Jeff. *Day Trading Options*. Upper Saddle River NJ: FT Press, 2010.
———.*Trading Options at Expiration: Strategies and Models for Winning the Endgame*. Upper Saddle River, NJ, FT Press, 2009.
Bittman, James B. *Options for the Stock Investor*. New York: McGraw-Hill, 1997.
Bulkowski, Thomas J., *Encyclopedia of Candlestick Charts*. Hoboken, NJ: Wiley, 2008
Crane, John. *Advanced Swing Trading*. Hoboken, NJ: Wiley, 2003
Farley, Alan S. *The Master Swing Trader*. New York: McGraw-Hill, 2001.
Kaeppel, Jay. *The Option Trader's Guide to Probability, Volatility, and Timing*. Hoboken, NJ: Wiley, 2002.
Kyle, Scott G. *The Power Curve*. New York: Nautilus Press, 2009.
McMillan, Lawrence G. *Options as a Strategic Investment*. 4th ed. New York: New York Institute of Finance, 2002.
———. *Profit with Options*. Hoboken, NJ: Wiley, 2002.
Natenberg, Sheldon. *Option Volatility & Pricing*. New York: McGraw-Hill, 1994.
Pring, Martin. *Technician's Guide to Day and Swing Trading*. New York: McGraw-Hill, 2003
Schaeffer, Bernie. *The Option Advisor*. Hoboken, NJ: Wiley, 1997.

Index

Accumulation Distribution (A/D), 59
automatic exercise, 11

Bollinger Bands, 59
breakeven return, 66–67

candlestick:
    abandoned baby, 148–149
    basics, 53–55
    black crows, 31, 32, 54
    charting, 133–137
    confirmation, 59
    continuation, 133, 152–163
    doji, 31, 126, 130, 140–142
    doji star, 150–153
    engulfing, 31, 32, 53, 100, 138
    evening star, 150
    gap filled, 161, 163
    hammer, 127, 139–140
    hanging man, 127, 139–140
    harami, 31, 142, 143
    harami cross, 142–144
    in neck, 155–157
    inside patterns, 146–147
    inverted hammer, 144–146
    long-legged doji, 130, 140–142
    morning star, 150
    on neck, 154–156
    outside patterns, 147–148
    reversals, 12, 133, 137–152
    separating lines, 154, 156
    side-by-side lines, 157–161
    spinning top, 126–127, 130, 142
    squeeze alert, 150, 151
    tasuki gap, 161–162
    thrusting lines, 153–154, 155
    white soldiers, 31, 32, 53–54

Chaikin Money Flow (CMF), 59
chartists, 32–33, 44
confirmation, 31, 54–59. 137–138
contrarian trading, 4, 29

diversification, 8, 30–31
double top and bottom, 12, 32, 45, 54, 59, 100
Dow Theory, 33

Eastern technical analysis, 138
ex-dividend date, 179–183, 270–271, 340–341
extrinsic value, 15

falling range, 37
Federal Reserve, 78
Fibonacci Sequence, 111–115
Financial Industry Regulatory Authority (FINRA), 96

head and shoulders, 44–45, 54, 100
herding, 27
high-frequency trading (HFT), 1–2
horizontal range, 35

implied volatility, 15, 91–94, 165–166
Internet, 32
intrinsic, value, 14–15

leverage, 8, 24–25

margin:
    advantage, 79–80
    calls, 78–79
    CBOE Margin Manual, 64, 84
    collateral, 296–297, 309

margin—*Continued*
  Federal Reserve, 78
  interest, 11–12
  maintenance, 77–78, 87
  management, 82–84, 91
  Regulation T, 78
  risks, 80–81
  trading (options), 86–88
  trading (stock), 65–78
momentum oscillators, 12, 50, 59, 127
Moving Average Convergence/Divergence (MACD), 59

New York Stock Exchange (NYSE), 97

On Balance Volume (OBV), 59
option:
3-2-1 iron butterfly, 336–337
1-2-3 iron butterfly, 330–331
75 percent rule, 193–195, 214–215
  at the money (ATM), 17
  basics, 8–11, 22–24
  box spread, 86
  butterfly spread, 86
  closing, 20
  collateral, 296–297
  covered call, 13, 20, 229–230, 234–235
  delta, 44, 134
  dividend effect, 270–271
  exercise conversion, 189–191
  exercise, 19–20, 215–216, 250–251, 258–259
  expiration, 11, 20, 165–166, 235–236, 248–249, 257
  flexibility, 8
  gamma, 44, 134
  Greeks, 44, 134
  hedge matrix, 331–332
  in the money (ITM), 17
  iron butterfly, 327–330
  leverage, 24–25, 88–94, 297–298
  long and short, 11–14, 22–23
  margin collateral, 64, 90, 91
  moneyness, 247–248, 256–257, 318
  out of the money (OTM), 74
  proximity and time, 166–175, 216–218
  put, covered and uncovered, 13–14, 234–235
  qualified covered calls, 186–187

ratio calendar spreads, 23, 307–308, 324–326
ratio put spreads, 272–274
ratio writes, 23, 187–188, 246–251, 249–250, 257–258
reconstructed hedge matrix, 334–336
risks, 8, 61–62
rolling techniques, 19–22
spreads, 23
straddles, 23–24
strike, 9–10, 235–236
synthetic, 23
theta, 134
types, 9
uncovered call, 13
value, 14–19
variable ratio write, 188, 256–259
vega, 134
OTC Bulletin Board Securities, 78

pattern day trading, 96–98
price gaps, 12, 32, 35, 45, 54, 59, 100
pump and dump, 3

Regulation T, 78, 97
Relative Strength Index (RSI), 59, 103, 127
rising range, 37
risk:
  awareness, 8
  diversification, 30–31, 68, 71–72
  expiration, 72–74
  goal-setting, 62–64
  increments, 339–340
  information, 62
  knowledge, 62, 94–96
  leverage, 67–68, 85–86
  long option, 309–310
  lost opportunity, 64–65
  margin, 64, 80–81
  market, 12
  multiple option, 309–314
  option, 61–62
  pattern day trading, 96–98
  reduction, 8
  rules, 341
  self-discipline, 62–64
  short call 283–284, 310–314
  short put, 271–272, 285–287
  stock shorting, 68–69

swing trading, 69–72
synthetics, 295–296, 304–306
tax, 65–66
time decay, 72–74
tolerance, 8
weighting swings, 315–320
worst-case analysis, 340

Securities and Exchange Commission (SEC), 97
shorting stock, 12, 13
Stochastic Oscillator, 59
StockCharts.com, 133–134
support and resistance, 12, 34–43, 137
swing trading:
   basics, 27–30, 43–44
   channel analysis, 104–111
   coiled markets, 115–119
   cup and handle, 123, 124
   defensive strategies, 195–197
   diversification, 200–202
   ex-dividend date planning, 179–183
   exercise likelihood, 183–185
   expanded iron butterfly, 327
   Fibonacci Sequence, 111–115
   flexibility, 308–309
   leverage, 200–202
   long or short, 175–177
   long put offset to short risk, 202–204
   long-option strategy, 193
   long/short call strategy (covered short), 227–229
   long/short-call strategy (ratio write on short), 245
   long/short-option strategy (uncovered short), 213–214
   long/short-put strategy, 267–268
   multiple contracts and weighting, 307–308

narrow-range day (NRD), 43, 98, 99
predictability, 230–234
price spike reversal, 124, 125–127
profit limitations, 287–288
puts in place of calls, 268–269
ratio calendar spreads, 324–326
ratio put spreads, 272–274
retracement and pullback, 111–115, 320–324
reversal day, 43–44, 98, 101–104, 119–122
risks, 69–72, 247–251
short stock risk, 218–219
short-option strategy, 281–283
short-term price cycles, 32–34
stock and option combinations, 185–188
strategy tests, 7, 341–346
strike peg, 177–178
synthetic stock positions, 298–304
time and cost problems, 197–200
timing, 30–32, 180–183
volume spike, 44, 98, 100, 120
weighting methods, 314–315

technical analysis basics, 44–52
time value, 15
trading range flip, 43
triangles, 12, 32, 37, 50, 59, 111

underlying security, 9, 18

volatility, 18–19
volume, 12, 59

wedge reversal, 37
wedges, 32, 59, 111
Western technical analysis, 32, 54, 59, 123, 138